SKEPTICISM AND IDEOLOGY

SKEPTICISM
&
IDEOLOGY

SHELLEY'S POLITICAL PROSE AND
ITS PHILOSOPHICAL CONTEXT
FROM BACON TO MARX

Terence Allan Hoagwood

UNIVERSITY OF IOWA PRESS · IOWA CITY

PR
5442
P64
H63
1988

University of Iowa Press, Iowa City 52242
Copyright © 1988 by the University of Iowa
All rights reserved
Printed in the United States of America
First edition, 1988

Typesetting by G&S Typesetters, Inc., Austin, Texas
Printing and binding by Thomson-Shore, Dexter, Michigan

Library of Congress Cataloging-in-Publication Data

Hoagwood, Terence Allan, 1952–
Skepticism and ideology: Shelley's political prose and its philosophical
context from Bacon to Marx/by Terence Allan Hoagwood.—1st ed.
p.   cm.
Bibliography: p.
Includes index.
ISBN 0-87745-218-0
1. Shelley, Percy Bysshe, 1792–1822—Political and social views.
2. Shelley, Percy Bysshe, 1792–1822—Prose.   3. Political science—
Philosophy.   4. Skepticism.   I. Title.
PR5442.P64H63   1988
821'.7—dc19   88-17270
                                                      CIP

FOR BARBARA HOAGWOOD

If the concepts of the mind are not realities, reality cannot be thought.
Gorgias of Leontini

Instruction transforms a man, and in transforming, creates his nature.
Democritus of Abdera

It is the same thing to think and to be.
Parmenides of Elea

Pure mind . . . is a myth.
Gorgias

All that we see while slumbering is sleep.
Heracleitus of Ephesus

Horses would draw pictures of gods like horses, and oxen of gods like oxen.
Xenophanes of Colophon

Whatsoever thy hand findeth to do, do it with thy might; for there is no work, nor device, nor knowledge, nor wisdom, in the grave, whither thou goest.
Ecclesiastes

When the bastard can do no more—neither see more minutely, nor hear, nor smell, nor taste, nor perceive by touch—and a finer investigation is needed, then the genuine comes in as having a tool for distinguishing more finely.
Democritus

CONTENTS

Contents

ACKNOWLEDGMENTS

Research for this book and much of the writing were supported by a Summer Stipend from the National Endowment for the Humanities and a West Virginia University Summer Grant for Research. A grant from the College of Liberal Arts and Department of English at Texas A&M University facilitated completion of the last stages of work on the volume. The Library of Congress, Research Facilities Office, assigned to me a splendidly situated study for extended periods of research in that library's peerless collections. Librarians at the Library of Congress Rare Book Room and General Reading Room generously facilitated my access to those collections. The staffs of the Folger Shakespeare Library and of the Carl H. Pforzheimer Shelley and His Circle Collection provided access to rare materials that were valuable and even essential in the course of this project.

For allocation of time for research and writing, funds for travel, and various other forms of support, I gratefully acknowledge the help of Kjell Meling (Pennsylvania State University, Altoona), Rudy Almasy (Chair of the Department of English at West Virginia University), Dean Tom Knight (now at Colorado State University and formerly Dean of the College of Arts and Sciences at West Virginia University), Hamlin Hill (Head of the Department of English at Texas A&M University), and the Interdisciplinary Group for Historical Literary Study at Texas A&M. At West Virginia University, Dean Gerald Lang and the Benedum Distinguished Professors also contributed materially to the completion of this project.

I hope that the notes to this volume record adequately my debts to published work, and I wish to acknowledge here the intellectual debts that I owe to three scholars and friends whose critical exchanges with me—numerous, long, and hard—lie behind the development of arguments in this book: among Romanticists, Daniel P. Watkins; among philosophers, Eugene Schlossberger; and among social scientists who write on ideology, Kimberly Hoagwood. I gladly acknowledge conceptual debts to Rod Jellema, no less for his work on Plotinus than his knowledge of Milton. Hilary Hoagwood was helpful in matters of bibliographical detail.

I wish also to acknowledge debts to former teachers—Joseph Wittreich, Jr., John Howard, the late John Kinnaird, and the late Gayle Smith, all of whom stimulated and developed my interest and education in the philosophy and politics of Romanticism—sine qua non.

At key junctures, E. B. Murray responded generously with textual advice and guidance on troublesome fine points. Donald H. Reiman answered queries, talked helpfully with me on matters Shelleyan and skeptical, and guided me to documents that I would not otherwise have known. Robert Boenig has been generously helpful in matters involving the classical Greek.

Members of graduate seminars that I conducted at West Virginia University and at Texas A&M University provided enjoyable and productive discussions of issues relevant to this book: Gale Acuff, Martina Domico, and Marjean Purinton were among them.

I want also to thank three audiences, critical and kind, for their responses to portions of this book's argument: the Washington Area Romanticists Group (especially Pat Story, Neil Fraistat, and Joseph Sitterson), the Southeastern Nineteenth-Century Studies Association, and the Interdisciplinary Group for Historical Literary Study at Texas A&M. According to Antiphon the Sophist, "One's character must necessarily grow like that with which one spends the greater part of the day." For good days of intellectual work, I thank colleagues in those organizations.

Several decades ago, Barbara Hoagwood, my mother, first puzzled me with some of the arguments from Descartes that are treated in this book—the dreamer hypothesis and the cogito argument. Through the years of this project, as before, she has been unfailingly supportive and encouraging, and to her this book is gratefully dedicated.

PROLOGUE

This book is a study of the ways of thinking that are embodied in Shelley's philosophical prose. Its narrower aim is to analyze Shelley's prose works; its broader aim is to articulate the larger philosophical spectrum in which his work takes an intelligible place. That larger philosophical spectrum is the skeptical tradition, involving a set of philosophical methods, tendencies, and procedures that I shall identify and illustrate in Chapter 1. Skeptical methods characterize, in one way or another, some of the most influential philosophical work from the pre-Socratics through the Renaissance. Skeptical argumentation also appears, though differently, in Descartes, Hume, Kant, Marx, and many philosophers of our own lifetime. That claim, however, must constantly be qualified by a principle that makes up one of the methodological assumptions of this book: that every articulation is conditioned importantly by its own historical specificity.

In fact, Marxist and contemporary ideological theories constitute a variety of skeptical methods. Shelley's philosophical prose, according to a subsidiary thesis of this book, articulates a conceptual and methodological position that mediates between Marxism and the older forms of skeptical argumentation.

The importance of skeptical methods and traditions for Shelley's thinking has been widely understood since 1954, when C. E. Pulos presented an argument for the centrality of skepticism in Shelley's thought. This book shares an aim with Pulos's—the narrower aim of a commentary on Shelley's philosophical prose. But recent scholarship on skeptical traditions and methods (by Myles Burnyeat, Benson Mates, Nicholas Rescher, Barry Stroud, and others) has generated a deeper and more accurate understanding of skepticism than was available to Pulos. Knowledge of the skeptical tradition is substantially different from what it was thirty years ago; our understanding of Shelley's philosophical work, and its relation to that tradition, is therefore also different now.

Major studies of Shelley—including books by Donald H. Reiman, Earl R. Wasserman, Stuart Curran, Timothy Webb, Angela Leighton, and many others—have made valuable applications of the skeptical orientation to the interpretation of Shelley's poems and poetics.

This book attempts no such literary application, however, offering instead a philosophical account of Shelley's philosophical work. It has seemed to me that such an approach has been warranted for a number of reasons: when Shelley writes of the problem of knowledge, of the thought/thing dichotomy, or of the structures of thought that are related to political and economic institutions, he does so with a keen intellectual skill that deserves attention independently of his poetry. And, second, the issues with which Shelley deals, and the methods by which he engages them, are far larger than his own work: they include conceptual problems and philosophical procedures that are still vitally important. To articulate the philosophical field in which his work belongs is to contruct arguments on philosophical problems; it is not simply to offer a reading of his texts.

This book accordingly has two aims: an exposition of an intellectual context defined by philosophical skepticism, and, second, an exposition of Shelley's philosophical prose within that larger context. Analysis of Shelley's philosophy, however, has been hampered in the past, or even prevented, by serious textual problems that have persisted to the present moment: many of Shelley's "essays" are in fact manuscript fragments with a troubled history of dispersal among collections in England and America. Published editions of Shelley's prose have been afflicted with problems of textual authority and integrity, largely because holograph manuscripts, transcriptions by others, and early printed editions do not always agree and are not always available. Assembling a "text" for interpretation has been a massive difficulty, recently (and still currently) being solved by the editorial work of scholars including Reiman, Webb, Kenneth Neill Cameron, and E. B. Murray.

Beyond textual problems, however, lie important conceptual issues that are still being worked out. Dismissals of Shelley's thought, by T. S. Eliot, F. R. Leavis, and others, were countered by Platonists (including James A. Notopoulos and Neville Rogers), by writers sensitive to Shelley's scientific knowledge (Carl Grabo, for example, and Desmond King-Hele), and by scholars—chiefly Cameron—who showed how Shelley's thought is related to political issues and conflicts of the period. Wasserman's studies of Shelley's poems, then, offered a learned, subtle, and contextual account of the poet's work within the framework of what Shelley called the "intellectual system."

Pulos's contribution, thus, was largely that he showed how skepticism as a philosophical orientation unifies all these elements in Shelley's thought and work. Shelley's treatments of immaterialism, Platonism, political radicalism, and even Christianity can be shown to be coherent because skeptical premises and aims are common to all of his discussions.[1] The maturity and cogency of Shelley's thought appear when the hostile charges of confusion are met with the kind of organizing vision that Pulos mapped out.

One of the most surprising things that has appeared to me recurrently, in the course of writing this book, is in fact the pervasiveness of those skeptical arguments. The extent to which natural science in Britain was built upon skeptical premises (as in the early Royal Society), the extent to which Plato's dialogues were long understood as skeptical texts rather than articulations of transcendental dogma, and the extent to which radical political thought and action during the Regency allied themselves with skeptical argumentation are even more impressive than Pulos had suggested.

Rather than attempting a summary pointing to the general orientation of skepticism, however, I have aimed in this book at a very different sort of project: a more rigorous analysis of Shelley's concepts and intellectual methods, in the context of skepticism as Shelley found it in the philosophical discourse of his contemporaries and their traditions.

The novelty of this approach in Shelley studies warrants some explanation. What I propose to analyze are concepts, not "texts" in the sense of independent verbal structures. Often statements and arguments by Shelley are available and intact, even when his texts are not. Beyond that practical consideration lies a theoretical distinction. The sort of exposition that consists of a summary, paraphrase, and discussion or appreciation of a text or texts is very different from an analysis of relevant concepts. The state of Shelley's texts makes the expository paraphrase misleading, in many cases, or even impossible; and further, such an expository paraphrase begs important questions about the nature of Shelley's philosophical project. Such a procedure assumes, for example, that Shelley produced essays to be approved as completed articulations of positions, or even to be revered (to judge from the language of some commentators). Alternatively, Shelley can be understood as offering and employing a philosophical methodology: that is, an analysis of intellectual procedures and aims, or a set of such procedures and aims. Further, the concepts that he raises for discussion are assumed, by the expository paraphrase, to be expressed in the essays or texts; alternatively, they could be nominated for analysis. To assume the independence and coherence of a text is to presuppose the working-out of positions; skeptical discourse often works in another way, undermining and obviating such positions. A critical method that presupposes the presence of doctrine (however tentatively affirmed) can misrepresent the nature of some skeptical procedures.

Some kinds of literary explications often manifest another tendency that is inimical to skeptical argumentation. When the ultimate aim of a critical act is the disclosure of what a text *says* (e.g., the establishment of Shelley's doctrine of probability or his concept of the "One Mind"), commentators can be inhibited from a genuinely critical analysis of those concepts. Philosophers tend to proceed in such matters differently from literary critics: philosophers commonly respect texts, but not to the point of blinding themselves to the implications of concepts articulated within those texts. One sometimes has the sense, reading literary studies of Romanticism, that their writers and readers care not at all about the problems of time, space, or personal identity but care intensely and reverently for what Wordsworth or Shelley *said* about time, space, or personal identity. The evidence of Shelley's prose shows repeatedly that he did care about those problems and others (including the mind-body problem, the dialectic of freedom and determinism, and the problem of metaphysical assumptions inscribed in the language of discourse).

Using the methods of conceptual analysis and procedures belonging to the traditions of skeptical dialectic, I have sought in this book to offer an argument about how Shelley's philosophical work can be approached (i.e., a methodology) and, second, a clarification of the philosophical cruxes to which he returns repeatedly. The context of that methodology and of those crucial arguments is defined largely by skeptical discourse, including work by David Hume, Sir William Drummond, and, behind them, the continually changing tradition of skepticism that arises in ancient Greek philosophy. Aided by the recent philosophical scholarship that I have mentioned above and by a fresh examination of the central philosophical texts on which Shelley relied (Drummond's *Academical Questions,* for instance), I have tried to analyze Shelley's arguments from a vantage point within their own philosophical context.

That project has involved another methodological feature that distinguishes this book from others on related topics: this book is not about poetry or poetics, nor does it presuppose the supremacy of poetry or poetics as a goal of all Shelley's work. It seeks instead to analyze Shelley's philosophical arguments as though they had philosophical importance.

Among the clear and original studies of Shelley's prose, one—Michael Henry Scrivener's *Radical Shelley*—offers a useful example of the kinds of contributions that have been made by studies that assume Shelley's poetry or poetics as an ultimate end. Writing of the *Defence of Poetry,* Scrivener says that for Shelley "poetry is the source of social creativity." Poetic theory is thus assumed as a centerpiece for Shelley's social philosophy. That choice assigns poetry a place in the conceptual foreground, where it would not necessarily belong if his philosophical prose were considered on its own terms. With every justification, students of Shelley have been led by an admiration of his poems and of his poetics; and Shelley does say, in the *Defence,* many things that warrant an assertion like Scrivener's. Similarly, P. M. S. Dawson's *Unacknowledged Legislator* offers important interpretations of Shelley's poems in the light of his political thinking (and, along the way, important textual scholarship on Shelley's prose as well). But the assumed teleology of poetic discourse, whereby Shelley's career takes on coherence as everything in it points toward a poem or poetics, and whereby commentary on Shelley is also bound to treat poetry and poetics as an ultimate end or aim, is unnecessary. Valuable results can follow from other assumptions.

In point of fact, it is not the case that Shelley's philosophical prose was designed to enhance his poetic products. Methodologically, the foregrounding of poetry and poetics in every discussion of Shelley's work aligns perspective with a bias. For example, the argument of the *Defence of Poetry* involves a particular rhetorical occasion, an instance of debate, and within that situation Shelley allows his discourse to be tilted toward the aims that he has immediately in view (including especially his ongoing debate with Peacock). But it might be a mistake to subordinate Shelley's political and metaphysical arguments in *other* essays to his sentences about poetry in the *Defence.* That subordination is what occurs whenever Shelley's sentences about poetry are allowed to serve as a summary of his thinking on politics or metaphysics. To assume any conceptual centerpiece other than poetry is to realign perspective entirely on Shelley's arguments. The *Defence of Poetry* is not the only, or even the most philosophically interesting, prose work of Shelley's, and its specific purposes do not necessarily dominate his philosophical discourse generally. To approach that philosophical discourse on its own terms is to generate insights that are not available within an assumed teleology of the poetic product.

My work is indebted to Dawson's and to Scrivener's, and also to another important study of the *Defence of Poetry,* John W. Wright's *Shelley's Myth of Metaphor.* But Wright also assumes poetry and poetics as an ultimate aim and end of the discourse; this assumption mandates certain narrow limitations on the arguments and conclusions that Wright can offer. For Shelley, Wright says, "culture is intrinsically and entirely poetry for the mind"; bluntly, "metaphor must be the basic unit and genetic principle of the world poem which constitutes reality for the mind." Wright's analysis of Shelley's concept of the synthetic imagination is insightful, and there is ample warrant for his conclusions about the *Defence;* but if poetry and the *Defence of Poetry* function as commanding centerpieces, the resulting worldview will be limited by poetic purposes.

More extremely, recent applications of what is called deconstruction in Shelley's criticism go farther toward a reductive view of Shelley's works, until they are said to be chiefly or solely about themselves. Jean Hall, not a deconstruction critic, to be sure, nevertheless reflects this tendency when she says that "poetry must become all in all for him [Shelley]," slighting thus the poet's political and ideological commitments. The reductive individualism of this approach appears when Hall celebrates Shelley's "creation of a poetic universe that everywhere embodies himself." This fantasy of selfishness distorts Shelley's thought; the supposition of a universe as an extended self is monstrous, Shelley says. The issues with which Shelley characteristically engages his work entail society more than self, ideology more than psychology, and political argument rather than narcissistic projection.

Another form of critical reduction takes places in the kind of deconstruction that limits discourse to intertextuality: Julia Kristeva, for example, says that a text "situates itself at the junction of many texts of which it is at once the rereading, the accentuation, the condensation, the displacement, and the profound extension." It is a premature contraction of that extensiveness, however, to say, as Tilottama Rajan does, that texts of Romantic literature are limited to "the restless process of self-examination." To confront the ideological issues engaged by Shelley's prose is to pass beyond what Rajan calls the "search of a model of discourse which accommodates rather than simplifies its ambivalence toward the inherited equation of art with idealization." Shelley's philosophical prose is not about his poems, nor about itself; to lay down as a presupposition that all texts are about themselves and other texts is to blind oneself to the conceptual range of that prose and to trivialize its issues by reducing them to narcissistic preoccupations. Skeptical discourse reaches outward toward engagement as well as inward toward reflexivity.

Shelley does write of language, but his concept is a constructive epistemological principle and an important social insight as well. One sort of deconstruction treats indeterminacy of meaning as a sign of self-reference (I am thinking of Paul de Man's essay "Shelley Disfigured"); in contrast, Shelley acknowledges (as I have said elsewhere) that meanings are inventional, free, fictional, indeterminate, and variable. But Shelley makes a political tool of that principle, with which he can counter material oppression and whereby human beings can forge a new social order. The internality of self-reference is a dogma as foreign to that political project as the tyrannous reifications of the past.

Shelley's sentence about language and freedom in the *Defence*— "Language is arbitrarily produced by the imagination and has relation to thoughts alone"—surely implies, as William Keach has said, that "language is created by a voluntary act of mind"; I would say further that Shelley assigns language purely mental reference as well. And I agree with Keach that Shelley here suggests simultaneously that the individualistic sense of freedom and voluntariness is mitigated by a larger perspective, whereby speakers and writers "inherit a language produced by previous arbiters, a language fraught . . . with the despotic, capricious arbitrariness of dead metaphor." The idea that language is mental production does not imply that language is free play for each private individual user; in fact, the notion of code, which depersonalizes utterance, politicizes the issue; internalized and personalized constructions of self-reference are foreign to the theory that Shelley articulates, which instead assimilates the arbitrariness and mentalistic ontology of language with paradigms of reification and tyranny in the political and social world.

Furthermore, outside the *Defence* Shelley's philosophical prose

xix

deals with those politicized manifestations of reification and tyranny directly, and not by way of their relevance to poetry. My conviction that Shelley's arguments have relevance on their own terms has been rewarded by a series of disclosures that would not have been available to me if I had assumed a poetic final purpose. As Cameron has argued, Shelley's *Philosophical View of Reform* offers one of the most advanced political arguments of his time; the significance of that argument is simply invisible when all one wishes to do is to offer another interpretation of *Prometheus Unbound*. So many complexities and ranges of significance arise within the philosophical arguments themselves that it is useful—perhaps needful—to examine those arguments in their own terms before converting them to a gloss on the poems.

For those reasons, I have excluded Shelley's poems from the subject matter of this book. I would not be misunderstood as denying their importance or relevance to Shelley's skepticism, but in the figurative discourse of poetry and in the rhetorical occasion of the *Defence of Poetry,* skeptical methods take very specific forms, and I have become convinced increasingly, while working on this book, that even an elementary understanding of those basic methods is not yet to be had within published commentary on Shelley.

I have also moved toward a conviction that Shelley's arguments often have persisting relevance for philosophical discourse. To mention only two examples: his work can offer a bridge between the epistemological projects of the ancient Greeks (philosophers on whose systems Karl Marx began his own career) and the ideological theories of Marx, Engels, and their successors. Second, Shelley's arguments on sign theory take on special interest when they are seen in the dual context of earlier theories of language and modern developments in the theories of signs and significance. A book like Eugene Goodheart's *Skeptic Disposition in Contemporary Criticism* (which does not mention Shelley) can be understood as in part a gloss on the same issues and methods with which Shelley worked. In a highly generalized way, Jonathan Culler calls attention to the relevant cluster of issues: writers as diverse as Roland Barthes, Harold Bloom, René Girard, and Shoshana Felman concern themselves less with meanings of texts than with the enabling structures and processes, political, psychological, or philosophical, that produce both texts and meanings. This tendency obviously connects the theoretical projects of those writers with the work of Marxist and ideological critics, including Raymond Williams, Fredric Jameson, Terry Eagleton, and Jerome J. McGann. In important ways, an often unacknowledged scaffolding of skeptical procedures, transforming themselves from antiquity, connect these contemporary projects with Shelley's skeptical discourse.

Like the methods of most of those contemporary theorists, Shelley's methods of argument characteristically involve a dialectical conception of history. Premises and procedures associated with this way of thinking affect virtually every argument that he makes. I have tried to be as persistent as Shelley in pressing the implications of this sort of theory, and a word is due here about the kind of philosophy that I have thus undertaken.

Shelley employs (in *A Philosophical View of Reform,* for example) both a philosophy of history and a history of philosophy: contextual methods are essential to his arguments, because he affirms a constant, active, and reciprocal relationship between (1) human beings, along with their cultural products, and (2) their natural and social environments. This way of thinking about philosophy is commonly associated, now, with Marxism: in Engels's *Anti-Dühring* a related set of methodological assumptions is articulated, relevant arguments appear in *The German Ideology* by Marx and Engels, and the historical materialism of *Capital* assumes the centrality of historical context in the production of culture. Behind Marx and Engels lies Hegel's philosophy of history, and as Lukács has pointed out in *History and Class Consciousness,* the Marxist transformation of Hegel's idea of cultural self-consciousness into a concept of class consciousness is actually a refinement of the dialectical and conceptual methods and assumptions of the earlier philosophical system. Shelley was largely or wholly uninfluenced by the German philosophy of history, but his own thinking exhibits everywhere a relationship to the skeptical tradition of dialectical thought that also lies behind Hegel as well as Marx and Engels. (Marx and Engels point out the skeptical nature of Hegel's methods, as I show in the second chapter, below.)

Shelley's preface to *Prometheus Unbound* illustrates this kind of historicism: Shelley says, "Poets, not otherwise than philosophers, painters, sculptors and musicians, are in one sense the creators and in another the creations of their age." Human beings and their artistic or intellectual products stand in a dialectical relationship with natural and social environments, as I have said. To quote Albert William Levi, whose *Philosophy as Social Expression* deals with this same methodological issue, "The argument in favor of contextualism implies that the very nature of a philosophy as such is that to discuss it apart from its author and its age is to falsify and misunderstand it." In illustration, Levi cites R. G. Collingwood's "profound skepticism with regard to the historical continuity of meaning":

> If there were a permanent problem P, we could ask, "What did Kant, or Leibniz, or Berkeley, think about P", and if that question could be answered, we could then go on to ask, "Was Kant, or Leibniz, or Berkeley, right in what he thought about P?" But what is thought to be a permanent problem P is really a number of transitory problems p1, p2, p3 . . . whose individual peculiarities are blurred by the historical myopia of the person who lumps them together under the one name P.

The answers to philosophical questions that are offered by Plato, Shelley, Kant, or Marx cannot possibly (so this argument implies) be identical; historically specific conditions define the questions, which, like the answers, are therefore different for the different writers. For Shelley, the problem reaches across space as well as time, so that European Christianity is an entirely different sort of system, charged with entirely different sorts of values, when it is articulated in India as opposed to England.

A recurrent methodological assumption of my own in this book, with which I have sought to explicate and analyze related arguments of Shelley's, is perhaps less absolutist than Collingwood's dogma of irreducible difference: I have sought to identify recognizably paradigmatic arguments and also the differences conditioned by their historical occasions. Again to quote Levi, "New problems arise, but older problems persist, and it is generally possible in the history of philosophy to recognize and to discriminate the individual twists from the ancient residues." The contextual method allows both sorts of investigation and both kinds of interpretive claim.

McGann has laid it down as a rule of his "historical criticism" that "any criticism which abolishes the distance between its own (present) setting and its (removed) subject matter—any criticism which argues an unhistorical symmetry between the practicing critic and the descending work—will be, to that extent, undermined as criticism." To adopt or reproduce ideological assumptions of the works we study—without even acknowledging their problematic and ideological status—is to fail in the critical task: in our difference from the past lies our knowledge of the past; in large measure our knowledge of the present can also be said to depend on our knowledge of that difference from the past. With a change in the setting of an articulation, an essential change is wrought in the articulation itself. Accordingly, McGann commends afresh a methodological principle of Arthur O. Lovejoy: that criticism consists in large part in defining differences, in discriminating a plurality among "dynamic factors in the history of thought and art."

Lovejoy's method, however, is articulated not in the famous essay on Romanticism, which McGann cites, but rather in the polemical essay with which Lovejoy begins his retrospective collection, *Essays in the History of Ideas*. It is following Lovejoy's own method to press here for a discrimination between his history of ideas and the kind of ideological analysis that this book employs. Lovejoy writes of an "idea-complex" (he happens to use "nature" here, but another would do for the methodological point) that it exhibits a fundamental identity across the centuries—in the third century (in Tertullian) and the eighteenth (in English writers): "The fundamental identity of the idea, and of the logic of the reasonings to which it gave rise, is not annulled by the dissimilarity of the concomitant ideas with which it was associated, nor from the differing preoccupations and temperamental biases of the writers into whose thinking it entered."

I would discriminate, as Lovejoy does, between "the identity *in* the differences, and the differences against the background of the identity"; that principle is one of his most important contributions to theoretical inquiry. But ideological criticism differs from this now-traditional history of ideas in an important way. The historian of ideas posits a fundamental identity of the idea, conditioned by idealistic variety ("concomitant ideas") or by sheer individualism ("temperamental biases"); ideological criticism resists dislocating the idea from its historical context, as a fundamental identity that survives local differences. Marx and Engels characterize such a dislocation as inversion, as I shall be showing below; McGann reduces *The German Ideology* to that central principle.

The difference in method between traditional history of ideas and contemporary ideological criticism is brought to focus in some forms of what is called discourse analysis. Here I will mention two examples: the linguistic arguments of Teun van Dijk, on "the relations of verbal features and social acts," and Roger Fowler's treatment of literature as social discourse. The dialectical relationship between language and social structure, as Fowler seeks to show, appears in literary as well as nonliterary discourse. The foregrounding of the social context of any utterance prevents a reification of a supposed fundamental identity of the idea across centuries. Differences are conditioned not only by ideational and individualistic vagaries but also radically and originally by the social and historical context of utterance.

A different set of assumptions, however, underlies another sort of procedure that I have used in this book: conceptual and linguistic analysis (associated with philosophers such as Ludwig Wittgenstein and J. L. Austin). This method has tended often to isolate itself from historical methods altogether. Whereas, for contextualists, historicity invades the nature and determines the character of a philosophical utterance or system, for some analytical philosophers the entire history of philosophy offers no more (it sometimes appears) than a list of potential solutions to allegedly permanent problems.

These two kinds of philosophical work—that which is based on contextual and historical procedures and assumptions and that which is based on analytical assumptions of conceptual independence—have historically split American philosophy in two. What is called history of philosophy is treated sometimes as a discipline almost utterly distinct from what is called analysis of concepts. Kant is the last major thinker for whom these two schools share an admiration. Generally, historicists tend to admire and discuss Hegel, and often Marx; analytical thinkers tend to cite Wittgenstein, Hume, and sometimes no one.

In contrast, John B. Thompson has recently argued that methods of discourse analysis provide a useful framework for the analysis of ideology. From its historical origins (among the French Ideologues and then with Marx and Engels), ideological theory has been marked by controversy, but, says Thompson, "it is only in recent years that this theory has been enriched and elaborated through a reflection on *language*." This integration of linguistic and conceptual analysis with a historical framework enriches (I would argue) both forms of philosophical practice; as Thompson says, "To explore the interrelations between language and ideology is to turn away from the analysis of well-formed sentences or systems of signs, focusing instead on the ways in which expressions serve as a means of action and interaction, a medium through which history is produced and society is reproduced."

Behind both analytical and historical methods in philosophy lie skeptical procedures and arguments, and so powerful are these skeptical arguments that both schools are empowered by them to undermine and virtually invalidate the exclusive character of each other's projects. The principles of historical relativity that appear everywhere in Marx and Engels derive from ancient tropes of relativity that are codified in Sextus Empiricus' *Outlines of Pyrrhonism* (among other works). The critical methods of conceptual and linguistic analysis and the dialectical elenchus whose refinements constitute analytical arguments are also skeptical procedures with an ancient history. The dogmas of historical materialism (including the strongest senses of the word "determine," amounting to a concept of cause) are liable to a skeptical critique, and so are the hypostatic autonomous concepts that make up the materials of some analytical philosophy. Skeptical procedure like Shelley's is capable of restoring the contexts in which concepts are inexorably to be located and employed.

This book, then, proceeds through three sections that are designed to be useful independently and yet also integrally related. An account of the skeptical paradigm of argument opens this book, because it is within the intellectual context here defined that Shelley's work is composed. Here my organization is roughly historical, though conflicts and transformations among issues are more central to the argument than assumed chronological progression. It is in fact part of my argument that the assumption of a steady coherent progress of ideas over time is a methodological feature that has dangerous implications.

The second section of this book then offers an analysis of the central concepts in a dialectical theory of history and in an ideological criticism. Such theories, including Shelley's, involve complex relationships among concepts like superstructure, determine, and (among the French Ideologues and then Marxists) ideology. I have therefore tried to approach Shelley's thought according to a more rigorous analysis of these concepts than I have been able to find anywhere outside professional philosophical scholarship.

Finally, the third section of this book offers a sustained analysis of

A Philosophical View of Reform. I have chosen this work because in it the arguments (metaphysical, epistemological, and immediately political) that Shelley formulates elsewhere come together in his most comprehensive (though still fragmentary) philosophical work. To treat this work, with its own identifiable political urgency and philosophical methods, as a culmination of the analysis is an expository device that places Shelley's concerns, methods, and accomplishments in a very different perspective from that which emerges from the more narrowly poetic concerns of earlier studies.

Readers who are primarily interested in what Shelley said, rather than in philosophical analyses of the problems involved, may want to proceed directly to this third section. But the issues involved in that conceptual analysis are sufficiently sophisticated that I have thought it worthwhile to examine those issues and arguments with some rigor and in some detail.

The organization of this book, however, reflects one of its arguments: I proceed from skepticism to ideological theory to Shelley because of conceptual linkages among those systems. Several different concepts of ideology are now current and sometimes vitally important in political philosophy and in discourse analysis. Many of these concepts of ideology reflect arguments from skeptical philosophical tradition. It is not always clear what a given theorist means by the word "ideology," and conflicting senses of that word are sometimes wholly incompatible. What are in my judgment the most powerful among those critiques of intellectual systems that go under the rubric of ideological theory, however, are demonstrably forms of skeptical arguments with an ancient pedigree; history and circumstance condition the theoretical constructs, and this methodological assumption in fact belongs to skeptical tradition. This linkage of ideology with philosophical tradition is sufficiently important to warrant a fairly extended analysis, and I offer one in the second part of this book. The task was especially urgent, I felt, for two reasons. First, theorists who do not offer precise definitions of the term "ideology" are often using that word to talk about entirely different things; identical statements thus mean opposite things, and in heated polemic the confusion worsens. Second, some ideological theorists (Karl Marx among them) have sought self-consciously to obscure or to deny the fact that their own dialectical arguments are rooted in skeptical tradition; it is a matter of historical record that Marx had mastered and practiced these ancient forms of argument.

The nature of ideological criticism is fundamentally different from the sort of scholarship that used to be called "source studies." For an argument about the importance in Shelley's work of passages from the *Symposium,* it is germane that he translated that Platonic dialogue in July 1818 and that he turned to a Latin translation by Ficino when he had difficulty with passages in the Greek. But for ideological criticism, even when this criticism employs concepts articulated by Marx or Engels or Godwin or Plato, it is often irrelevant whether the author of a work under analysis was acquainted with the theories employed. Ideological theory locates a critic outside the conceptual framework of a work under analysis; it is a way of talking about the work from a vantage point outside its own ideological absorption. The fact that Marx had read and admired Shelley is no doubt interesting, but that fact is also irrelevant to the sort of argument that I have undertaken here.

Two points of method that I have assumed and employed throughout this book, therefore, I shall state here, and then I shall be content to let these methods be judged by their fruits. First, skepticism furnishes a method of talking critically about systems of ideas, attitudes, value apprehensions, and behavioral systems. The sort of critique that has come to be called "ideological criticism" is a recognizable version of this generic form of critical argument. Second, no claim is put forward in this book to the effect that direct influence obtains among Shelley, Marx, Engels, and Marxists; instead, the intellectual systems analyzed and employed by Shelley, Marx, Engels, and Marxists are independently related to forms of argument older than the Platonic dialogues. This assertion does not deprecate but opens up the significance of transformations that these writers effect in the earlier and codified formulations.

NOTE ON TEXTS

For some of Shelley's prose works very good texts are readily available; for others, good texts have been more difficult to establish. Much of Shelley's prose remained fragmentary in manuscript at the time of his death, and textual problems accordingly appear among published editions. For example, what is sometimes treated as a unitary work, *Treatise on Morals,* is elsewhere presented as two separate series of manuscript fragments, entitled *Speculations on Metaphysics* and *Speculations on Morals.* What are sometimes presented as two separate works, *On the Christian Religion* and *On Miracles,* are elsewhere edited as one unitary *Essay on Miracles and Christian Doctrine.* The conventional kind of study that would offer a set of readings of Shelley's "essays" would have to assume a text of each essay. Many of the texts are problematic, and so such a study would, in many cases, face serious difficulties.

Such problems have been adequately solved, however, in some particular cases. For *A Philosophical View of Reform,* the text that appears in the long-standard Julian edition (by Roger Ingpen and Walter E. Peck) presents the uncanceled portions of Shelley's text adequately, as Reiman has said in the introductory matter published with his own impeccable transcription of Shelley's manuscript (in *Shelley and His Circle*). *A Philosophical View of Reform* is the only essay of Shelley's for which I offer in this book a sustained analytical commentary depending upon an edited text. Otherwise, my study concerns Shelley's philosophical methods and statements, but my argument does not, in any other case, rest on a single editorial construction of a particular text.

I have used the conventional titles for Shelley's works (explaining my choice in each case in which an essay has had alternative titles); I have consistently respected the assignment of dates of composition as precise as the evidence will allow, and I have taken quotations from the editions and manuscript transcriptions that are indicated below. I have not used one single edition as a source of all quotations from Shelley's prose because so far no one edition offers the best text of all of Shelley's prose.

With one important limitation, however, a good text of every passage of Shelley's prose cited in this book is available. That limitation concerns matters of total textual integrity—the ordering and coherence—of some of Shelley's fragments. I have thus avoided arguments depending, in those cases, on assumptions of such a textual integrity. Even where those problems are most severe (in the *Treatise on Morals* or *Speculations on Metaphysics* and *Speculations on Morals*), an exact transcription of Shelley's holograph manuscripts makes available an accurate text of Shelley's statements, though not necessarily a definitive ordering of them. In cases where good texts of the essays are readily available—for example, the edition by Reiman and Powers of *On Love, On Life,* and *A Defence of Poetry,* and *A Philosophical View of Reform* as it appears in the Julian edition and in manuscript transcription in *Shelley and His Circle*—even that limitation has been adequately overcome.

My quotations from Shelley's works have been taken from the following sources. Notes on the dates and textual sources of these works appear with first references in the body of this book.

A Philosophical View of Reform: The Complete Works of Percy Bysshe Shelley, eds. Roger Ingpen and Walter E. Peck (London: Ernest Benn, 1926–30), 7:3–55. I have also used the transcription of Shelley's holograph manuscript that appears in *Shelley and His Circle,* ed. Donald H. Reiman (Cambridge, Mass.: Harvard Univ. Press, 1973), 6:945–1066.

On Love, On Life, and *A Defence of Poetry: Shelley's Poetry and Prose,* eds. Reiman and Sharon B. Powers (New York: Norton, 1977).

Treatise on Morals (*Speculations on Metaphysics* and *Speculations on Morals*): My documentation refers to the location of each cited passage in the Ingpen and Peck edition. I have, however, used for my text the manuscript transcriptions that appear in the following publications: For the portions of the manuscript that are located in the Bodleian Library, Oxford, Tatsuo Tokoo, "Bodleian Shelley Mss. Re-examined: A Re-edited Text of Some of Shelley's Prose Works in the Bodleian Mss.," *The Scientific Reports of the Kyoto Prefectural University,* No. 33 (1981):16–53. For the portion that is located in the Carl H. Pforzheimer Library, I have used the manuscript transcription by Kenneth Neill Cameron that appears in *Shelley and His Circle,* ed. Cameron

(1970), 4:734–37. Although this machinery of multiple documentation for each passage may at first appear complex, in fact, it provides readers of this book with the ease of a ready reference while also assuring the accuracy of the text of each quotation.

Essay on Miracles and Christian Doctrine: "A New Shelley Text: Essay on Miracles and Christian Doctrine," ed. Claude Brew, *Keats-Shelley Memorial Bulletin,* 28 (1977):22–28.

Letters: The Letters of Percy Bysshe Shelley, ed. Frederick L. Jones, 2 vols. (Oxford: Clarendon Press, 1964).

For Shelley's other prose works, citations refer to the Ingpen and Peck edition.

ABBREVIATIONS

Ac.	Cicero, *Academica,* trans. Horace Rackham (London: William Heinemann, 1933). (The Loeb Classical Library edition.)
AQ	Sir William Drummond, *Academical Questions* (London: W. Bulmer, 1805).
DL	Diogenes Laertius, *Lives of Eminent Philosophers,* trans. R. D. Hicks, 2 vols. (1925; rpt. London: William Heinemann; Cambridge, Mass.: Harvard Univ. Press, 1972–79). (The Loeb Classical Library edition.)
I&P	*The Complete Works of Percy Bysshe Shelley,* eds. Roger Ingpen and Walter E. Peck, 10 vols. (London: Ernest Benn, 1926–30).
Letters	*The Letters of Percy Bysshe Shelley,* ed. Frederick L. Jones, 2 vols. (Oxford: Clarendon Press, 1964).
PH	Sextus Empiricus, *Outlines of Pyrrhonism (Pyrrhonistic Hypotyposes),* trans. R. G. Bury (1933; rpt. Cambridge, Mass.: Harvard Univ. Press; London: William Heinemann, 1939). (The Loeb Classical Library edition.)
R&P	*Shelley's Poetry and Prose,* eds. Donald H. Reiman and Sharon B. Powers (New York: Norton, 1977).
SC	*Shelley and His Circle,* eds. Kenneth Neill Cameron and Donald H. Reiman, 8 vols. to date (Cambridge, Mass.: Harvard Univ. Press, 1961–86).

I

SHELLEY AND
PHILOSOPHICAL
SKEPTICISM

SKEPTICAL METHODOLOGY

Shelley's philosophical prose treats such a variety of topics—metaphysics, morality, politics, poetry, love, and life—that the unity of such a corpus can hardly be a set of recurrent doctrines. Shelley does suggest that another kind of unity belongs to his philosophical work: he calls it "the intellectual system" or "the intellectual philosophy" (R&P, pp. 476, 477).[1] This unifying system is a methodology rather than a set of beliefs or doctrines. That is, the intellectual system includes methods, procedures, and postulates useful for analysis of problems. In a secondary sense, a methodology is a critical analysis of such a set of procedures. Shelley characterizes his methodology in this way: it is a "strict scepticism concerning all assertions" (I&P, 7:62).[2] This sort of skepticism, then, is a critical procedure for the analysis of concepts; it concerns assertions rather than things or the world. Shelley can and does write about things and about the world, as I shall be showing in some detail; but his philosophical method involves a rigorously dialectical analysis of assertions about such things.

In its classical form, skepticism comprises paradigmatic arguments that appear (with differences) in several ancient texts. Foremost among the ancient skeptical works are Diogenes Laertius' *Lives of Eminent Philosophers,* Sextus Empiricus' *Outlines of Pyrrhonism,* and Cicero's dialogues, especially the *Academica.* Shelley was familiar with the skeptical arguments from these texts: he annotated Diogenes' work, for example, and said of Cicero that he "is, in my estimation, one of the most admirable characters the world ever produced."[3] Shelley's use of skepticism is more, however, than a case of his using particular sources such as these: issues and ways of arguing that are expressed in these works recur (though often with significant differences in form and application) throughout European and British philosophy, and Shelley was well read in this philosophical literature.[4]

As Pierre Couissin, David Sedley, and other historians of philosophy have shown, the skeptical arguments ("tropes," they are sometimes called) were for the ancients what they are again for Shelley: not so much a body of doctrines as a dialectical method for debate.[5] Skeptical arguments are intended to undermine the authority of a dogmatist; they are not designed to produce an alternative dogma. Thus, skeptical argumentation is a largely negative procedure, as Shelley emphasizes in *On Life*.

In that essay, Shelley cites Sir William Drummond, whom he elsewhere names "the most acute metaphysical critic of the age" (*Letters, 2*:142). Drummond was a contemporary whom Shelley had met and whose *Academical Questions* was evidently Shelley's favorite work of modern philosophy.[6] That book, taking its title from Cicero and from the skeptical tradition that Cicero explained and defended,[7] offers a skeptical critique of several philosophical systems, using the dialectical methods of the ancient writers and adding others from modern philosophers including David Hume. The paradigmatic arguments and methods that recur over history, with specific changes conditioned by their historical occasions, make up a recognizable skeptical tradition.[8] Throughout this book, I shall be showing that Shelley's philosophical prose belongs to this tradition, though the arguments are transformed in his work, as they are within every specific expression. The world of the ancients was not the world of Regency England; in fact, it will be a subsidiary thesis of this book that historical conditions always transform the inherited systems of thought expressed within them. The relevance, application, form, and even conceptual substance of a philosophical system are changed by the circumstances of the expression, philosophy, like all discourse, being subject to conditions that are time- and place-specific.

Here, it will be useful to summarize at the outset what sort of arguments they are that make up this skeptical tradition.

The common topic of *isostheneia* is essential to the dialectical form of skeptical argument. The word denotes a balancing of arguments on both sides of a question. What results from the conflict of arguments and counterarguments, when they are equally cogent, is not (as in Hegel's dialectic) a new synthesis or resting place. Instead, what is called the equipollence of arguments produces for the skeptic *epochē,* "suspension of judgment" (*PH*, I,8,26). The only sort of outcome formally possible, therefore, for a strictly skeptical dialectic, is more dialectic: *isostheneia* discloses only what is called *ou mallon*, "the case is no more that than this." What results from argument is therefore never, for the skeptic, final belief but rather *epochē* and further dialectical argument.

One codification of the skeptical tropes that lead to *epochē* is a list of ten paradigmatic arguments. These tropes, attributed to Aenesidemus, appear in Diogenes (IX, 79–88) and in Sextus (I, 36ff.).[9] These tropes consist of arguments about the relativity of knowledge and the undecidability of some kinds of questions. In critical response to their dogmatic (and specifically Stoic) opponents, the ancient skeptics argue that absolute truth of knowledge is not apparent and not determinable. Stoics (led, in Athens, by Zeno) had argued that some thoughts or perceptions are manifestly and certainly true, in the most absolute sense; such a perception is a *katalepsis*. Their skeptical critics, including Arcesilaus and, later, Carneades (successors of Plato in the Athenian Academy), argue instead that no perception has any such guarantee. By definition, a perception of *x* is not equal to *x* itself, and that gap persists even when we have reason to think that the perception is much like *x*. In any case, the perception cannot properly be said to include more than a perception, and so the gap remains as an epistemological problem. The skeptics call this critique *akatalepsia,* the impossibility of perceiving in a perception anything more than a perception, and specifically the impossibility of perceiving in a perception its own absolute truth.

One distinction maintained among the ancient skeptics becomes important enough in Shelley's arguments that it is worth emphasis here: the ability to *know* reality (to perceive with absolute certainty the truth of *x*) is a different problem from the problem of the *existence* of such a thing as reality. In the words of Cicero, skeptics "do not deny that some truth exists but deny that it can be perceived" (*Ac.* II, 73); that is, Sextus denies the *phantasia katalepsia,* the perception that confirms its own absolute truth.

No skeptic, ancient or modern, Cicero or Shelley, is immobilized or even slowed down by the resulting suspension of judgment. "*Skepsis*" means "inquiry," and the dialectical procedures that are used to produce *epochē* are also used to generate and to serve vigorous intellectual inquiry. Cicero states the reason for this empowering potential: "We possess our power of judgment uncurtailed, and are bound by no compulsion to support all the dogmas laid down for us almost as edicts by certain masters" (*Ac.* II, 8). It is this kind of skepticism, of Cicero's *Academica,* of which Drummond says, "Philosophy, wisdom, and liberty, support each other" (xv).[10] Freedom of inquiry and freedom of action are so closely related that, in his *Letter to Lord Ellenborough* and again in his letter to the *Examiner* on the trial of Richard Carlile, Shelley produces skeptical arguments in the service of immediate political action.[11] In *A Philosophical View of Reform,* Shelley shows (with a remarkably comprehensive argument) how the critical, intellectual forms of skepticism are related to the most concrete kinds of political liberty and ethical action.[12] Part of what links the classical *skepsis* with the modern political activist is precisely this emphasis on the value of freedom.

Some forms of skepticism, however, are associated with conservative positions in politics or religion, as I shall show; such is the fideism of Erasmus and Montaigne, a religious position that relies on faith in the absence of rational certainty. For others, including Cicero, Drummond, and Shelley, the ability to live and act without dogmatic certainty and the ability to oppose every dogmatic assertion with a counterargument can together stimulate revolutionary activity in intellectual matters and sometimes in politics as well.

A distinction is conventionally made between two forms of skepticism, Pyrrhonism and Academic skepticism. I have not honored that distinction in this summary because it will be part of my argument to show that the distinction is largely impertinent. Academic skeptics are said to profess a doctrine of probability, and Pyrrhonists (chiefly Sextus and his school) are not. But Shelley's sources (including Diogenes among the ancients and Pierre Bayle among the moderns) deny the distinction.[13] The alleged doctrine of probability may also be an impertinent attribution.

A skeptical methodology is, however, recognizable. I do not mean to say that Shelley uses mechanically the exact rules specified in the numbered lists of tropes that appear among ancient texts; he knew them, but he also knew and used so many other philosophers (Drummond most of all, but also Hume and others) that direct usage of one particular skeptical text will seldom be the focus of my own discussion. Instead, I shall be showing how that methodology appears in his philosophical prose, taking "methodology" in both senses, as a set of methods for analyzing problems and also as an analysis of such methods.

It is often the case, however, that studies of Shelley's thought, including the most enlightened among them, seek among Shelley's essays a final doctrine. In the history of European and British philosophy, skepticism has regularly been treated as a crisis, an emergency, a danger to be overcome; to seek a final doctrinal resting place is a popular tendency with powerful appeal. It is no insult to say of Shelley scholars that like Plato, Saint Augustine, Descartes, Kant, and F. H. Bradley, they express and exhibit exactly this tendency. And it is often alleged that Shelley's later poems (and I am thinking of Earl R. Wasserman's influential reading of *Adonais*[14]) represent Shelley's quest for, or discovery of, such a doctrinal resting place.

My argument in this book will proceed otherwise. A thorough analysis of Shelley's poems, including *Adonais,* according to the skeptical paradigm that I shall be working out, will form the matter of other books. Here, I mean to show that Shelley's philosophical prose does not arrive at any such doctrinal resting places and that Shelley's arguments do not seek to do so.

The difference in method and assumption on which I mean to insist arises most clearly from a contrast of Shelley's statements with those of critics who are nearest to his own skepticism. I am aware of a paradox here, but analyses of Shelley's thought that are based on principles utterly alien to Shelley's skeptical framework can do little to refine conceptions of that skepticism. Studies like those by Wasserman and Pulos, alternatively, which do articulate a relevant framework, are of greater utility in this connection. My own methods will have at least this much in common with the skeptical paradigm that I discuss: my analysis will be most specifically critical of those arguments that are most germane. Conceptual analysis proceeds by an elenchus, a progressive refinement of definitions, rather than by a transmission of already formulated positions—hence the paradox that this book will be evidently most critical of those books among Shelley studies to which it is most indebted, having little to say of those works of Shelley criticism with which it has less in common.

One of the most influential of the commentaries germane to this book is Wasserman's, which offers this list of Shelley's philosophical concerns: "Is there a substantive reality independent of the mind? Or is the 'external' world only the mind's perceptions? Is there a sense in which all the thoughts of the mind are real existences?" This list of yes-or-no questions falsifies the nature of Shelley's philosophical project. It does so because it reifies "a special brand of idealism rooted in a persistent epistemological skepticism."[15] That is, Wasserman's formulations misrepresent the character of skepticism itself; skeptical argument is a procedure that is "not meant to establish the truth or falsehood of some thesis" but rather "to show that the opponent is no authority on the matters in question," as Michael Frede has recently said.[16] Skepticism such as Shelley's is a method of undermining doctrine; it is not an attempt to answer questions such as those in Wasserman's list.

Accordingly, Shelley says of the "intellectual system" that "it establishes no new truth" (R&P, 477); it leaves a "vacancy" of doctrine, and not a presence.[17] The difference, therefore, between Shelley's dialectical philosophy and the sort of paraphrases that have attempted to reify doctrines for him is thus largely theoretical. Disputes over particular positions—whether Shelley affirms, intuits, discerns, endorses, advocates, or expresses a doctrine of Beauty, God, Power, or Necessity—are irrelevant precisely because the framework of affirmation is irrelevant to the analytical project. Shelley says that metaphysical propositions (i.e., statements belonging to the intellectual philosophy) do not and cannot have reference to objects of conception (God, or the world); "They are about these conceptions" (I&P, 7:62). A statement about x must be distinguished from a statement about the statement-about-x. To put the point in another way: the subjects of philosophical discourse are the terms of the discourse itself, and not hypostatized objects supposedly existent external to the discourse. Shelley's definition of his philosophical project thus anchors it directly in skeptical dialectic: the gap between x and appearance-of-x is reproduced as a gap between a conception and the object of conception. The distinction is between an epistemological method (Shelley's skepticism) and a set of ontological claims (answers to Wasserman's questions).

The most influential book on the subject of Shelley's skepticism is Pulos's *The Deep Truth;*[18] since its publication, books on the topic have taken their start from Pulos, and mine will in this respect be no exception. I shall take up, in the following sections of this book, two philosophical cruxes on which Pulos had also focused his exposition of Shelley's thought. These issues are probability and the question of the existence of external objects. With Pulos, I agree that these issues and Shelley's handling of them both derive from skeptical tradition. I depart from Pulos's analysis, however, at just the point at which I depart also from Wasserman's and from the entire approach of literary critics like Lloyd Abbey, and that is at the point of a commitment to a presence of doctrine, affirmed however tentatively. With Abbey's comments I am not directly concerned, because his attempt to paraphrase poems has little to do with philosophical analysis, and he simply relies on others on such points.[19] But Pulos's important book calls attention to what are, in my view, exactly the most pertinent issues, backdrops, and contexts for interpretation, and so the sort of elenchus that I have described can be most fruitfully applied to arguments such as his.

Pulos handles the skeptical crux of probability as a doctrine. He handles the skeptical questions about the existence of external objects as a denial of such existence. I shall be pointing out that the skeptical approach to these problems differs significantly from whatever approach it is that leads to these doctrines. Sextus speaks for the skeptics generally when he says that "we neither deny nor affirm anything" (*PH* I, 10). *Isostheneia* produces *epochē,* a suspension of judgment, and not a doctrine at all.

THE CONCEPT OF PROBABILITY

Shelley articulates a concept of probability with which he proposes to test doctrinal and dogmatic knowledge claims. Such claims would include those of Christianity, for example, or the atheistic doctrines of materialism found among such eighteenth-century French philosophers as Baron d'Holbach. These bodies of doctrine are said to be dogmatic (see, e.g., *On Life,* in R&P, 476), because they affirm the absolute truth of what appears, just as it appears, and just as it is affirmed. Possessed of an impression, or a perception, or an idea, of *x,* a dogmatist claims to know with infallible certainty that *x* (outside the perception) is exactly as the perception represents it. The dogmatic knowledge claim does not concern only the appearance of *x* or an idea about *x;* it concerns *x.* Sextus, for example, defines "dogma" in this way: "assent to one of the non-evident objects" of inquiry (*PH* I, 13). What appears is evident (the appearance is immediately present). A

7

dogmatic claim concerns what is nonevident, such as the invisible and underlying cause of a visible perception.

In a document that Claude Brew has reconstructed and entitled *Essay on Miracles and Christian Doctrine,* Shelley mentions probability as an outcome of logical analysis when such analysis is applied to a dogmatic claim: [20]

> A doctrine pretending to be divine and therefore true may assert the most extravagant positions, and as there is no test of it except a miracle, of which it appears it is itself the test, it follows that there can be no test at all.—A doctrine pretending to be true may be brought to the test of logic and dialectics, which though not infallible often leave us in possession of a probability sufficiently strong to warrant us in conforming our actions and sentiments to it (25).

A divine doctrine asserts its own truth, pointing to miracles as evidence; but the divinity of the doctrine is the only authority for the truth of the miracle, and so (left to its own terms) the divine doctrine is a self-confirming system, immune to testing but irrelevant outside its own discourse. In contrast to an uncritical absorption in such a self-confirming system of dogma, Shelley proposes that logic and dialectics furnish tests that, though they cannot necessarily produce a truth, can produce a probability that will be sufficient to warrant us in doing certain things according to it. Whether this probability represents another doctrine (as Pulos says) or something else is a question requiring some conceptual analysis.

At the beginning of such an analysis, it is important to notice that the definition of "probability" is exactly a statement of how probability is essentially different from truth. Probability is not a version of truth, or a kind of truth, but a different sort of criterion altogether. Where truth is treated as absolute, probability is a relative property: the phrase "a probability sufficiently strong" implies a flexible range or scale of degrees of strength. And what is perhaps more important, "true" applies to a doctrine, a claim about how things are; "probability" applies instead to the guidance of "actions and sentiments." Truth concerns the nature of a thing in itself (God, in Shelley's example); probability concerns instead an internally conditioned response.

Shelley emphasizes in the *Treatise on Morals* that these analytical polarities or antitheses are themselves heuristic; they are useful rather than true. But because they are useful, a schematization of the conceptual parallels may help to summarize what has been said so far.

	Dogmatic Account	Skeptical Account
Gap 1	*x:* material or spiritual object in external space. God, or a stone that nobody perceives.	Perception or impression of *x;* idea of *x* or physical sensation (sight) of *x*. Called *phantasia* in Greek accounts.
Gap 2	*x*-in-itself.	An account of *x*, a statement about *x*, a concept to explain *x*. Opinion, called *doxa* in Greek accounts.
Gap 3	truth.	Probability; *to pithanon* in Greek accounts.

It is sometimes said that probability, as Shelley uses that word and concept, is a tool for bridging these gaps. According to this popular account, probability is a way to determine whether the appearance-of-*x* really is like *x*-in-itself. Probability so understood is a way of testing for truth or at least for the likelihood of truth.[21] But this is in fact not Shelley's sense of probability at all. By definition—every definition that he offers of the concept—probability belongs to appearance, and never to supposed objects antecedent to appearance or beyond appearance. Probability, as Shelley defines it in the passage from *Essay on Miracles and Christian Doctrine* that I have quoted, is a mental condition; and our "actions and sentiments," which are to be guided and formed by probability, are equally limited to our awareness, because experience is coextensive with awareness. That is, our actions, sentiments, and probability judgments are *ours,* phenomenal rather than absolute.

To show how the concept of probability works in Shelley's prose, it

9

will be helpful to show how related concepts appeared in accounts of skepticism generally. In 1929, Pierre Couissin clarified and emphasized the distinction to which I refer here, correctly describing the *pithanon* statements of the ancient skeptics as utterly nondogmatic, essentially opposed to all claims of truth.[22] But an earlier understanding, whereby the *pithanon* statements were taken as approaches toward truth claims, persisted until recently in philosophical scholarship and criticism. Neither Shelley nor any of his sources—Drummond, Hume, Cicero, Diogenes—so misunderstood the Academic skeptics. Shelley's definitions indicate a more accurate understanding of the *pithanon* as a criterion of statements.

The skeptical arguments arose in a context of debate. The ancient Stoics, led by Zeno, had argued that some persons (notably the special sort of individual known as the Sage) could and did have ideas that were infallibly and universally true (*phantasia katalepsia*). The Sage knew that they were so, because of properties belonging to the ideas themselves; no criterion was applied, because the Sage's perception was itself the criterion of its own truth. Subsequently (in the third century B.C.), Arcesilaus, the first great skeptical leader of the Platonic Academy, met those claims with criticism. The sole purpose of Arcesilaus' philosophical arguments was to show "that knowledge, as the Stoics conceived it, apprehension (*katalepsis*), which is their criterion of truth, does not exist."[23]

Arcesilaus' critique was dialectical: he defied the Stoics to produce an example of a *phantasia katalepsia,* an idea that could not possibly be false. An argument could be presented to show at least the possibility of the falsehood of any statement whatsoever; although this procedure did not show that nothing is true or that truth does not exist, it did indicate that our conceptions and statements cannot be shown to be exactly and infallibly true. And the second part of Arcesilaus' argument, therefore, was that assent (belief and the bestowal of belief) is given to propositions and only propositions. Sometimes the ancients use the words "proposition" and "presentation" ("perception") interchangeably; Arcesilaus' argument was, therefore, that belief attaches not to things but to impressions or representations of things. And no such impression or representation can be shown to be infallibly true, even if some are so in fact; we do not have a criterion to assure us which of them are true and which are not.[24]

And yet we live and act, as Arcesilaus noticed. He did not think that a know-nothing argument should lead to a do-nothing attitude. Purposeful action should be founded on intelligent choices, intelligent discriminations among presentations and perceptions. How, then, could these perceptions be sorted, if not according to truth? Arcesilaus' answer was the *eulogon,* the "practical criterion": one followed that proposition that one had more reason to believe than to disbelieve. One need never forget that the *eulogon* (sometimes called "the reasonable") is a presumption and only a presumption, a characteristic of a belief and therefore a property belonging to a fallible thought rather than to infallibly true things.

Arcesilaus died in 241 B.C., and his dialectical methods were carried on by his successors in the Platonic Academy. One of those successors, Carneades, pressed the argument further by proposing a different criterion for action and for the choices on which actions are based. His criterion was *to pithanon,* usually translated as "what is probable." One reason that *pithanon* is translated as "probable" is that Cicero, in his Latin account of Carneades' concept, puts the Latin word *probabilis* for the Greek word *pithanon.* But in Greek *pithanon* does not mean "probable"; it means "persuasive." It is the word, for example, that Aristotle uses throughout the *Rhetoric* to mean "persuasive." What Carneades said of this criterion, therefore, was that it could discriminate among statements and perceptions according to how convincing they are. The characteristic *pithanon* belongs to the proposition or perception, ascribing to it force in the subjective field of belief and conviction; it has nothing to do with the supposed truth, or lack of it, belonging to the object about which a belief is offered. It describes the belief, in other words, and not the object of the belief. As Couissin says, "Carneades describes as persuasive [*pithanon*] the presentation which appears true, and this does not mean that which resembles the true (a meaningless phrase) but that which in a natural way persuades us (*peithein hemas pephuken* [Sextus Empiricus, *Against the Dogmatists,* I, 169]) and which draws us to assent (ibid. 172)." [25] The word that is commonly translated as "probability," therefore, does not describe a relation between the proposition and reality; it describes a relation between the proposition and us, and our action. It leaves aside the question of truth and has nothing to do with "likely truth" (in Wasserman's terms) or resemblance of truth. [26]

The fact that what appears true is not equal to what "resembles the true" is acknowledged in a passage of Shelley's in which he sets forth a graduated scale of probability: "But the intensity of belief, like that of every other passion, is precisely proportioned to the degrees of excitement. A graduated scale, on which should be marked the capabilities of propositions to approach to the test of the senses, would be a just measure of the belief which ought to be attached to them. . . . That is believed which is apprehended to be true" (*A Refutation of Deism*, I&P, 6:39).[27] This remark is psychological rather than metaphysical: it is about "intensity of belief." The scale of probability that Shelley recommends does not discriminate propositions according to their resemblance to the truth but according to "the capabilities of propositions to approach to the test of the senses." What belongs to the senses are perceptions, not allegedly anterior objects of perceptions.

Because Shelley's statement includes the word "true," it might mislead some readers by suggesting that the scale of probability that Shelley here recommends concerns truth rather than the psychological properties of persuasion, but Shelley's distinction is exactly that of Carneades: he writes of that "which is apprehended to be true" and not that which *is* true or that which is likely to be true. Belief is a psychological state belonging to the believer; it is not a property of the thing believed.[28]

The notion of degrees of persuasiveness, and of a graduated scale, also derives from Carneades, by way of Sextus, Diogenes, and Cicero. (The fullest account of this scale is in Sextus, *Against the Dogmatists*, I, 176–89.) Carneades distinguished three stages of progressively persuasive presentations: (1) perceptions or propositions that are simply persuasive, (2) perceptions or propositions that are persuasive and are not opposed by a contrary persuasion (i.e., a presentation is more persuasive when no *isostheneia* has been applied to it), and (3) perceptions or propositions that are persuasive, are not opposed by a contrary persuasion, and have also been subjected to a detailed scrutiny (see Couissin, p. 48). As Shelley's scale refers to the senses and intensity of belief, so too the ancient model of Carneades' distinguishes degrees of *to pithanon* according to the internal properties of conviction.

One might wonder, then, how the widespread mistake arose, confusing *pithanon* as a category of perception with probability as a category of likely truth. The answer (like so many answers in the history of dialectical philosophies) lies in historical circumstances. In the first century B.C., the leadership of the Academy in Athens fell to Philo of Larissa; continuing to talk of the *pithanon,* Philo was understood by many of his followers to deviate nonetheless from the more rigorous skepticism of his predecessors Arcesilaus and Carneades. One of the followers, Aenesidemus, responded to what looked to him like a new form of dogmatism (reifying the *pithanon* as a criterion of truth) by defecting from the Academy. Founding a new school of skepticism, Aenesidemus sought to distinguish it from Philo's Academy. One way in which he did so was to treat the Academic *pithanon* as a positive guide meant to warrant the truth content of statements. The Academy, he said, is culpable of dogmatism; the *pithanon* as Philo uses it (so the argument goes) is really no more than a truth claim. Aenesidemus charged Philo's predecessors with the same lapse of skeptical rigor; he said that Carneades' use of the *pithanon* was dogmatic in the first place. His charge was a manifest distortion; Philo did veer toward dogmatic use of the *pithanon* in the first century B.C., but there is no direct evidence at all that Carneades had ever done so in the second century B.C., when he introduced that skeptical concept in the New Academy.

Aenesidemus, however, could warrant the formation of his new school and claim that in it he and his followers practiced a more rigorous skepticism than the pseudoskeptical philosophers of Philo's Academy. He distinguished the alleged probabilism of the New Academy from the teachings of another skeptical philosopher, Pyrrho of Elis (c. 360–270 B.C.). Pyrrho, he said, preserved *epochē* ("suspension of judgment") in contrast to the Academic skeptics, who collapsed (with their alleged doctrine of probability) into dogma. That is why the school of Aenesidemus came to be known as the Pyrrhonistic skeptics. Pyrrhonism is (by its own self-representation) more strictly skeptical, but its self-representation was clearly heuristic, serving to differentiate and to warrant Aenesidemus' new school. And the distinction includes a plain distortion of historical fact, charging Philo's predecessors with a vice original with Philo.

The two most influential texts of ancient skepticism were written, then, by a follower of Aenesidemus: in *Outlines of Pyrrhonism* and *Against the Mathematicians* (a compilation that includes the books cited conventionally as *Against the Dogmatists*), Sextus Empiricus codified Aenesidemus' self-representation. In fact, Sextus' chapter "Wherein Scepticism [Pyrrhonism] Differs from the Academic Philosophy" is the locus classicus for the theory of probabilism spuriously attributed to the earlier Academic skeptics, and especially Carneades. Solidified in subsequent accounts of the history of skepticism, the fiction continued to dominate even modern accounts until quite recently.

Cicero, meanwhile (also in the first century B.C.), had studied at the New Academy and learned there the concept of the *pithanon*. His teacher, however, was not Philo but Antiochus, Philo's predecessor; the doctrine of probabilism had not yet been invented, but a dialectical procedure closer to Carneades' was what Cicero learned. Returning to Rome, Cicero then codified this earlier conception of the *pithanon* in a Latin work with which he sought to make available the philosophy of the skeptical Academy to his contemporary Romans; this book is the *Academica,* and concepts in it appear also in other philosophical dialogues of Cicero. For *pithanon* Cicero uses the Latin *probabilis,* as I have said, but that Latin word has, in rhetorical contexts, exactly the sense of "persuasion" that belongs to the *pithanon.* Cicero was first and foremost a rhetorician, and it is exactly in this rhetorical sense that he uses *probabilis.* It is a matter of verbal ambiguity, a homonymic confusion, that takes Cicero's word "persuasive," or "convincing," for the utterly alien concept of probability as an approach to truth content. But this merely homonymic confusion was given great historical force by the contemporary arguments that were going on in Greek; when Sextus' works were translated into Latin, then, in the Middle Ages, *pithanon* became *probabilis,* and *probabilis* (persuasive) became *probabilis* (approaching to truth content).

Shelley's understanding of the skepticism of the New Academy, however, was not based on Sextus' account (which is Aenesidemus' account); it cannot even be shown that Shelley ever read that account. What he did read was Cicero (in the Latin, whose *probabilis* Shelley was competent to construe as "persuasive"); he read Drummond's account, in *Academical Questions,* and Drummond was a philologist as well as a skeptical philosopher, taking his title from Cicero and his concepts from the ancient Academy; and he read Hume, whose skepticism Shelley calls "the accurate philosophy of what I may be permitted to term the modern Academy."[29]

Hume's argument is more complex but precisely compatible with the skeptical construction of the *pithanon* as persuasiveness having nothing to do with the alleged truth of the object: "Knowledge and probability are of such contrary and disagreeing natures, that they cannot well run insensibly into each other."[30] Hume produces an argument of infinite regress that undermines equally the efficacy of knowledge and probability as approximations of truth: "In every judgment, which we can form concerning probability, as well as concerning knowledge, we ought always to correct the first judgment, deriv'd from the nature of the object, by another judgment, deriv'd from the nature of the understanding" (pp. 181–82). We ought to modify judgment A about an object by judgment B about our own faculties for making that judgment. We might have made an error in judging, and this possibility, derived from the nature of our faculties rather than the nature of the object, should qualify our judgment about that object.

We might, however, be mistaken in our judgment about our own faculties. A new judgment, judgment C, is called for, to qualify our certainty by noticing that our assessment of our own abilities might be mistaken. Obviously, each stage of doubt will be further weakened by another doubt, for the same reason. Soon we have disappeared from A altogether, into an attention to our own faculties, and from there we are led by inexorable logic to a series of progressively worsening doubts about the accuracy of our faculty to assess the accuracy of our faculty, "and so on *in infinitum.*" The certainty that we thought we were in search of, checking to see whether we knew something certain about A, has become unattainable; "No finite object can subsist under a decrease repeated *in infinitum.*"[31] Probability has gone the way of all consciousness in Hume's account; it becomes an intensional entity (belonging to conceptions and not to external objects).

That Shelley follows this Humean concept of probability, into questions of internally conditioned impressions and away from questions of external objects, is indicated explicitly in the *Treatise on Morals.* Shelley began this essay after finishing *A Refutation of Deism,* where the "graduated scale" appears. Now, when he assumes degrees of belief or conviction, his argument is more obviously psychological. Apparently universal beliefs include beliefs in the existence of other living creatures and of a Power causing all we perceive. Shelley internalizes the grounds of these beliefs; that is, he analyzes them according to B, our faculties, and not A, the alleged objects: "The laws of mind almost universally suggest[,] according to the various dispositions of each[,] a conjecture[,] a persuasion, or a conviction of their existence" (Tokoo, p. 19; I&P, 7:59). This three-part scheme of intensities of belief is (I repeat), like Carneades' earlier three-part

15

scheme, a psychological description of the internal impressions and not an assertion about the relation of those impressions to something that is not an impression.

Here, in the *Treatise,* Shelley emphasizes that point by articulating (almost as a negative dogma) a position that he will later qualify: "Beyond the limits of perception and of thought nothing can exist" (Tokoo, p. 20; I&P, 59). Realizing that his claim is not properly about what exists or not, but rather about perception and assertion, Shelley qualifies that statement even here: he does not positively affirm that nothing exists beyond the limits of perception and thought; more precisely he says that what he has just shown "adds force to the conclusion" that nothing so exists.[32] That sentence, like the probability statements, concerns degrees of force of conviction, and not truth. Later, he qualifies the claim even further, removing the issue to more utterly psychological space: "All things exist as they are perceived; at least in relation to the percipient" (*A Defence of Poetry,* R&P, p. 505). The relations of a perception are with other perceptions; it is within this circle, whose circumference Shelley defines as "the limits of perception and of thought," that the concept of probability operates.

What is sometimes called "the probabilism of the New Academy,"[33] then, is a doctrine that never existed in Shelley's work, or in Hume's, or in Cicero's, or in the arguments of the skeptical Academy. Hamstrung by a political distortion effected in the first century B.C. and misled by a homonymic confusion inhering in the Latin language, interpreters of Shelley's skepticism have sometimes taken a wrong turn at this crossroads; the error is not originally theirs, I am arguing, but rather it is lodged in the histories of philosophy on which the literary critics relied. They took the wrong turn because they were given faulty directions when they asked the local experts. The error has recently undergone correction in the philosophical community,[34] and Shelley studies are therefore in a position to catch up.

Another crux at which Shelley's methodology prevents a wrong turning is the question of the existence of external objects, to which I proceed in the next section of this book. Some of Shelley's statements run perilously close to a denial of the existence of external objects; when he is charged with having made such a denial, Hume, Drummond, and the ancient skeptics are usually produced as his authorities. The concept of causation is closely related to this issue of external objects: since external objects are usually understood to be the

16

causes of perceptions, the denial of the existence of external objects seems to involve a denial of that kind of causation. On this issue, too, Hume, Drummond, and the ancient skeptics are often produced as alleged authorities for Shelley's alleged denials. But I shall be arguing that (as in the case of probability) Shelley's arguments do not affirm or deny any such thing but rather constitute a "strict scepticism concerning all assertions" about them. Shelley applies no dogmatic denial but rather what his methodology requires: *skepsis*.

THE PROBLEM OF EXTERNAL OBJECTS AND THE CONCEPT OF CAUSE

Shelley's fullest discussion of the question of the existence of external objects appears in the *Treatise on Morals*. His comments on the problem are consistent with a set of skeptical arguments that had already been formulated by Berkeley, Hume, and Drummond. Their arguments, in turn, are related to earlier work by Descartes and other seventeenth-century writers, but behind all of these modern formulations of the question lie ancient skeptical procedures and doubts. Shelley had read all the modern accounts of the problem, as well as major texts of ancient skepticism; it is not my purpose, however, to rehearse all their arguments and their relationships but rather to focus (as Shelley does) on some central assumptions that have conditioned discourse on the problem.

Skepticism is sometimes treated as an answer to the question of whether a material reality exists independently of the mind.[35] Accordingly, it is sometimes said that skeptics, and specifically Hume and Shelley, "deny the existence of external objects."[36] But no skeptical argument, Greek or British, asserts any such position on the question of external objects. We can say of Hume or of Shelley exactly what Sextus says of one of their ancient precursors: "We do not find him making any assertions about the reality or unreality of anything" (*PH,* I,232). A point of conceptual analysis is worth clarifying here, because it conditions both Shelley's statements and critical treatments of them.

Shelley complains that the language of philosophy imposes conceptual problems. The word "metaphysics," he says, is "very ill adapted" for the purpose to which it is put: "to express the science of mind"

(I&P, 7:62). The word itself "asserts a distinction between the moral and the material universe which it is presumptuous to assume" (7: 62). This assumed distinction is one of the "obstinate preconceptions" that afflict discourse: philosophers (specifically Locke and his followers) "mistake . . . a name for a thing" (7:63). What Shelley says, thus, is not that external objects exist independently of the mind, or that they do not so exist. What he says is that the distinction of mind and matter is an assumption inscribed in the language of metaphysical discourse.[37] That of which Shelley is critical is the embedded conception rather than the supposed ontological entity in question.

Accordingly, the passage of Shelley's in the *Treatise on Morals* that contains the words "external objects" does not deny their existence. It classifies a distinction of concepts.

> It has commonly been supposed that those distinct thoughts which affect a number of persons, at regular intervals during the passage of a multitude of other thoughts, and which are called *real,* or *external objects,* are totally different in kind from those which affect only a few persons, and which recur at irregular intervals, and are usually more obscure and indistinct, such as hallucinations, dreams, and the ideas of madness. No essential distinction between any one of these ideas or any class of them is founded on a correct observation of the nature of things, but merely on a consideration of what thoughts are most invariably subservient to the security and happiness of life (Tokoo, p. 20; I&P, 7:59–60).

I have quoted this passage at length because in it lie two important conceptual bases: one is the relation between Shelley's philosophical thought on this question and the thought of his mainstream predecessors, Hume and Berkeley (and then Drummond as well); but another is a principle that moves Shelley from metaphysics to morals (in the *Treatise*) and then to politics (in *A Philosophical View of Reform*). That Shelley politicizes the problem is a fact that distinguishes his treatment of it from the similar treatments by all those predecessors. But that difference must depend on an exposition of the similarities, and that exposition requires at least a summary account of the arguments as they appear in Berkeley and Hume.[38]

In the *Principles of Human Knowledge,* Berkeley articulates the skeptical formulation of the problem (the existence of external objects). He points out first that "everybody will allow" that thoughts, passions, and ideas formed by the imagination do not exist outside the mind. On that point all are agreed. It would be possible for external objects to exist outside the mind, corresponding to our perceptions and ideas of them; "yet how is it possible for us to know this?" The existence of such external objects is one thing; our knowledge about them is another matter altogether.[39]

"Either we must know it by sense or by reason," Berkeley says. But by the senses we have knowledge only of sensations, and these (everyone has agreed) do not exist outside the mind. Reason, too, will furnish no such knowledge; it is also "granted on all hands (and what happens in dreams, frenzies, and the like, puts it beyond dispute) that it is possible we might be affected with all the ideas we have now, though no bodies existed without resembling them."[40]

One part of Berkeley's argument is therefore exactly what Shelley was later to affirm (and, as I shall be showing, the same idea appears in Descartes and Drummond as well): dreams, hallucinations, and the ideas of mad persons do not imply anything about external objects. But no essential distinction can be produced between the two sets of ideas (or perceptions). If external objects were required to account for sensations, then dreams and hallucinations would not be (as they universally are) understood as entirely internal to the mind. Neither Berkeley nor Shelley is here saying that he thinks that physical objects exist only in his mind, or in your mind. Berkeley is not even (so far) saying that they exist in the mind of God. His concern is with the account given of those physical sensations, the concept of their existence, the explanation of the thing, and not the thing itself.

What Berkeley has shown has recently been summarized expertly by Benson Mates:

He is saying to his opponents: Look here. According to your own account of the mechanism of perception, it is impossible to know that that account is true, and, further, your account implies that, even if it weren't true, you could have all the same reasons for believing it that you do now. This amounts to a demonstration that it is impossible to know that the received account (R) is true. For if R implies that R is not known to be true, we have the result that, if R *is* known to be true, then R is *not* known to be true. Hence R is not known to be true; and, since this has now been proved without using any factual premises [which would introduce contingency], we can conclude that it is *impossible* that R be known to be true.[41]

Again I want to emphasize what Mates's exposition has shown: what is denied is not the existence of external objects; what Berkeley shows to be impossible is, instead, knowledge that the received account of external objects is true. Whether it is in fact true or not is another matter, largely impertinent to the question of whether our knowledge about that account is certain.

As in the case of probability, the widespread misunderstanding concerns what the discussion is about. And also, as in the case of probability, the misunderstanding concerns not Shelley alone but also antecedent British philosophy. Berkeley and Hume have also been accused of denying the existence of external objects, as Shelley has; but a perception of Shelley's agreements and departures from those thinkers requires a more accurate assessment (like Mates's) of what exactly the argument is about. Philosophical scholarship includes several such assessments,[42] but the influential accounts of Shelley's skepticism were written when literary critics were still being told that Berkeley and Hume engaged in dogmatic denials. That Shelley scholarship reproduces that misconstruction is (like the misconstruction of probability) therefore a difficulty arising in others' having misdirected them.[43] Scholarship on the skeptical philosophers is, however, now more than adequate for the correction of some earlier errors, and so it is probably worthwhile to summarize some relevant arguments from Hume as well as Berkeley, as part of the backdrop against which Shelley's passage (quoted above) should be placed.

Hume's argument concerning external objects is a development of a question: "What causes induce us to believe in the existence of body?"[44] Wasserman's question about the existence of substance is, according to Hume, "vain to ask." Instead, he analyzes critically the conceptions involved (body, external, independence) and the construction of those conceptions.[45] A relevant theoretical point has recently been raised by Spencer Hall, who suggests that Shelley critics use the word "skepticisms" in the plural, to avoid reifying a single position and to acknowledge relevant distinctions.[46] Philosophers tend to be more precise in such matters, and Robert J. Fogelin offers an apt distinction in his account of Hume's skepticism: a theoretical skepticism embodies the principle "I. There are no rational grounds for judgments of kind A"; in contrast, a prescriptive skepticism is expressed by the principle "II. One ought not to assent to judgments of kind A."[47] Hume's theoretical skepticism is, as Fogelin argues, wholly unmitigated; it has nothing in common with a third principle, that objects do not exist. Such a proposition expresses in fact a judgment of kind A (to use Fogelin's formula); skepticism, theoretical or prescriptive, includes arguments designed to resist such judgments.

What can be understood as Hume's conceptual starting point is a psychological observation:

It seems evident, that men are carried, by a natural instinct or prepossession, to repose faith in their senses; and that, without any reasoning, or even almost before the use of reason, we always suppose an external universe.[48]

In the same psychological mode, and with the same skeptical qualifiers, Hume says, "It seems also evident, that, when men follow this blind and powerful instinct of nature, they always suppose the very images, presented by the senses, to be the external objects" (p. 151). The slightest philosophy undermines that "universal and primary opinion" (i.e., the opinion that images of objects equal the objects). Philosophy "teaches us, that nothing can ever be present to the mind but an image or perception," so that the intercourse between mind and object is not "immediate"; it is the perception that is in the mind, and not the object (p. 152).

So far this argument is consistent with Berkeley's; he has not denied the existence of anything but has rather observed that as a matter of psychological fact, the evidence for the opinon is not immediately in the senses. Reasoning apparently intervenes. Hume asks, then, "By what argument can it be proved, that the perceptions of the mind must be caused by external objects?" (pp. 152–53). To paraphrase: the opinion of such existences does seem to exist among human beings; this opinion is not founded immediately on the evidence of the senses; on what reasoning, then, *is* the opinion founded? The mode of criticism is psychological, and its subject is opinion, not objects. Shelley expresses this conjuncture of a psychological mode of criticism with a conceptual subject matter: "How came many of those facts to be called indisputable? What sanctioning correspondence unites a concatenation of syllogisms?" (I&P, 7:63). The conclusion to which both Hume and Shelley bring their arguments is the "negative truth" that, Shelley says, belongs to metaphysics (Tokoo, p. 18; I&P, 7:71). Hume's version of the negative conclusion emphasizes that this conclusion (like the entire argument) has concerned a supposition:

> It is a question of fact, whether the perceptions of the senses be produced by external objects, resembling them: how shall this question be determined? By experience surely; as all other questions of a like nature. But here experience is, and must be entirely silent. The mind has never anything present to it but the perceptions, and cannot possibly reach any experience of their connexion with objects. The supposition of such a connexion is, therefore, without any foundation in reasoning (p. 153).

It is this conclusion upon which Shelley mounts his further claim that the distinction between (allegedly external) objects and (admittedly internal) ideas arises not from "a correct observation of the nature of things." Like Hume, he says neither that this supposed distinction is true nor that it is false; both skeptics discuss instead where the supposition comes from, rather than its truth.

Shelley and Hume are not alone in this epistemological focus: Drummond also focuses his critique of the received opinions in that way. Rather than deny any existences, Drummond says that "it would be absurd to say, that a difference in our sensations is a difference in an external object" (*AQ*, pp. 24–25). It is the statement that Drummond challenges, not the object; and Drummond's formulation is even closer to Shelley's than is Hume's. Both Shelley and Drummond indicate that a distinction between ideas is not equal to a distinction between ideas and objects. That distinction between distinctions obviously arises from the earlier arguments of Berkeley and Hume, but it is Shelley and Drummond who put it in these terms.

As Berkeley had done, Drummond identifies Locke with the conventional opinions of the existence of external objects (the received account, as Mates says):[49] "It is observed by Locke, that sensation convinces us, that there are solid and extended substances. I shall examine the truth of Locke's assertions." Rather than seek to answer Wasserman's question about the existence of material substance, Drummond seeks "to show, that it cannot be admitted upon the principles of [Locke's] own system" (*AQ*, p. 33).

It should be obvious that what Drummond expresses here is a commonplace among British skeptical writers: grant the dogmatists their received account; will the conclusion *R* follow from the premises and definitions of *R*? Unanimously, Berkeley, Hume, Drummond, and Shelley answer no; but their negative answer concerns assertions rather than matters of fact. Like their skeptical authorities among the ancient philosophers (Diogenes, Sextus, and Cicero all make the same point), Hume, Drummond, and Shelley articulate a method of analysis "owing to which we neither deny nor affirm anything" (*PH* I, 10).

There are positive or constructive elements in Shelley's statement on the problem, however, that warrant attention. One I have already mentioned: he proceeds from metaphysics ("the science which regards those laws by which the mind acts" [I&P, 7:62]) to morals (the science that "regards simply the determination of that arrangement of [ideas] which produces the greatest and most solid happiness" [Tokoo, p. 18; I&P, 7:7]). It will be for him an even easier leap, subsequently, from morals to politics, because both morals and political philosophy concern action and prescription. The more difficult connection for him to establish is that between the descriptive analytical task (metaphysics) and the value-based prescriptions of morality.

Shelley establishes that more difficult connection, however, shortly and swiftly. He inserts a moral principle—the utilitarian principle—into his critical analysis of the distinction between thoughts and things. Rather than an essential difference in the nature of things, Shelley says, this commonplace distinction arises from "a consideration of what thoughts are most invariably subservient to the security and happiness of life." Of course he is not here advocating that distinctions be founded on the utilitarian principle; in his metaphysical argument he says simply that this particular distinction is in fact founded upon the utilitarian principle. But the insertion of that principle binds his metaphysics to his moral discourse, where (in the *Treatise on Morals*) he says for example that

The object of the forms according to which human society is administered is the happiness of the individuals composing the communities which they regard, and these forms are perfect or imperfect in proportion to the degree in which they promote this end (Tokoo, p. 24; I&P, 7:72).

In this transition from the epistemological argument (much like Hume's or Drummond's) to the moral argument, Shelley politicizes his discourse. I shall be analyzing his political philosophy in a later chapter of this book, but here I want to point out this particular element of its basis, in Shelley's metaphysical writing.

Another positive and constructive assertion that Shelley makes in the *Treatise,* about the thought-thing dichotomy, encloses that problem within a linguistic frame of reference. This time, he ascribes the dichotomy to the terms and structure of discourse in such a way as to discredit the extralinguistic significance of that dichotomy:

It imports little to inquire whether thought be distinct from the objects of thought. The use of the words *external* and *internal* as applied to the establishment of this distinction [has] been the symbol and the source of much dispute. This is merely an affair of words (Tokoo, p. 22; I&P, 7:65).

Again in *On Life,* Shelley makes the same point, and here (like Arcesilaus, Carneades, Sextus, Hume, Drummond, and virtually every other rigorously skeptical writer in the tradition) he identifies his own statements as critical responses intended to undermine an element in the received and conventional account of things: "The difference is merely nominal between those two classes of thought which are vulgarly distinguished by the names of ideas and of external objects" (R&P, p. 477). I shall subsequently have much more to say about what "nominal" means, because Shelley is able to make of it a powerful critical concept and an equally powerful constructive tool. Both usages of "nominal" come to fruition in *A Philosophical View of Reform,* where again Shelley politicizes the critique of doctrines. Here, it is enough to say that where Shelley encloses knowledge within the circumference of ideas (thoughts or perceptions), he also encloses the issue very specifically within the structure of the discourse itself.

Shelley's complaint about the language of metaphysical discourse is precisely that such language traps criticism within doctrinal parameters, which it is the task of skepticism to resist and to overcome: where the skeptic would analyze conviction, his language threatens to entrap him in conviction. Wittgenstein has expressed a similar problem:

> If I were to say "It is my unshakeable conviction that etc.", this means . . . that I have not arrived at the conviction by following a particular line of thought, but that it is anchored in all my *questions and answers,* so anchored that I cannot touch it.[50]

Skeptical methodology seeks to elude this entrapment by the fictions inscribed in its own discourse. As George Santayana says, "The skeptic is not committed to the implications of other men's language."[51] These implications include the falsely exclusive dichotomy of affirmation and denial, and the supposed "inevitability of entertaining opinions."[52] Shelley admits that these presuppositions are inscribed in the language of the debate, but he aims his dialectic toward ovecoming their authority.

The same argument that Shelley applies to the question of external objects is extended then to two other subjects of debate. One of these other subjects is personal identity, or the problem of the existence of the individual mind. Here Shelley follows Hume (though Berkeley and Drummond make little of the issue). Shelley's account is quite brief, he seldom returns to it, and it contributes little to the substance of his larger arguments.[53]

Hume had extended Berkeley's critique of the conventional account of external objects in such a way that other sorts of opinions were found to be equally without rational grounds. Just as the presence of a perception alone includes no warrant for a knowledge claim about external objects, so too the presence of perceptions includes no warrant for a knowledge claim about the person, identity, or mind that "has" the perceptions: "I can never catch *myself* at any time without a perception, and never can observe anything but the perception" (*Treatise,* p. 252). The conventional form of assertion about persons affirms, beyond the perceptions that the persons "have," something else distinct from the perceptions and having them. But only perceptions are perceived. So how could anyone know of the existence of the thing that is not a perception, since it is by nature imperceptible or at least unperceived?

I may venture to affirm [of human beings], that they are nothing but a bundle or collection of different perceptions, which succeed each other with an inconceivable rapidity, and are in a perpetual flux and movement (*Treatise*, p. 252).

Rather than a positive claim about what exists, Hume makes it clear that his argument concerns a limitation on knowledge about what exists:

They are the successive perceptions only, that constitute the mind; nor have we the most distant notion, of the place, where these scenes are represented, or of the materials, of which it is compos'd (*Treatise*, p. 253).[54]

Shelley's treatment of the problem, in *On Life*, follows Hume conceptually, to the extent of linking it similarly to the critique of knowledge claims about external objects:

Pursuing the same thread of reasoning, the existence of distinct individual minds similar to that which is employed in now questioning its own nature, is likewise found to be a delusion. The words, *I, you, they*, are not signs of any actual difference subsisting between the assemblage of thoughts thus indicated, but are merely marks employed to denote the different modifications of the one mind (R&P, pp. 477–78).

A person who has a perception of others has but a perception. To point out that fact is not to make "the monstrous presumption, that I, the person who now write and think, am that one mind" (R&P, p. 478); the name for that monstrous presumption is solipsism, and Shelley's philosophy has nothing to do with that doctrine. Instead, Shelley simply draws the same limiting circle around what is known of his one mind, and of other minds, that had already been drawn around the other question, what is known about external objects. Premises of empiricism, taken from materialists themselves, lead to the skeptical deconstruction of both concepts.

A third issue, causation, is subject to similar treatment, and Shelley, like Hume and Drummond, extends the same kind of critique to the concept of causation. The opinion of the existence of such a thing as a cause is almost universal, but such a thing was never a subject of sensation (was never perceived); rather, it was internally conditioned ("the laws of mind . . . suggest" the entity).[55] In *On Life*, as later in *A Defence of Poetry*, Shelley defines "cause" as an internal state of the mind: "Cause is only a word expressing a certain state of the human mind with regard to the manner in which two thoughts are apprehended to be related to each other" (R&P, p. 478). "We know no more of cause and effect," he says in the *Defence of Poetry*, "than a constant conjunction of events" (R&P, p. 489).

In the *Treatise of Human Nature* Hume says that forming the idea of a cause, "the mind goes beyond what is immediately present to the senses" (p. 73). In fact, the concept of cause is the only device we have that "informs us of existences and objects, which we do not see or feel" (p. 74). But "cause," Hume says, names nothing we can perceive at all; it names instead a relation between perceptions. This is Hume's first definition:

[Cause is] an object precedent and contiguous to another, and where all the objects resembling the former are plac'd in a like relation of priority and contiguity to those objects, that resemble the latter (*Treatise*, p. 172).

That definition is followed immediately in the *Treatise* by another, which moves the concept yet further into psychological space:

[Cause is] an object precedent and contiguous to another, and so united with it in the imagination, that the idea of the one determines the mind to form the idea of the other, and the impression of the one to form a more lively idea of the other (p. 172).

In the first definition, cause is a relation of objects of perception; in the second definition, cause implies an internally determined movement of the mind. In neither case is it a known, externally existent entity.

Both definitions appear also in Shelley: the first concept of cause is expressed in *On Life* and again in the *Defence of Poetry*, the second in the *Treatise on Morals*. Their importance in Shelley's philosophical work is related to two kinds of dogma that the conventional concept of cause is used to support. Shelley, persistently seeking to undermine dogmatism, uses Hume's critique. Thus, for example, in the essay *On a Future State*,[56] Shelley argues that the conventional Christian doctrines about "God, and a future state of rewards and punishments, are totally foreign to the subject" of human beings' living after death. And in the analysis of the possibility of knowing such a thing, as whether human beings do in fact live after death, Shelley's arguments are repeatedly skeptical: for example,

> To say that the principle of life *may* exist in distribution among various forms, is to assert what cannot be proved to be either true or false (I&P, 6:206, 208).

Similarly, the principle of life may be a particular substance: "It *may be;* though it is sufficiently unphilosophical to allege the possibility of an opinion as a proof of its truth" (6:208–209). And most centrally, Shelley states the critical conception of cause in a way that challenges the religious explanation of reality: "For when we use the words *principle, power, cause,* &c., we mean to express no real being, but only to class under those terms a certain series of co-existing phenomena" (6:208).

God is defined so often as "cause" or "power" that the efficacy of this critique is obvious: in a world where cause is "no real being," assertions of religious belief are dogmatic and "sufficiently unphilosophical." In *A Refutation of Deism*, Eusebes makes the antitheological force of the argument explicit:

> Hume has shewn, to the satisfaction of all philosophers, that the only idea which we can form of causation is derivable from the constant conjunction of objects, and the consequent inference of one from the other. We denominate that phenomenon the cause of another which we observe with the fewest exceptions to precede its occurrence. Hence it would be inadmissible to deduce the being of a God from the existence of the Universe; even if this mode of reasoning did not conduct to the monstrous conclusion of an infinity of creative and creating Gods, each more eminently requiring a Creator than its predecessor (I&P, 6:55).

Here Shelley paraphrases Hume's conception of cause as a mere inference from the constant conjuction of ideas, and he simply adds an obvious argument of infinite regress.

A second application that Shelley makes of the critique of the concept of causation involves politics rather than religion. In the *Proposals for an Association of Philanthropists*,[57] Shelley applies the critique to the concept of social determinism in connection with the French Revolution. In place of a dogmatic explanation whereby persons or ideas are said to cause a particular event, Shelley puts a nondogmatic expression of conjunction, using Hume's argument again:

> I do not deny that the Revolution of France was occasioned by the literary labors of the Encyclopaedists. When we see two events together, in certain cases, we speak of one as the cause, the other the effect. We have no other idea of cause and effect, but that which arises from necessary connection; it is therefore, still doubtful whether D'Alembert, Boulanger, Condorcet, and other celebrated characters, were the causes of the overthrow of the ancient monarchy of France.[58]

I delay until a later chapter the analysis of this concept of social and historical determinism and its implication in political theory. Here, I want only to point out that it has such implications, and that Shelley insists on them. From the beginning of his philosophical career (with *The Necessity of Atheism*, which is an essay about the conditions of belief), Shelley regularly contextualizes his own arguments. The principle of utility links his metaphysical analysis to his moral theory and to his political philosophy: the critique of the conventional account of external objects leads to the critique of the concept of causation, and with that critique Shelley engages his arguments with issues as practical as the revolution in France, the abolition of the state religion, and, later, political reform or revolution in his own community.

Most of the arguments about causation that I have cited from Hume could have been cited also from Drummond's *Academical Questions,* a book that Shelley knew and admired at least as well as he knew and admired the works of Hume. I have chosen Hume in this particular connection because it is Hume whom Shelley cites on the issue of causation; but he cites Drummond often enough (in *On Life* and elsewhere) to make the following observation pertinent here: Drummond's critiques of concepts such as power and cause were also related to the political contexts that Shelley was to address more directly. Drummond's extensions of these arguments into their political contexts are much more oblique, partly because he separates the metaphysical issues (analyzed in *Academical Questions*) from the religious and political issues. In the post-revolutionary war years, and one year after the execution of Louis XVI, Drummond published *A Review of the Governments of Sparta and Athens,* which is in fact a work in praise of democracy. In the following year he published *Philosophical Sketches of the Principles of Society and Government* (1795), but he did so anonymously, and many of his arguments in *Philosophical Sketches* appear cautious and conservative in comparison with other expressions of social-contract theory from the period.[59] Drummond was a statesman as well as a philosopher, and he had reasons for these oblique and cautious forms of political argument. During his lifetime and Shelley's, reform advocates as moderate as Leigh Hunt spent years in prison, and not only authors but publishers were jailed and fined (like Richard Carlile, of whom Shelley was to write a defense). But Shelley's prose—that which was published in his lifetime and that which was not—makes clear what even Drummond's works only hint: that the historical and political conditions in which the skeptical arguments were composed and promulgated have much to do with the selection and the nature of those arguments themselves. Even the apparently abstract metaphysical problems at which I have been looking take on concrete political importance.

One obvious point of contact between skeptical metaphysical arguments and, for example, the French Revolution has been suggested already: both challenge authority. Both go farther than simply opposing an opponent's position on an issue, seeking instead to undermine the entire foundation of conviction and justification on which the opponent's position is based. Central to the metaphysical and French Revolutionary projects, as well as other crucial and revolutionary events in the history of modern Europe, including the Reformation, is the issue of the criterion of authority. Monarchy and dogma rest alike upon a claim for absolute certainty and right. The skeptic and the revolutionary, in Shelley's particular moment of historical crisis, can simultaneously attack both bases of authority, and even (as

Shelley does in his later and longer essays) argue that these contexts of authority are vitally interrelated to begin with.

It is to the question of the criterion of authority, then, that I turn in the next section of this book. The organization of that discussion will be broadly historical; ideas do not have a history, as Marx once said, because it is the human makers of the ideas who live and act; but in the history of human beings the repetition of paradigmatic structures of ideas and confrontations discloses how the historically specific occasions transform those ideas. Shelley's relationship to the skeptical tradition is always a matter of likeness and difference, the difference arising in part from his situation in his particular time. But the likenesses and differences unfold only under an exposition of the related works. Therefore, as I look at the development of these arguments over the criterion of authority, I shall try always to place them within their historical conditioning occasions. For the purposes of exposition, Shelley's later and longer essays—and especially *A Philosophical View of Reform*—will be treated then as a culmination of the progressive debates and struggles, conceptual and concrete, that lie behind them.

THE EPISTEMOLOGICAL CIRCLE AND
THE CRITERION OF TRUTH

Skeptical arguments characteristically employ a historical methodology. The dialectical character of the Socratic elenchus shows in microcosm how this procedure works. A participant in a dialogue offers a definition; the next speaker seizes a part of that formulation and discards other parts; a redefinition takes place. The process continues, sometimes (as in Plato's *Euthyphro*) never reaching a conclusion at all.[60]

The Socratic form of dialectic is thus a kind of conceptual backstitch: a speaker loops backward to take up a thread from an earlier formulation and moves the argument along in a line that is momentarily recursive but generally progressive. And skeptical philosophers (from Arcesilaus through Sextus, Cicero, Drummond, Shelley, and Benson Mates) extrapolate this elenchus out of conversation and into historical progressions.

Thus Arcesilaus cites Socrates, Plato, Parmenides, and Heracleitus.[61] These figures and others are produced as forerunners with a difference. Carneades does the same, adding Arcesilaus to the antecedent elenchus. So does Cicero, then (*Ac.,* II, 18–23), and Sextus uses the same device repeatedly. Favorite passages of the ancient skeptics, used as historical backdrop, include these:

We know nothing in reality; for truth lies in an abyss.
(Democritus)

None of us knows anything, not even whether we know or do not know, nor do we know whether not knowing and knowing exist, nor in general whether there is anything or not.
(Metrodorus of Chios)

I only know one thing, which is that I know nothing.
(Socrates)

And I don't even know that.

(Arcesilaus)[62]

In each instance, the procedure is revisionary. As Arcesilaus points out, for example, even Socrates' statement "I only know . . . that I know nothing" is dogmatic and self-contradictory: if it is true, it is not true. But the earlier formulations offer each skeptic a loop of thread that he can then pull forward.

That method is one way in which Drummond's *Academical Questions* is so valuable: his critique reaches backward to the pre-Socratics, Plato, the Academic skeptics, Cicero, Sextus, Descartes, Spinoza, Leibniz, Locke, Berkeley, Hume, Holbach and the Encyclopaedists, and Thomas Reid and the Common-Sense school. His aim is not expository but profoundly critical, and Shelley follows him in his use of the historical method. In *A Philosophical View of Reform* Shelley begins with a historical argument, winnowing earlier philosophical systems; he brings the argument forward to his own temporal crux, but (like Drummond) he implies no schematic end. The defining primacy of the historical context precludes a finality of assertion.

The particular issue whose historical transformations I shall be examining here is the problem of the criterion of truth; it is important because it opens onto virtually all the other issues in skeptical argument. I shall offer first a summary of the problem (introducing, I realize, an expository backstitch into this book) because its conceptual form is complex. Then I shall show its occasionally recursive but generally progressive development into Shelley's lifetime.

All of the skeptical arguments summarized in the preceding section of this book—on external objects, personal identity, and causation—imply an epistemological circle, which is a mentalistic or phenomenal limit to the truth content of knowledge claims. (What are known are ideas, sensations, impressions, perceptions, notions, concepts, and so forth.) Often a dogmatist will offer, against this epistemological limit, a criterion of truth. This criterion is a tool for leaping over the limit: it would enable us to say, beyond "*x* appears *y*," that "*x* really is *y*, even outside our awareness." Skeptics (Sextus, Berkeley in the first part of his *Treatise,* Hume everywhere, Drummond, and Shelley) routinely point out to the dogmatist that his assertion of a criterion fails. The entire assertion, its terms and its structure, exists wholly within a linguistic frame. It exists therefore within the epistemological circle, language being a human invention and being afflicted furthermore with the additional problems of nominal properties, intensional reference, and so forth.

Shelley's claim for the epistemological circle is a strong one: it is "the character of all life and being." And in *On Life* he defines the circle in these terms: "Each is at once the centre and the circumference; the point to which all things are referred, and the line in which all things are contained" (R&P, p. 476). In *On Life* the enclosure of all objects of knowledge within a mental field is an epistemological principle; in *Treatise on Morals* it is ethical as well. Knowledge is "bounded by perception," as in *On Life;* the moral corollary follows: "The only distinction between the selfish man and the virtuous man is that the imagination of the former is confined within a narrow limit, while that of the latter embraces a comprehensive circumference" (Tokoo, p. 23). This comprehensive circle that includes all is, I emphasize, the imagination.

Further, the linguistic basis of the epistemological circle is more powerful than at first it appears: metaphysics is a kind of word game, though an entirely serious one; it is the science relating to the "just classification, and the assignment of distinct names to its ideas"

33

(Tokoo, p. 18; I&P, 7:71). By definition, the entire project is helpless to leap over the epistemological limit.

The concept of probability cannot help: probability is a matter of persuasiveness (*pithanon*), not truth or likely truth; probability, Shelley says, belongs to logic, and logic is "the science of words." Alternatively, logic can be said to belong to dialectics, but Shelley defines "dialectics" as a method of solving problems by analysis of propositions.[63] Probability is lodged firmly within the epistemological circle, then, as a subset of logic and dialectics, which also belong entirely within that circle. If truth is conceived as lying outside that epistemological circumference (i.e., if truth is understood as that which is, in distinction from that which appears), no means of getting to it have ever been discovered.

Within the epistemological limits, however, we are in a much better position: "The science of mind possesses eminent advantages over every other with regard to the certainty of the conclusions which it affords," because we are ourselves "depositories of the evidence of the subject which we consider" (I&P, 7:63).[64] This assurance, however, has hardly satisfied most thinkers, in Shelley's time or before or since. The history of human thinking has been largely a matter of people seeking and desiring a correspondence between what they think and what is really so, and these people usually want to be sure about these things. They do not want only to know that they have an idea; they also want to know that it is true, and they usually take truth to require leaping over the limit of the epistemological circle. Some skeptics, Shelley among them, respond differently; they move truth to a location within the epistemological circle, where it can be got at.

What is called truth, according to an argument that Shelley puts in *A Refutation of Deism,* is a relation between elements in a cognition and not a relation between cognition and something else: "Truth is the perception of the agreement or disagreement of ideas" (I&P, 6:31–32). Knowledge claims do not and cannot refer to anything "beyond the limits of perception and of thought"; that is why "the view of life presented by the most refined deductions of the intellectual philosophy, is that of unity" (*On Life,* R&P, p. 477).

Shelley knows the classical loci of the skeptical arguments, as I have said, but in *On Life* he locates the discussion in the context of arguments formulated during his own lifetime; he says, "Perhaps the most clear and vigorous statement of the intellectual system is to be found

34

in Sir W. Drummond's Academical Questions." These arguments, he says, are "sufficiently familiar" to his audience, "those enquiring minds whom alone a writer on abstruse subjects can be conceived to address." He pronounces his verdict on a current debate: "Examined point by point and word by word, the most discriminating intellects have been able to discover no train of thoughts in the process of its reasoning" that does not lead to Drummond's conclusions (R&P, pp. 476–77).

Drummond indicates repeatedly that his own book is a new statement in an ongoing debate over the criterion of truth. Arguments similar to Drummond's appear first in Hellenistic philosophy, in a specific dispute where the issue of the criterion concerns what belongs to the individual "wise man." When those same arguments appear in Renaissance debates (as between Luther and Erasmus), what is at issue includes more, becoming a matter of religious principle and institutional church authority. Finally, in the lifetime of Drummond and Shelley, the question is distinctly political.

Drummond's challenges to the authority of truth criteria appear in the wake of ideological turmoil surrounding the French Revolution. When he published a book contrasting the claims of monarchical authority with the structure of democracy, England was at war with the Revolutionary French government, and so too again when he published *Academical Questions* in 1805. Drummond was directly and personally involved in England's foreign affairs; Lord Nelson expressed concern about "the intended purity of our cabinet" when he commented on the fact that Drummond was British ambassador to the Sublime Porte of the Ottoman Empire.[65] I am not arguing that these events are expressed directly in philosophical works by Drummond or Shelley, but it is important to recognize that these writers' challenges to traditional claims occur within a particular ideological crisis.

George Stanley Faber, a contemporary of Drummond's and a correspondent of Shelley's, says that "a revolution . . . unparalleled in its consequences, has suddenly burst upon an astonished world." Joseph Priestley argued that the French Revolution and its aftermath, in which Drummond involved himself as author and as statesman, were to "make a totally new, a most wonderful, and important aera in the history of mankind," representing "a liberating of all the powers of man."[66] This context conditions the skepticism of Drummond and Shelley in radical ways. Both writers draw an epistemological circle around their claims, as I have said, but at the same time the historical context within which they write invests the argument itself with political importance. It is under political pressure, and not in an abstracted freedom of disinterestedness, that Shelley takes up the problem of the criterion of authority. The dialectic of dogma and doubt proceeds in a spiral, not a straight line, toward Shelley, its transformations responding to individual pressures operating concretely around him.

The conflict between two schools—the Stoics and the Academic skeptics—dominates the history of Hellenistic philosophy, as Michael Frede has said.[67] The Stoics, following Zeno of Citium, had maintained that a criterion of truth existed and that it belonged to the Sage (wise man) of their school. They called it *katalepsia*, as I have pointed out in my introductory summary above—"a cognition that is true" or "an infallible belief." Led by Arcesilaus, the skeptical Academy challenged this dogma specifically. Cicero's philosophical dialogues are evidently Shelley's favorite accounts of that debate (*Letters*, I : 30), and Cicero makes it clear that the issue is the possibility of knowledge—that is, not whether a particular doctrine or set of doctrines is true but rather whether a criterion of truth exists. Cicero claims to speak for the Academic skeptics (he had studied at the New Academy in Athens) when he says that skeptics "do not deny that some truth exists but deny that it can be perceived" (*Ac.*, II,73). Cicero distinguishes the claim of Democritus, who "flatly denies that truth exists at all," from the skeptical position. The latter, he indicates, is closer to that expressed by Metrodorus of Chios ("None of us knows anything, not even whether we know or do not know"). Applying the common rhetorical tactic, Cicero claims the authority of other ancients; he says that Parmenides, Xenophanes, Socrates, and Plato, among others, "held that nothing can be known" (*Ac.*, II,74).

Cicero locates the argument specifically in the local debate between the Athenian rivals, Zeno and Arcesilaus: Zeno maintained that the wise man never held a mere opinion (*doxa*, fallible belief) precisely because a criterion of truth did exist, distinguishing true from false impressions (and this, again, was the *katalepsis*).

"What then was this?" asked Arcesilaus. . . . Zeno defined it as follows, a presentation [or impression] impressed and sealed

36

and moulded from a real object, in comformity with its reality (*Ac.,* II,77).

It is clear that according to the Stoics, such an infallible cognition is "perceived as such by its own intrinsic nature" (*Ac.,* I,40). Arcesilaus responded that no such perception was possible if a true impression "had such a character as even a false one might have," and he went on "to show that no presentation proceeding from a true object is such that a presentation proceeding from a false one might not also be of the same form" (*Ac.,* II,77–78).[68]

The Stoic criterion of truth, then, is a cognitive impression, i.e., one that is impressed from a real object, conforms to the reality of the object, and is of such a nature that "a presentation proceeding from a false [object] might not also be of the same form."[69] The skeptical critique is entirely epistemological: how, given only the impression's internal properties, could we know its external relations with a real object? Cicero cites with approval a principle of the Cyrenaics: "They maintain that nothing external to themselves is perceptible [i.e., kataleptically perceptible], and that the only things that they do perceive [infallibly] are the sensations" (*Ac.,* II,76). Neither Arcesilaus nor Cicero is denying the existence of the real objects; rather, they are questioning the availability of a criterion to distinguish the impressions of it; they are also challenging the authority of the Stoic wise man who claims to have what he cannot exemplify: a perception such that, given only its internal properties as a mental event, it is an infallible presentation of the truth.

Nicholas Rescher has recently summarized a common form of the argument as it appears among the ancient skeptics: the Wheel Argument (*diallelus*). The skeptics responded to the Stoics' claim of a criterion in this way:

How are you going to validate your criterion itself? Surely not on its own ground, in terms of itself? That's just begging the question. In terms of another? But that just starts an infinite regress—like the ancient myth about supporting the earth on the back of an elephant, and this on the back of an alligator, and so on. The choice before you is an unattractive one—that between a vicious circle or a vitiating regress. Either way, you have no adequate means to support the truth-criterion which lies at the foundation of your cognitive enterprise.[70]

Sextus expresses the critique in this way:

> To decide the dispute which has arisen about the criterion we must possess an accepted criterion by which we shall be able to judge the dispute, and in order to possess an accepted criterion, the dispute about the criterion must first be decided. And when the argument thus reduces itself to a form of circular reasoning [*diallelus*] the discovery of the criterion becomes impracticable, since we do not allow them to adopt a criterion by assumption, while if they offer to judge the criterion by a criterion we force them to a regress *ad infinitum*. And furthermore, since demonstration requires a demonstrated criterion, while the criterion requires an approved demonstration, they are forced into circular reasoning (*PH*, II,20).

This line of argument goes far beyond conventional appeals to the fallibility of particular senses. Sextus argues that the composition of the eye affects visual perception, so that "sufferers from jaundice see everything yellow, and those with blood-shot eyes reddish like blood" (*PH*, I,126). The dialectical argument of the Academic skeptics transcends such testable error. The argument of the *diallelus* shows not merely the possibility of error or distortion in a given instance; it shows the indefensibility of the (Stoic) claim to possession of a special kind of cognition, whereby the Stoic wise man claims knowledge qualitatively different from the *doxa*, mere opinion, of the multitude. No such criterion exists, say the skeptics, capable of supporting such a distinction.

In its Hellenistic context, then, the debate over the criterion escalates a particular rivalry between two schools; the points of conflict are what is worthy of a wise man, and what authority and distinction he can claim in the field of knowledge. The skeptical dialectic is thus understood as a liberating procedure: "We are more free and untrammelled," not bound by the edicts of a wise man or masters (*Ac.*, II,8). It is the distinction of infallibility, the qualitative superiority of the Sage's knowledge, asserted by Zeno and his followers, which Hellenistic skepticism undermines.[71]

An effect of the dialectic, paradoxically, is a virtual constraint on the discourse: the supposed real object is no longer available for examination but only its "presentation," i.e., mental data that may or may not correspond exactly to such a real object. The truth content of a statement, as Cicero makes plain, is limited to appearances (*phantasia*); the relation of an appearance to a real object beyond what appears is indeterminable. Sextus makes the same point; "We do not overthrow the affective sense-impressions which induce our assent involuntarily; and these impressions are 'the appearances.' [But] we question whether the underlying object is such as it appears" (*PH*, I, 19). A circle is thus drawn around the reference of knowledge claims; this is the epistemological circle that Shelley defines in the *Treatise on Morals,* with its "eminent advantages . . . with regard to the certainty of the conclusions" that arguments can reach. Mental data, Shelley says, are the only "facts which cannot be disputed" (Tokoo, p. 19; I&P, 7:342n.).

Nothing, however, in the skeptical formulations—Cicero's, Sextus', or Shelley's—would rule out discourse about matters that fall outside the epistemological circle thus defined. On the contrary, practical action in the natural and social world is a focal preoccupation for all these writers. Thus Shelley insists, "Important distinctions of various degrees of force indeed are to be established [among subjects of discourse], if [they were,] as they may be[,] subjects of ethical or economical discussion" (Tokoo, p. 20; I&P, 7:60). But what the skeptical arguments would restrain are assertions of absolute certainty regarding what is not in fact evident: Cicero insists that answers to questions of action are possible within the parameters of the skeptical method, "provided that we answer without actual assent" (*Ac.,* II, 104), where Cicero's "assent" (*adsensu*) has the sense of "assertion of absolute certainty." The epistemological criterion for certainty is quite distinct from ethical and political criteria for action, not for Shelley alone but also within the classical occurrences of the paradigmatic argument.

Whereas, for Zeno and Arcesilaus, the matters at issue were the character, privilege, distinction, and beliefs of the individual Sage, particular Renaissance debates involved questions of narrowly religious doctrine and, specifically, challenges to the authority of the institutional church. As Richard H. Popkin has shown, non-Christian challenges to church authority "struck at the very heart of human certainty";[72] Jean Bodin's dialogue *Colloquium heptalomeres,* for example, presents a debate between adherents of various religions, including critiques of Christianity so profound that a Jew and a believer in natural religion actually win the debate.

Bodin's dialogue is one clear formal antecedent of Shelley's dialogue on natural religion, *A Refutation of Deism,* but the relationship is generic rather than unique. Pierre Bayle's influential account of skepticism, in the *Dictionnaire historique et critique* (published in translation in London, 1734–38), includes such a skeptical dialogue; Hume's *Dialogues Concerning Natural Religion* (published posthumously in 1779) is an obvious example of the same genre of skeptical debate, and so is the dialogue on natural religion that Drummond includes in *Academical Questions* (pp. 218–81). Bodin juxtaposes views of a Jew, a Christian, and a proponent of natural religion; Hume places a spokesman for orthodox Christianity in conflict with a deist and an outright skeptic; Drummond narrates a debate between Hylus, who endorses the naturalism of Spinoza and the ancient Stoic philosophy, and Theophilus, who speaks for orthodox Christianity. Shelley, then, produces a dialogue between a deist and a conservative Christian fideist. All these dialogues look back obviously to Cicero's *De Natura Deorum,* a theological debate between a spokesman for Epicurus' theology, a Stoic, and an Academic skeptic.

My point about this genre, the skeptical dialogue on religion, is twofold. First, these works share an ideological principle from classical skepticism: as Gisela Striker expresses this principle, "nothing can be found out about the real nature of things because of what is alternatively and indiscriminately called the undecidable conflict between mutually inconsistent views or the relativity of all impressions."[73] Striker goes on to refine the distinction between undecidability and relativity, but the relevant point here is (again) generic: the juxtaposition of conflicting views is a formal element that accords with the ideological commitment—a suspension of judgment. A second point I would emphasize here is that non-Catholic challenges to Church authority in the Renaissance arose in part from the material conditions of exploration and commercial expansion. The new science, colonialism in the New World, the flight of Jewish scholars from Spain and Portugal, the importation of Islam into Europe through the Turkish invasions of the sixteenth century, and the rediscovery of classical texts (including Sextus' works, published in 1562)—all these developments contributed to a literal and material clash of viewpoints. This sort of ideological conflict accords exactly with the skeptical tropes of relativity and undecidability (*PH* I,36–163; *DL* IX,79–88). The formal structure of the dialogue in turn embodies the resulting suspension of judgment. (In Drummond's dialogue, Eugenius concludes the debate by declaring it undecided.)

Religious controversy of the Renaissance thus makes up a context in which arguments over the epistemological circle are especially germane. As Karl Mannheim has said, it is a context of ideological conflict that forces "persons to reflect not merely about the things of the world, but about thinking itself and even here not so much about truth in itself, as about the alarming fact that the same world can appear differently to different observers."[74] Such problems become general, according to Mannheim, "in an age in which disagreement is more conspicuous than agreement," and in such a context it becomes an intellectual norm to turn "from the direct observation of things to the consideration of ways of thinking" (p. 6). Whether or not Pyrrho's voyage to India did (as is commonly said) precipitate his skeptical relativism in the Hellenistic period, it is clear that novel ideologies clashing in the Renaissance often generated skeptical dialectic, and their focus is typically religious.

Martin Luther focused his own challenges to the authority of the church institution precisely on the question of the criterion: both at the Leipzig Disputation (1519), where his opponent was Johann Eck, and again in his refusal to recant at the Diet of Worms (1521), Luther specifically attacked the principle of papal and ecclesiastical infallibility, setting forth what Popkin calls "his new criterion of religious knowledge, that what conscience is compelled to believe on reading Scripture is true."[75] Erasmus was responding directly to this criterion of Luther's when, in his *De Libero Arbitrio* of 1524, he suggested a "sceptical basis for remaining within the Catholic Church" (Popkin, p. 5). Erasmus tried to show that Luther had dogmatically handled an issue "so complex that no human could really find a satisfactory solution to the problem." He offers instead the fideistic and conservative position: "He preferred to recognize the inability of man to discover adequate answers to such theological problems and to rest content with the decisions of the church on such matters," as Popkin says elsewhere.[76]

It is in the context of this conservative position of the Counter-

Reformation, then, that Erasmus invokes the skeptical arguments of the Hellenistic New Academy, arguments that he had been commending since 1509: "Human affairs are so obscure and various that nothing can be clearly known. This was the sound conclusion of the Academics, who were the least surly of the philosophers."[77]

A series of paradoxes thus occurs: Luther, seeking to deny the absolute authority of the Pope and Councils, produces a new criterion of truth; radical reform is thus tied to a new dogmatic criterion. Erasmus had been one of the more forceful advocates for Church reform (attacking, for example, the dogmas of Scholasticism), but under pressure to defend the Church and to justify remaining within the Church, Erasmus produces the skeptical arguments against dogmatic criteria. The radical reformer (Luther) turns to a form of dogmatism; the defender of the church institution (Erasmus) is a reformer offering skeptical arguments.[78]

The name usually applied to a religious faith maintained on a skeptical basis is "fideism." Eusebes, in Shelley's *Refutation of Deism*, articulates such a position. Such an application of the skeptical arguments was widespread in the Renaissance, finding perhaps its most influential expression in Montaigne's *Apology for Raimond Sebond*. Montaigne had studied the classical skeptical arguments (including the 1562 edition of Sextus' *Outlines of Pyrrhonism*), and in the *Apology* (written c. 1576) he advocates a conservative fideism, which he defends by invoking old skeptical arguments about both the relativity of perception and also the *diallelus* (or Wheel Argument). He aims to show that no criterion of truth is accessible:

> To adjudicate among the appearances of things we need to have a distinguishing method; to validate this justifying argument we need the very method at issue. And there we are, going round on the wheel.[79]

Human reason and sense failing to offer a criterion of truth, Montaigne argues that pending absolutely divine revelation of truth, the only reasonable course is to remain within the customary and traditional religion.

That apparently conservative position, however, belongs to the context in which Erasmus and Montaigne construct their arguments

and not to the skeptical arguments themselves; that which would preserve the local structures of authority, in their arguments, would undermine authoritarian positions in, for example, Academic skepticism in the Hellenistic context.[80] More recently, too, "religious
scepticism has been grounded in philosophical scepticism, but so has
fideism," as Kai Nielsen has said.[81] Two points therefore require emphasis. First, skepticism offers a methodology, but the positions with
which it deals are movable counters, in no way fixed by the parameters of the methodology itself. Second, criticism—literary or philosophical—falsifies its own assertion when it lifts the arguments out of
their historical occasions; the fiction of an abstract space where positions retain integrity over time is belied by the skeptical arguments
themselves, and also by the history of their particular articulations.

Long after Erasmus, Christian philosophy continued to align itself
with skepticism. Shelley's assignment of skeptical arguments to a
Christian (in *A Refutation of Deism*) and his own linkage of Scripture
with strict epistemological limits (in *Essay on Christianity*) is a dual
strategy with a long-standing authority.[82] In England (particularly in
the climate of conflicts within which the Civil War approached), these
conflicts became increasingly conspicuous. Thomas Goodwin, for
example, was for a time vicar of Trinity Church, Cambridge; "Becoming dissatisfied with the terms of conformity," Goodwin re-
signed his church position, fled from England during the period of
William Laud's power, and only returned at the beginning of the
Long Parliament.[83] In the course of these theological disavowals and
political conflicts, Goodwin composed *The Vanity of Thoughts Discovered* (1638),[84] in which he aligns skepticism with Scripture. Though
no specific documentary evidence shows that Shelley had read this
volume, its representative arguments are worth looking at briefly, because they typify a form of critical thinking that Shelley then reproduces (with even greater irony and critical distance) in what he
perceived as the new revolutionary context of his own time, in the
years of the Regency.

Goodwin takes a scriptural text as an authority for his skeptical argument, as Shelley was to do in *Essay on Christianity:* "How long
shall thy vaine thoughts lodge within thee?" (Jeremiah 4.14). Goodwin amplifies the skeptical power of that biblical sentence: first,
by making it inclusive (arguing "that [all] our thoughts are vaine"

[p. 8]); second, by defining "thoughts" inclusively ("all the *internall* acts of the minde of man, of what faculty soever, all those reasonings, consultations, purposes, resolutions, intents, ends, desires, and cares of the minde" [p. 9]); and third, by defining "vanity" inclusively, assigning several senses to the term, including "unprofitablenesse," "inconstancy," and "folly" (pp. 20–24).

By claiming scriptural authority for his critique of knowledge and by extending its definitions so broadly, Goodwin produces a strong critique of all claims for certainty; truth is not a property of thought, according to Goodwin's definitions, and this negative argument is given greater rhetorical force as Goodwin claims the authority of Scripture: not only Jeremiah but also Solomon (pp. 7–8), Isaiah (p. 9), Ezekiel (p. 10), and Genesis (p. 10) are adduced for additional examples.

When Shelley argues that the meaning of the beatitude "Blessed are the pure in heart, for they shall see God" is that "virtue is its own reward," he is doing two things that dissenting thinkers like Goodwin had done in earlier revolutionary periods. He imposes an epistemological limit on the terms of the discourse, so that the scriptural sentence refers to acts of the mind; and he unseats any and all claims for the absolute authority of knowledge claims. His definition of "thought" is as broad as Goodwin's (see, e.g., *On Life*, R&P, pp. 477–78), and yet "thought" so broadly defined contains no possible criterion of truth.

The most famous and influential reproduction of the paradigmatic argument of the criterion—Descartes's account of "clear and distinct ideas"—reverses the ideological positions again. Where, for Erasmus and Montaigne, skepticism had served to protect the authority of the church institution, Descartes devotes his entire philosophical project to the task of protecting that authority by overcoming the skeptical arguments. Descartes produces arguments with obvious parallels to the ancient discussions of *katalepsis*,[85] but while Luther used the criterion of truth to challenge Catholic authority, Descartes uses it primarily to defend the Catholic concept of God. The context in which Shelley later challenges the criterion of truth is defined in part by specific responses to Descartes, and so it is important to examine the Cartesian application of the arguments here.

DESCARTES AND THE CRITERION OF TRUTH

In Shelley's polemical dialogue *A Refutation of Deism,* Theosophus puts forward what a conflict of apparent truths always demands—a criterion for judging:

> The intensity of belief, like that of every other passion, is pre-cisely proportioned to the degrees of excitement. A graduated scale, on which should be marked the capabilities of propositions to approach to the test of the senses, would be a just measure of the belief which ought to be attached to them (I&P, 6:39).

Theosophus' criterion stops short of dogmatism, because it remains limited to appearances, impressions ("the test of the senses"), and does not allege access to truth external to this epistemological limit. Similar efforts had long appeared in skeptical philosophy, to articulate a criterion for the discrimination of tenable, probable, persuasive propositions, in a world of human experience in which truth con-ceived as an externality is not accessible. The problem of the criterion reappears in Shelley, as in the *Treatise on Morals:*

> A scale might be formed, graduated according to the degrees of a combined ratio of intensity, duration, connexion, periods of recurrence, and utility, which would be the standard; according to which all ideas might be measured (Tokoo, p. 20; I&P, 7:60).

Again the criterion measures and discriminates among ideas. The cri-terion is not a means of distinguishing ideas from truth. This idea-tional property of Shelley's criterion characterizes Drummond's for-mulation as well: "The conviction of the philosopher . . . has no support but from itself. Each must ultimately trace what he calls cer-tainty to his own mind" (*AQ,* p. 152). The criterion for judging the certainty of propositions is a mental measure and not a correspon-dence that leads legitimately from subjectivity to its referent in exter-nal space.

Drummond's statement appears in one of the most important sec-tions of *Academical Questions,* the critical account of Descartes's phi-losophy. More than any European philosopher, perhaps, Descartes had struggled explicitly with the extremities of skeptical thought, seeking and claiming to construct a positive dogma, immune to doubt, from the abyss of skepticism. The problem of the criterion is the pivotal issue in Descartes's arguments; thus Drummond focuses his response in turn on that problem. Shelley's formulation—in his own voice and in his character's—takes shape in the context of this ongoing argument, and an exposition of the Cartesian formula and Drummond's response can show the determining limits of Shelley's claims.

Many facts lend support to the view of Descartes that Popkin has articulated, "as a man who tried to reinstate the medieval outlook in the face of Renaissance novelty."[86] One important piece of evidence is his suppression of his own scientific work: when he learned of the condemnation of Galileo for teaching the same Copernican system that Descartes had taught in *Le Monde,* Descartes had his own book suppressed.[87] This controversy involved more than astronomy; it was a matter of skeptical doubt that was central to Copernicus's work. The foreword to Copernicus's *Six Books on the Revolutions of the Heavenly Spheres* states a methodological condition of skepticism, one that Descartes was later explicitly concerned to overcome: an astronomer "cannot in any way attain to the true causes" of the motions he observes; therefore "he will adopt whatever suppositions enable the motions to be computed," but "these hypotheses need not be true nor even probable" but only heuristic.[88]

This fictionalist philosophy of science did not at all accord with Descartes's commitments. In 1628 (six years before finishing *Le Monde*) Descartes engaged in a debate with a chemist, N. de Chandoux. Chandoux argued that science could be founded only on probabilities; Descartes responded with a vigorous defense of absolute certainty, which, he argued, could alone assure a basis for human knowledge.[89] For this defense of absolute certainty—that is, for his attack on skepticism—Descartes was commended by a cardinal (Bérulle), who encouraged him to develop his system.

It was under these conditions that Descartes composed his treatments of the skeptical arguments, in the *Discourse on Method* (1637) and *Meditations on the First Philosophy* (1641). The *Meditations* contain Descartes's most radical presentation of the skeptical argument, and yet that volume also makes his reactionary aims obvious. He dedicates his *Meditations* to "the Dean and Doctors of the Sacred Faculty of Theology of Paris." This commitment to church authority is not at all nominal but a real feature of his argument in the *Meditations:* "When the reasonings contained in it, by which the existence of God and the distinction of the human soul from the body are established, shall have been brought to such a degree of perspicuity as to be esteemed exact demonstrations," Descartes implores the church officials to "condescend to accord them the authority of your approbation." This authority is exactly, he says, "the strongest support of the Catholic Church," and added to his arguments such support will effect this end: "There will no longer be any one who will venture to doubt either the existence of God or the real distinction of mind and body."[90]

The paradox of Descartes's account of skepticism is thus what Burnyeat has expressed:

> The First *Meditation* is a rehash of ancient skepticism, deriving (directly or indirectly) from Cicero and Sextus. Descartes' aim . . . is to ground positive knowledge on his examination of skepticism. . . . In virtue of this novel strategy Descartes claimed to be the first philosopher in history to refute "the Skeptics." What he in fact achieved was to bring about a permanent enlargement of our conception of the power and scope of skeptical doubt, with the result that Hume, for example, lists "Cartesian doubt" as a species of skepticism alongside, and more fundamental than, Pyrrhonism and "the Academical philosophy."[91]

Further, Descartes's dubitative procedures are extended to even greater scope in Drummond's *Academical Questions,* where Shelley found doubt so radical that it accomplished what even Hume had not: a direct overturning of Descartes's first principles. Drummond effects this overturning of Descartes's principles by placing them within their classical context, which is the Stoic argument of *katalepsis* and the criterion of truth.

The skeptical arguments that Descartes rehearses in the *Discourse* and again in the First Meditation express three levels of doubt, but the formulations differ significantly. In the *Discourse,* the first level of doubt is the classical one distrusting the senses: "As our senses deceive us at times, I was ready to suppose that nothing was at all the way our senses represented them to be" (*Discourse*, p. 20). The second level is doubt of rational faculties: "As there are men who make mistakes in reasoning even on the simplest topics in geometry, I judged that I was as liable to error as any other, and rejected as false all the reasoning which I had previously accepted as valid demonstration" (pp. 20–21). The third level is the ancient dreamer hypothesis: "As the same precepts which we have when awake may come to us when asleep without their being true, I decided to suppose that nothing that had ever entered my mind was more real than the illusions of my dreams" (p. 21). One classical locus of this dreamer hypothesis is Cicero's *Academica* (II,88): "When he had woken up he was able to think those appearances dreams, as they were, but he accepted them as real while he was asleep, just as much as he would have done if awake."

In the *Meditations,* the first level of doubt is still the argument from sensory errors, but the dreamer hypothesis is made the second level rather than the third.[92] What he now puts as the third and most extreme level of doubt is the most powerful and radical skeptical hypothesis he ever articulated: he supposes "that some malignant demon [or evil genius], who is at once exceedingly potent and deceitful, has employed all his artifice to deceive me" (p. 116). This hypothesis is stronger than the second level of doubt in the *Discourse,* according to which reasoning sometimes errs; this suggestion of the "malignant demon" leads to the supposition that "all external things are nothing better than the illusions of dreams" (p. 116). Rather than occasional error, this hypothesis (which Descartes called hyperbolical doubt) suggests that one is always deceived and that it is possible that no external world exists at all.[93] As Popkin has said, this hypothesis of the malignant demon presents "the most radical and devastating of skeptical possibilities, that not only is our information deceptive, illusory, and misleading, but that our faculties, even under the best of conditions, may be erroneous." Popkin correctly places the problem in its classical context: "Any criterion, any test of the reliability of what we know, is open to question."[94]

Descartes begins his solution to this crisis of doubt with what is probably the most famous passage in all of his work:

> But I soon noticed that while I thus wished to think everything false, it was necessarily true that I who thought so was some-

thing. Since this truth, *I think, therefore I am,* was so firm and assured that all the most extravagant suppositions of the sceptics were unable to shake it, I judged that I could safely accept it as the first principle of the philosophy I was seeking (*Discourse*, p. 21).

However, as Bernard Williams has shrewdly observed, the task that Descartes has actually set himself is not in fact discovering what is true; it is rather discovering things that are certain, that cannot be doubted.[95] That is, he seeks not what exists but rather a criterion whereby one can know a thing to be true and certain. Accordingly, he uses the cogito argument ("I think, therefore I am") not as a premise from which to deduce other truths but as an example of a certainty, wherein the criterion of certainty can be discovered:

Next I considered in general what is required of a proposition for it to be true and certain, for since I had just discovered one to be such, I thought I ought also to know of what that certitude consisted. I saw that there was nothing at all to this statement, "I think, therefore I am," to assure me that I was saying the truth, unless it was that I saw very clearly that to think one must exist. So I judged that I could accept as a general rule that the things which we conceive very clearly and very distinctly are always true (*Discourse*, p. 21).

This, then, is Descartes's criterion of truth: clear and distinct ideas. The similarity of this criterion to the Stoic *katalepsis* is obvious (the noticeable difference being, as Williams has said, that "the Stoic kataleptic presentations were paradigmatically some particular kinds of sense-perceptions [whereas for Descartes] the kataleptic impression is intellectual"[96]).

Having thus established the new criterion of truth (or rather resuscitated the ancient one), Descartes then rebuilds the world that radical skepticism had threatened to dismantle, beginning, as his dedication to the theological faculty might suggest, with God: "Among these my ideas, besides that which represents myself, respecting which there can be here no difficulty, there is one that represents a God; others that represent corporeal and inanimate things," and others sufficient to reconstitute the world according to Catholic dogmatism, completely and doubtless to the satisfaction of his good patron the Cardinal. There is no need here to rehearse Descartes's version of the ontological proof, a case that he erects only after he has settled the question of the criterion of truth; our concern and that of his critical successors as Shelley knew them is more fundamentally the question of the criterion itself. It is important to emphasize, however, as we pass to Descartes's critics, that the theological framework of his argument reflects the institutional crisis that his church was undergoing as he wrote.

The critic of Descartes whose arguments are most important in Shelley's prose is Sir William Drummond, but I would not wish to obscure the fact that Descartes's work was met with objections instantly on its publication. Many of his contemporary critics feared his apparently skeptical presentations rather than his dogmatism. His *Meditations* were published in what was itself a format of dialectical argument: to them were added six sets of Objections by writers including Thomas Hobbes, Antoine Arnauld, and Pierre Gassendi; these Objections were in turn answered in the same publication by Descartes's Replies.[97] But the arguments of Drummond, Shelley's contemporary, were closer to Shelley for many reasons, and only one of them is his more rigorous skepticism, amounting to a more critical application of the skeptical tropes than even Descartes's own. The ideological crisis of the nineteenth century was not that of the seventeenth; new problems for church authority had arisen, but joined to them were the literally political challenges to the authority claims of the counterrevolutionary monarchies of Britain and Europe. The shape of the skeptical dialectic in Shelley's time, therefore, both in its modes of attack and defense, is more complicated and yet still recognizably a repetition of the long-standing paradigms of debate.

DRUMMOND'S CRITIQUE OF DESCARTES: THE ARGUMENT OF RELATIVITY AND THE CRITERION OF TRUTH

Drummond begins by acknowledging that the history of the argument over certainty has a dialectical character: the dogmatism of Greek philosophers, especially Plato and Aristotle, "had imposed upon the credulity of mankind" (*AQ*, p. 2). Skeptical critiques did follow the establishment of dogma, but the ancient doctrines were then restored, as "the bold spirit of the dogmatic philosophy was, indeed, never satisfied with uncertainty" (p. 3). Again, in modern philosophy, some writers "have rejected many of the rash surmises of the Greeks" (p. 3), but then those surmises reaffirm themselves, as in Descartes's reproduction of the *katalepsis* (p. 144). "There may," therefore, "be reason to fear, that the spirit of dogmatism is still the same, though it speak by other oracles" (p. 3). Drummond meets that reaffirmation of dogma with a new (or newly recomposed) critique. The epistemological circle that Shelley assumes for a starting point (in *On Life*) is actually a result, in turn, of Drummond's critical construction, as Shelley says in his essay.

Drummond's account of Descartes is systematic and thorough, including treatments of the demon hypothesis (pp. 136–37, 151) and of Descartes's affirmations of God (e.g., p. 159). He starts, however, with what Descartes called "the first principle of the philosophy I was seeking"—the cogito argument, "I think, therefore I am." Drummond confronts this alleged certainty with three refutations. First, he points out that "Descartes commences his system of philosophy, with proposing to doubt of all things. He soon makes the reflection, however, that that which thinks must exist" (p. 136). But if "I have hitherto had no distinct perception . . . and I have not before perceived very distinctly, that I have soul, or that I have even a being," then how "with this troubled perception, this clouded vision, this indistinct understanding of any thing, shall I venture to say, *I think?* Some certain knowledge is required in the man, who makes this assertion" (p. 142).

This argument—that the assertion of one's own identity presupposes prior certainties—lies behind Shelley's complaint that "thought can with difficulty visit the intricate and winding chambers which it inhabits" (Tokoo, p. 21; I&P, 7:64). The concept of one's own identity is by no means simple or directly apprehensible: "Mind cannot be considered pure" (I&P, 7:61); its very unity depends on the conceptualization of "events or objects" as "diversities," and that conceptualization is an admitted fiction. "With what semblance of reason, then, can such an affirmation as this [the cogito] come from him, who has doubted of everything?" (*AQ,* p. 142). The cogito fails at that which it was proposed to accomplish:

In vain shall I be told, that an illustrious philosopher broke the spell of universal skepticism, by affirming, that he thought, and therefore was. If Descartes, the brightest genius of his time, really doubted of every thing, until he exclaimed, *I think,* it seems scarcely possible, that he should have understood his own words (p. 142).

Drummond's second and third refutations of the cogito argument thus involve accordingly the analysis of the assertion "*Ego cogito, ergo sum.*" "Something [*cogito*] is affirmed of a subject [*ego*], by which the existence [*sum*] of this subject is to be proved." Drummond questions the coherence of the predication: "How can anything be affirmed of a subject, of the existence of which we are not yet convinced?" (p. 143). The reference of each clause is merely to the other, and thus no warrant for a knowledge claim exists ouside the syntax of the statement: "The certainty of [A] my existence is inferred from something, which [B] I affirm I do," but the priority of A is an illusion, resting on the prior assumption of B: "until I know, that I exist, I cannot positively affirm, that I do anything" (p. 143).

Third, Drummond applies what he calls "a yet more severe *analysis*" to the assertion "*Ego cogito, ergo sum,*" and that is an analysis of logical form. "Is not that, which is here intended to be proved in the conclusion [*ergo sum*], already taken for granted in the premises [*ego cogito*]?" (p. 143). It was Descartes who invoked the logic of deduction, a test that his principle cannot survive; "Descartes has told us, that he exists as a thinking being, and that therefore he exists" (p. 143). This reasoning is tautology, but not proof: "The logic must be allowed to be simple enough, which assures us that we are, because we are" (p. 143), but such logic furnishes no knowledge—"He, who employs it, takes the thing for granted, which he had proposed to prove" (p. 143).

Thus Drummond asks of the cogito what Shelley later asks of all modern dogmas: "What sanctioning correspondence unites [the] concatenation of syllogisms?" Following Descartes's allegation of certainty, philosophers "have professed indeed . . . to deduce their conclusions from indisputable facts." But the dialectician asks, "How came many of those facts to be called indisputable?" (I&P, 7:63). The circularity of the cogito argument and others like it simply alleges what it sets out to demonstrate; "Logic, or the science of words[,] must no longer be confounded with metaphysics[,] or the science of facts" (I&P, 7:63). The relation of sentence elements to one another cannot be adduced as evidence of an extrastatemental verity. In the case of the cogito, as Drummond argues, the assertion seeks to belie its own circularity; the criterion it allegedly embodies is a fiction.

As I have already shown, Descartes produces the cogito only to establish a base from which to erect the criterion, i.e., clear and distinct ideas; having deconstructed the cogito, Drummond turns directly to the problem of the criterion. When Shelley then argues that criteria "are as various as those beings from whose opinions they result" (*A Refutation of Deism*, I&P, 6:52), he is repeating the trope of relativity and variety; and that is exactly the form of Drummond's attack on the criterion of clear and distinct ideas. The mere fact of ideological conflict is enough to undermine any ideology's claim to universal dominion, as I have argued in connection with the theological dialogues. Here again, Shelley's argument (following Drummond's) is threefold. One argumentative topos is historical: Descartes's criterion produced God, as soon as the criterion was itself produced; but "the invariable opposition which philosophy has ever encountered from the spirit of revealed religion" (*A Refutation of Deism*, I&P, 6:37), together with the fact of the small proportion of humanity actually believing in God, discredits the "universality of a belief in his existence" (I&P, 6:53).

Neither Shelley nor Drummond is arguing about God; rather each is arguing about this alleged universality of Descartes's criterion. The doctrine "wherein he pretends, that whatever is very distinctly perceived and understood must be true" is, Drummond says, a revival of the Stoic *katalepsis*. It is extraordinary "that Descartes should have hazarded an opinion, as an indubitable axiom, which had been so often called in question by the most illustrious men of antiquity" (p. 144). He cites Socrates' disclaimer, "*Scire se, nihil se scire*" ("I know only that I know nothing"); he repeats "that the New Academicians had not assented to the doctrine of the *katalepsis*"; and he cites Cicero's version of the refusal to assent, "*Nihil posse percipi*" ("Nothing can be perceived" as certainly true) (p. 144; cf. *Ac.*, II,40).

A second form of the relativity argument, applied to refute Descartes's criterion, is a variant of Cicero's argument of the dreamer or madman. Drummond turns the skeptical trope, used by Descartes, against Descartes:

A mathematician is convinced . . . that things equal to the same are equal to one another. It is impossible to make him think otherwise; and the Cartesian assigns the reason of this belief, by alleging, that the mathematician has a distinct perception of the truth, which he has affirmed. A lunatic takes his flock-bed for a throne, and his dungeon for a palace. I cannot persuade him to the contrary, for he assures me, that he has the clearest perception of what he has asserted (pp. 145–46).

This argument has even more force than that of relativity alone, because Drummond can show that the clear and distinct ideas of the mathematician and of the lunatic have exactly the same ground of authority: "A lunatic may be persuaded, that all mankind agree with him in the wildest fables, which his disordered imagination can fabricate. Nevertheless the conviction of the philosopher, like that of the lunatic, has no support but from itself" (p. 152). The certainty of each belongs to the mind of each; "How is the individual to assert, that one clear perception is more certain than another?" (p. 152).

Again, Shelley reproduces Drummond's argument, but he adds a political and ethical dimension that Drummond had not yet made explicit. As Descartes had used his doctrine of clear and distinct ideas to establish the real externality of the world, Shelley says,

It has commonly been supposed that those distinct thoughts which affect a number of persons, at regular intervals during the passage of a multitude of other thoughts, and which are called *real,* or *external objects,* are totally different in kind from those which affect only a few persons, and which recur at irregular intervals, and are usually more obscure and indistinct, such as hallucinations, dreams, and the ideas of madness (Tokoo, p. 20; I&P, 7:59).

Shelley's critique of this position is methodological rather than doctrinal:

No essential distinction between any one of these ideas or any class of them is founded on a correct observation of the nature of things, but merely on a consideration of what thoughts are most invariably subservient to the security and happiness of life (Tokoo, p. 20; I&P, 7:59–60).

If this, the considerations of the security and happiness of life, were the only application of the criterion, "the philosopher might safely accommodate his language to that of the vulgar"; but instead dogmatists reach for unwarranted authority, "to assert an essential difference which has no foundation in truth" (Tokoo, p. 20; I&P, 7:60) but which, as "violent dogmatism," does have "fatal consequences in morals" (*On Life,* R&P, p. 476).

Shelley thus elicits a progressive value from the dialectical procedure: to disclose the relativity of a view is to deny at once its universality and also its immutability. Again Drummond's exposition provides Shelley's backdrop: "The contradictions in our reasonings are as numerous and various, as in our characters and conduct" (*AQ,* p. 146). The contradictions appear even within an individual mind and life: "My experience furnishes me, as it probably does every other man, with examples of a total alteration in my own opinions, concerning things of which I entertained no doubts whatever" (p. 148); and this insight yields a readiness to "obtain new perceptions, by which you would see the error of some conclusions, which you now make without hesitation" (p. 153). This progress in the destruction of error can only be inhibited by the reification of what one perceives, at one moment, as an inflexible and eternal verity: "I fear to pronounce, that in me exists a standard of immutable truth" (p. 154). Shelley agrees about the ethical contribution of the skeptical method, both negatively ("it destroys error, and the roots of error") and also positively. But the positive contribution of the method has nothing to do with positive truth, or even with the likelihood of truth; even delusion can develop "the whole powers" of humanity, if the delusion is ethical and progressive rather than dogmatic and immutable: "Towards whatsoever we regard as perfect, undoubtedly it is no less our duty than it is our nature to press forward. . . . It is in politics rather than in religion that faith is meritorious" (*A Philosophical View of Reform,* I&P, 7:46).[98] Again for Shelley it is action that warrants our ideas, and not their alleged certainty as immutable truth.

Shelley's use of the skeptical arguments from relativity is in these ways like the later arguments of Marx and Engels, as I shall be showing below: Shelley takes the demonstration of individual and cultural variability as undermining absolutist claims of truth and right; and as Engels was to do (in *Anti-Dühring,* for example), Shelley makes of the epistemological circle a powerful tool for political analysis and argument.

UNIVERSAL CONSENT, FACTICITY, AND NOMINALIZATION

Both Drummond and Shelley expand the argument from relativity still further, until even universal consent cannot be alleged to warrant the truth content of any single claim to knowledge. Thus Shelley first invokes the variety of conceptions of God, for example, against an alleged universality of consent; but even universal consent, should it be found to exist, is no absolute warrant of any truth, because custom, habit, and temperament condition even shared beliefs:

> The word God cannot mean at the same time an ape, a snake, a bone, a calabash, a Trinity, and a Unity. Nor can that belief be accounted universal against which men of powerful intellect and spotless virtue have in every age protested (*A Refutation of Deism,* I&P, 6:55).

But the nonexistent universality of consent would constitute no trustworthy foundation for belief in any case: minds—even Jesus Christ's—"have been predisposed . . . to adopt the opinions of [their] countrymen" (*Essay on Christianity,* I&P, 6:229). "Every human mind has, what Lord Bacon calls its 'idola specus,' peculiar images which reside in the inner cave of thought" (*Essay on Christianity,* I&P, 6:241).

The discussion of Bacon's that Shelley cites helps to explain how even a universal consensus cannot warrant a claim to knowledge: Bacon identifies among the "deepest fallacies of the human mind" a kind of "predisposition . . . which as it were perverts and infects all the anticipations of the intellect." Even beyond the *idola specus,* which belong to "the individual nature of each man" there are what "I call Idols of the *Tribe,*" delusions "imposed upon the mind . . . by the nature of man in general."[99] Thus, Shelley says, "If we found our belief in the existence of God on the universal consent of mankind, we are duped by the most palpable of sophisms" (*A Refutation of Deism,* I&P, 6:55).

Again Drummond supplies Shelley's more immediate context: having rendered his critique of the alleged universality of belief, Drummond goes on to deny that were it allowed, such universality would have confirming power.

> The Cartesian makes a distinction between those truths, to which all men give assent, when the terms, in which they are expressed, are understood; and perceptions, about which the opinions of one individual may vary from those of another; or concerning which the individual himself may possibly entertain a different belief at different times (*AQ*, p. 152).

Drummond, like Descartes, acknowledges that the argument from relativity undermines the authority of the latter sort of truth, but he extends the criticism to the former kind as well: first, "the invariable assent of others proves nothing; since our conviction, that they are convinced, exists only in ourselves" (*AQ*, p. 152). That is, the universal consent is enclosed within the epistemological circle. Second, even the universal propagation of a belief in no way changes the foundations of it: "I will instruct the savage, say you, and he will have the same opinions with me. But to instruct him, is to give him new perceptions, and with them a new belief. It is to change the state of his intellectual being" (p. 153), not to adduce evidence of a relation between intellectual being and allegedly anterior truth.

Drummond argues that like any thinker, a Cartesian must "trace all his certainty to his own anterior conviction," since both conviction and certainty are intellectual; this condition imposes constraints on ontological claims, because "it is from [interior conviction] alone, that he can affirm the existence of any thing" (p. 154). Not even the appeal to universal consensus can overcome this circumscription of affirmations.[100]

Shelley and Drummond work their way back from this epistemological position into the world of action, with two concepts; I shall be calling these concepts facticity and nominalization. The importance of both concepts is that they enable the skeptic to formulate imperatives and to engage in materially efficacious action, without any of the dogmatism, even tentative or provisional, that skepticism has already undermined. Shelley identifies two dogmatisms that assume externality of objects: first, "the popular philosophy of mind and matter," which is dualism, and second, monistic materialism; as we have seen, he rejects both systems, aligning himself with "those philosophers, who assert that nothing exists but as it is perceived" (*On Life*, R&P, p. 476). What follows is by no means solipsistic quietism: solipsism, the doctrine that "I, the person who now write and think, am that one mind" in whose perceptions alone the world exists, is as Shelley says a "monstrous presumption" (R&P, pp. 477–78). Yet how, one might wonder, can Shelley assert that nothing exists but as it is perceived, without enclosing himself in such mere subjectivity?

Both Shelley and Drummond answer that question by acknowledging facticity. "When we desire to analyze what any thing is, which we denominate an external object, we always find, that it may be resolved into certain sensible qualities," says Drummond; as Locke, Berkeley, and Hume had argued, "sensible qualities of matter exist only as they are perceived"; it follows, says Drummond, that "if I be desired to explain, what I perceive . . . I can only repeat the catalogue of my own feelings" (pp. 24–25). This admission in no way suggests that the world is only ideas in one's head, so that one need not get out of the way of a careering carriage, or (as the dogmatist challenges in one of Hume's dialogues) as if a skeptic would as soon leave by an upstairs window as by the door. Berkeley, Hume, Drummond, and Shelley do make similar claims, limiting experience with ideas, but the philosophy of any of these thinkers would enjoin us actively to evade the carriage or safely to go out by the door. But where dualism (the mind-matter dogma) and materialism can only warrant that advice by hypostatizing fictional externalities, the skeptic notices that the real distinction is between perceptions that are subject to voluntary power and those that are not. "Thoughts and feelings [all sensations, including perceived carriages and broken collarbones] arise, with or without our will" (*On Life*, R&P, p. 475). Ideas (sensible data—carriages) of intellect or of imagination (chimeras, hallucinations) "do not always present themselves to the mind by an act of the will" (*AQ*, p. 13). The distinction is between what is given and what is willed, and this distinction does not depend upon (has nothing to do with) fictions of existence exterior to perception. "We do not overthrow the affective sense-impressions which induce our assent involuntarily," says Sextus, who may be allowed to speak on this point for these skeptics collectively; "we grant the fact that it appears [the carriage, the collarbone, the problem in industrial working conditions], and our doubt does not concern the appearance itself but the account given of that appearance" (*PH*, I, 19).

Facticity is the arrival unbidden of the object or event (carriage, armed platoon, rainstorm, headache) independent of our will. This concept has all the explanatory and practical power of the popular philosophy of external objects (enabling us to cry, "Look out!" or to campaign for Wendell Willkie) but none of what Shelley calls "the shocking absurdities" of that popular philosophy (*On Life*, R&P, p. 476).

The question arises, in philosophical literature and also in the streets: what causes the perceptions that arise thus unbidden and for which we must look out? Skeptics—Sextus, Hume, Drummond, Shelley—respond to that question by deconstructing the conventional assumptions of cause; they do not answer dogmatically (that is, with a negative or a positive dogma); "never satisfied with uncertainty," the multitude and the dogmatists alike rush desperately back toward the now-discredited dogmas, convinced that their rigidity is somehow safer than the suspension of judgment that skeptics, since Pyrrho and Arcesilaus, have repeatedly advocated and induced. Two of Shelley's accounts of the concept of cause summarize adequately the main lines of skeptical argument,[101] and I have written elsewhere of Hume's argument as it became important to Shelley.[102] Briefly, Shelley says that "cause is only a word expressing a certain state of the human mind with regard to the manner in which two thoughts are apprehended to be related to each other" (*On Life*, R&P, p. 478); he also identifies the argument's historical context:

Hume has shewn, to the satisfaction of all philosophers, that the only idea which we can form of causation is derivable from the constant conjunction of objects, and the consequent inference of one from the other. We denominate that phenomenon the cause of another which we observe with the fewest exceptions to precede its occurrence (*A Refutation of Deism*, I&P, 6:55).

To treat an object (appearance, perception, event, thing) as phenomenon does not commit one to the position known as phenomenalism—the assertion that nothing exists other than phenomena in their perceptual subjectivity. Shelley notices explicitly that the designation of the causal relation is an act of our nomination: we make the concept by constructing it and naming it. Rather than trivialize the process, Shelley spends much of his career celebrating the act of nominalization. Given his concept of facticity and his celebration of this constructive act of the mind,[103] Shelley can and does (consistently with his skeptical arguments) emigrate to Italy, knock down a German on a crowded boat, move heavy furniture, and eat meals. He also constructs both political and poetic theory; those theories, however, can be easily misunderstood, when criticism is guided by misconstructions of Shelley's conceptual framework. Characterizing that framework, I shall try to show how it is free of the reifications that may have been unhappily imposed on it in the past.

Confronted with the question of cause, the effective power that produces perception, some Shelley critics have moved inward into what is personal and perhaps even trivial: "He has found a way of talking to his own visionary self, and in loving nature, he has found a way to love his own conscious self," says Jean Hall.[104] What critics like Hall ascribe to Shelley is in fact the "monstrous presumption" that Shelley attacks, i.e., that "I, the person who now write and think," subsume existence. Alternatively, others have moved outward into the old and unintelligible dogmas of externality (unintelligible, that is, within the parameters of Shelley's skeptical discourse). Thus Wasserman predicates for Shelley a belief in an "eternal unmoved mover" named Power, which—though it is "unknown"— we allegedly know. It is "inaccessible" though we have access to it because it "enters into the realm of time." Wasserman's densely contradictory account becomes yet more interesting and important when it manifestly contradicts Shelley; not only do we have knowledge of this unknown Power, we have "knowledge of the absolute Power behind all worldly action, or, in more appropriately religious terms, of a transcendent and absolute divine Cause."[105] As I have shown, Shelley makes it clear that we have no such thing; what is more, Shelley deconstructs Wasserman's reification so pointedly that it is almost as if he had already read Wasserman's account and wished to refute it: "When we use the words *principle, power, cause,* &c., we mean to express no real being, but only to class under those terms a certain series of co-existing phenomena" (*On a Future State,* I&P, 6:208).

Shelley displaces Wasserman's hypostatized "absolute divine Cause" with the skeptical tropes of relativity and conceptualization:

> Mankind . . . have not failed to attribute to the universal cause a character analogous with their own. The image of this invisible mysterious being is more or less excellent and perfect . . . in proportion to the perfectness of the mind on which it is impressed. . . . Thus, the conceptions which any nation or individual entertain of the God of its popular worship may be inferred from their own actions and opinions which are the subjects of their approbation among their fellow-men (*Essay on Christianity,* I&P, 6:238–39).

Shelley's formulation is naturalistic and social in its framework: he says that practical change in social relations is associated closely with ideological transformation. Further, he provides a basis for the importance of such transformation: the conditions of living depend upon it.

SHELLEY, DRUMMOND, AND THE CONCEPT OF POWER

What Wasserman calls "more appropriately religious terms" are thus flatly disallowed by Shelley's analysis of "this invisible, mysterious being"; what is called "the universal cause" is a conception constructed within concrete social situations and is intelligible with reference to "actions and opinions" in those social situations. Rescher makes a pertinent distinction between kinds of knowledge claims: one kind involves "an unattainable ideal," but another (germane, I would say, to Shelley) is more limited. Such a limited assertion "must be construed in socially oriented terms as a real-life resource of the operative dynamics of communication."[106]

Shelley's argument has two parts: negatively, the power reified by religion (and by Wasserman) is "no real being" but rather a conceptual act of the human mind. Positively, the mental act of constructing this concept is intelligible as a psychological and social attribution. Both parts of this critical argument on deity-as-power are commonplaces in skeptical tradition. Carneades formulated them in his critique of the Stoic conception of the gods,[107] and Shelley found them in Drummond, in a form almost identical to his own: negatively, power is an "illusion of the mind"; positively, the construction of this illusion is explicable as social and psychological behavior. "When men first assumed the existence of power, in order to account for events, they seem always to have ascribed it to some being possessing will and intelligence" (*AQ*, p. 175).

As Shelley later does in the *Essay on Christianity* and in *A Refutation of Deism*, Drummond locates this act of construction within a historical framework:

In the first periods of society, rude and unlettered nations attributed every circumstance, for which they could not otherwise account, to the agency of visible, or invisible, beings, whom they called Gods, and adored either from fear, or from gratitude. The first opinions of men were transmitted to their posterity. . . . But the belief in the interference of Deities and Demons in human concerns, and in the order of nature, was gradually rejected, as the experience of men increased, and as their knowledge in physics extended. They retained, indeed, the ancient doctrine of active principles. . . . Powers were attributed to material as well as to incorporeal beings; and the nominal difference between physical forces, and mental faculties, concealed from the inattentive observer their common origin, and their real similitude (*AQ*, pp. 175–76).

For both Drummond and Shelley, anthropomorphism—the construction of fictions of deity after human patterns—has metaphysical implications as well as social. "The difference is merely nominal between those two classes of thought which are vulgarly distinguished by the names of ideas and of external objects," as Shelley says in *On Life* (R&P, p. 477); Drummond shows the importance of this "nominal difference" in the reifications that belong to religion (*AQ*, p. 176), as Shelley does, then, in *A Refutation of Deism*: "Barbarous and uncivilized nations have uniformly adored, under various names a God of which themselves were the model; revengeful, blood-thirsty, grovelling and capricious" (I&P, 6:34).

62

The act of nominalization that can institutionalize oppression can also furnish a basis for action; freedom follows from the demystification of the concept:

> Where we observe changes to occur, we assume the existence of power; we suppose the operation of causes; and we describe the physical and moral existence of things by their relative states of action and passion. But this illusion of the mind cannot alter the real nature of its perceptions; nor can it change the internal feeling into an external quality (*AQ,* p. 26).

Drummond's critique of the concept of power runs twenty-four pages (pp. 169–93), and it is important in his ethical applications as well as in his metaphysics. He locates his ethical insight in the context of classical skepticism when he says that "Cicero expressed the opinion of Plato, when he said . . . that the intellect sees and hears, and not external organs" (p. 53). When human beings acknowledge that they can and do construct systems of interpretation, that the conceptions according to which life is organized are made rather than caused by an unreachable absolute, then they are liberated and empowered to act: delusions, as Shelley says, can exercise and develop the powers of humanity. The effect of a transcendental or dogmatically materialist account of power is to enslave its believers; the effect of the skeptical dialectic is to relocate the construction of ideology within human activity.

SIGN THEORY: BERKELEY, DRUMMOND, SHELLEY, AND SKEPTICAL TRADITION

The act of naming is linked with metaphysics, for Drummond and Shelley as for the ancient skeptics, but it is also linked with politics. Skeptical sign theory—set forth, for example, by Sextus (e.g., in *PH* I,97ff.)—comprises not a set of linguistic propositions but a method for an analysis of worldviews. It is in this broader application that sign theory forms part of Shelley's philosophical context. He emphasizes its ideological importance when he defines the relation of sign theory to the intellectual system that he shares with Drummond; that system, says Shelley, "reduces the mind to that freedom in which it would have acted, but for the misuse of words and signs, the instruments of its own creation" (*On Life,* R&P, p. 477).

The definition of "sign" that Shelley then offers can clarify both his philosophical context and his special contribution to a traditional argument:

> By signs, I would be understood in a wide sense, including what is properly meant by that term, and what I peculiarly mean. In this latter sense almost all familiar objects are signs, standing not for themselves but for others, in their capacity of suggesting one thought which shall lead to a train of thoughts (*On Life,* R&P, p. 477).

Three features of that definition link it to the locus classicus for skeptical sign theory, in Sextus Empiricus. First, Shelley distinguishes suggestive signs for his discussion, as Sextus does; second, analysis of signs offers not a linguistic theory but rather a view of the world and of how we come to know it; and finally, Shelley's stance toward the implied view is critical—he writes of "the misuse of signs," and he denies signs independent ontological validity: they are "instruments of [our] own creation."

Sextus' distinction of suggestive signs from others involves a critique of some dogmatic assumptions of the Stoics. "Dogma" can be defined, says Sextus, as assent to what is nonevident; and Stoics had used a theory of signs to do precisely that. According to a Stoic argument that Sextus summarizes, objects that are nonevident "are apprehended by means of signs" (*PH,* II, 99; see also 97–98). Says Sextus, such a sign "is inconceivable" (II, 104). His distinction between suggestive and indicative signs is the formulation that Shelley then follows. A sign is "'suggestive' when, being mentally associated with the thing signified, it suggests to us the thing associated with it" (II, 100). As Shelley says, "Almost all familiar objects are signs . . . in their capacity of suggesting" other thoughts. Neither Shelley nor Sextus denies the importance of such signs: "For the suggestive sign is relied on by living experience . . . ; we even lend it our support by assenting undogmatically to what it relies on, while opposing the private inventions of the Dogmatist" (*PH,* II, 102). One of the inventions that the skeptics oppose is what is called an indicative sign.

Says Sextus, "An 'indicative' sign," according to the dogmatists, "is that which is not clearly associated with the thing signified, but signifies that whereof it is a sign by its own particular nature and constitution, just as, for instance, the bodily motions are signs of the soul" (*PH*, II, 101). This concept lies behind what Shelley calls the "violent dogmatism" of "the popular philosophy of mind and matter." For Shelley as for Sextus, dogmatism links this body-soul dichotomy with a theory of indicative signs. Sextus refuses to deny either doctrine, the body-soul dualism or the doctrine of indicative signs, and so too does Shelley. The skeptical critique of these concepts stops short of a negative and opposite dogma; philosophy, Shelley says, "leaves, what is too often the duty of the reformer in political and ethical questions to leave, a vacancy" (*On Life*, R&P, p. 477).

Related analyses of sign theory appear in Berkeley and Drummond, and in both cases, the problem involves the association of an apparent sign with an unapparent signified; the apparent is associated with body, and the unapparent with soul. The concept has a positive theological history that these writers set out to transform: Saint Augustine, reacting to skeptical challenge (in *Contra Academicos*), sets out to show that "a truth can be apprehended by signs."[108] Leslie Tannenbaum emphasizes "Augustine's idea that through the Incarnation the objects of sense are transformed into signs."[109] Vastly as Augustine differs from the skeptics, it should be obvious that the body-spirit dichotomy and the application of sign theory to "all familiar objects" are concepts common to Sextus, Augustine, and Shelley.

Closer to Shelley's argument, however, is Berkeley's: "Visible ideas," he writes, "signify . . . after the same manner that words of any language suggest the ideas they are made to stand for."[110] Berkeley, like Sextus and like Shelley, uses "sign" in the sense of "suggestive sign"—an idea associatively linked with another: "The connection of ideas does not imply the relation of *cause* and *effect,* but only of a mark or *sign* with the thing *signified*" (Berkeley, *Treatise,* par. 65). The body-soul dichotomy would break the associative link, because it would assert an absolute signification of what is nonevident. To such an assertion Sextus, Berkeley, and Shelley do not assent; each skeptic rejects such dualism as "violent dogmatism."

Drummond also treats sign theory as a metaphysical rather than linguistic construction. It is time and space that he takes as signs: "The parts in the simple mode of duration, *extension,* may be taken as signs for the parts in the simple mode of duration, *time;* and in this manner the one mode will serve as the measure of the other" (*AQ,* pp. 80–81). The fictionality of such constructions (and of the sign system generally) is suggested by Drummond but then stated outright by Shelley. Drummond points out that "we seek to attach ideas to mere abstractions, and to give being to pure denominations" (p. 166). That is, we affirm the reality of nonevident objects signified indicatively by evident signs. The act of free nominalization can, when it becomes passive and credulous, enslave the thinker who becomes "the dupe and often the victim of the illusions, which he himself has created" (*AQ,* p. 167).

Shelley states the point about signification and about dogmatic belief in the nonevident: dogmatism is "misuse of words and signs, the instruments of [the mind's] own creation." As Sextus, Berkeley, and Drummond had not done, Shelley embeds sign theory in precisely that principle of value that (in *A Philosophical View of Reform* and in *A Defence of Poetry*) becomes the radical basis of his philosophy— imaginative construction of ideological forms.

In skeptical contexts, arguments from consensus establish nothing, and in the case of skeptical sign theory the principle of conventional assent positively undermines the authority of knowledge claims (*PH,* I,214).

THOMAS REID: COMMON SENSE, CONVENTIONAL
ASSENT, AND POLITICAL POWER

In British philosophy in the period of Drummond and Shelley, the criterion of conventional assent was linked with sign theory by Thomas Reid, a Scottish philosopher of the Common-Sense school. Reid offers a definition of signs that resembles the classical skeptical definition in important ways, but he uses the concept to support his criterion of certainty. Drummond devotes the last chapter of *Academical Questions* largely to a critical attack on Reid's philosophy, designed to overturn the authority of this new version of the criterion of absolute certainty. When Shelley takes up Reid's definitions (specifically his definitions of signs), his relation to the Scottish philosopher is especially important because of its complex form. Shelley's concept of signs is formed after Reid's, but Shelley uses the concept to undermine the authority of Reid's knowledge claims.

That dialectical method had always characterized skeptical argument: Hellenistic skeptics, as Pierre Couissin reminds us, did exactly the same thing, opposing and undermining Stoic claims for certainty, but precisely with arguments drawn from the Stoics' own definitions and principles.[111] Drummond's full and explicit critique of Reid (in *Academical Questions,* pp. 383–404) is, like his critique of Descartes, pointed specifically at the authority of the criterion, which guarantees in turn the authority of Reid's knowledge claims. In the same essay in which he calls Drummond's book perhaps "the most clear and vigorous statement of the intellectual system" (*On Life,* R&P, p. 476), Shelley focuses the argument on sign theory by adopting a distinction from Reid's *Inquiry into the Human Mind.*[112]

Shelley's distinction between what is customarily meant by "signs" and "what I peculiarly mean" is formed after Reid's distinction between artificial signs and natural signs. Reid writes that "signs may be conceived to be of two kinds: First, such as have no meaning but what is affixed to them by compact or agreement among those who use them—these are artificial signs."[113] These artificial signs represent, for Shelley, "what is properly meant by that term" ("sign"). "Secondly," says Reid, there are signs that "previous to all compact or agreement, have a meaning which every man understands by the principles of his nature . . . natural signs" (p. 117). This second sort of sign includes, as Shelley says, "almost all familiar objects"; Reid indicates that all bodily sensations are "signs of external things" (p. 121) and that throughout the natural world, "what we commonly call natural *causes* might, with more propriety, be called natural *signs,* and what we call *effects,* the things signified" (p. 122). For Reid, it is a class of natural signs (bodily sensations) that gives us our knowledge of external objects. Apparently, so far, Shelley is simply agreeing by reproducing Reid's broadest definition of sign; but in fact he performs a skeptical deconstruction of Reid's formulation, as the passage in *On Life* continues.

For Reid, the sensation of hardness (a sign) conveys knowledge of a hard body (a signified). The effect (sensation) signifies a cause (material object). But for Shelley, this second kind of sign that includes "almost all familiar objects" does not point outward from perception to a world of external objects; each sign simply points to other signs, all of which belong equally in perception: a sign, for Shelley, is not a subjective datum (sensation) that signifies an objective datum (material object); it is simply a phenomenon, belonging to mind, which has the "capacity of suggesting one thought, which shall lead to a train of thoughts" (*On Life*, R&P, p. 477).

Shelley's skeptical approach to sign theory has this much in common with what is now known, in literary theory, as poststructuralism. As Terry Eagleton explains, "If you want to know the meaning (or signified) of a signifier, you can look it up in the dictionary; but all you will find will be yet more signifiers."[114] In contrast, a naive reader or a commonsense philosopher will be likely to feel assured of a stable signified thing, toward which the signifier points, but different in kind from it. The sign can belong to mental space, but the signified, for Reid, is an object in the external and material world. Shelley overcomes the distinction, enclosing the signified object in mental space with the signifying perception: "By the word *things* is to be understood any object of thought, that is, any thought upon which any other thought is employed" (*On Life*, R&P, p. 478).

The understanding that I have called naive is associated by Jacques Derrida with Rousseau's notion of the "supplement," in the influential argument in which Derrida revives the ancient argument without noticing its antiquity. Writing, in Derrida's reading of Rousseau, is a supplement to speech, and speech is a supplement to thought; the chain continues, as thought is a supplement to the object of thought, to the supposed thing itself. Says Derrida,

> Through this sequence of supplements a necessity is announced: that of an infinite chain, ineluctably multiplying the supplementary mediations that produce the sense of the very thing they defer: the mirage of the thing itself, of immediate presence, or originary perception.[115]

Derrida offers thus a critique of a regressive absurdity: signification is doomed if it rests upon an object that is always absent, always deferred. Shelley is also sensitive to the problem, but he eludes the infinite regress, rather than merely exposing it. For Shelley, a sign is to be understood as an idea with which another idea is associated. Enclosing both thought and thing, signifier and signified, within the same epistemological set, Shelley arrests the regression and eliminates the absurdity that, as Derrida points out, afflicts the more conventional notion of signification.

As the issues rise, from linguistic signification to the thought-thing dichotomy, implications increase. Related issues form the basis of the problem of personal identity, or the existence of individual minds. For Reid, natural signs provide knowledge (dogmatic, absolute, indubitable) of the existence of personal identity and individual minds. A passage from Reid's argument is worth quoting at some length because of its important relationship to the more skeptical arguments on personal identity by Hume and then Shelley. Says Reid,

> A . . . class of natural signs comprehends those which, though we never before had any notion or conception of the things signified, do suggest it, or conjure it up, as it were, by a natural kind of magic, and at once give us a conception and create a belief of it. . . . our sensations suggest to us a sentient being or mind to which they belong—a being which is still the same, while its sensations and other operations are varied ten thousand ways—a being which hath the same relation to all that infinite variety of thoughts, purposes, actions, affections, enjoyments, and sufferings, which we are conscious of, or can remember. The conception of a mind is neither an idea of sensation nor of reflection; for it is neither like any of our sensations, nor like anything we are conscious of. The first conception of it, as well as the belief of it, and of the common relation it bears to all that we are conscious of, or remember, is suggested to every thinking being, we do not know how (Reid, *Inquiry*, p. 122).

Reid is manifestly trying to refute Hume's arguments about personal identity; the first chapter of Reid's *Inquiry* includes a section devoted entirely to Hume, about whose skepticism Reid expresses a real fear:

> If this is the philosophy of human nature, my soul enter thou not into her secrets! It is surely the forbidden tree of knowledge; I no sooner taste of it, then I perceive myself naked, and stript of

all things—yea, even of my very self. I see myself, and the whole frame of nature, shrink into fleeting ideas, which, like Epicurus's atoms dance about in emptiness (p. 103).

Here is Hume's skeptical analysis of the concept of identity, an analysis that frightened Reid into his absolutism of common sense:

I never can catch *myself* at any time without a perception, and never can observe anything but the perception. . . . I may venture to affirm of the rest of mankind, that they are nothing but a bundle or collection of different perceptions, which succeed each other with an inconceivable rapidity, and are in a perpetual flux and movement. . . . The mind is a kind of theatre, where several perceptions successively make their appearance; pass, repass, glide away, and mingle in an infinite variety of postures and situations. There is properly no *simplicity* in it at one time, nor *identity* in different; whatever natural propension we may have to imagine that simplicity and identity. . . . They are the successive perceptions only, that constitute the mind.[116]

Reid would rather be given a belief in magic than try to live with that much uncertainty; he retreats into the dogmatism of *katalepsis,* in the guise of common sense. Hume, Drummond, Shelley, or any sophisticated skeptical writer would have been able to point out for Reid that if the mind he seeks to know is not "like anything we are conscious of," then we do not know it; or that if the conception of an ontologically independent mind is "suggested to every thinking being, we do not know how," then we may have ignorance, doubt, *epochē,* or folly, but certainly not knowledge. As Drummond says, "It is evident . . . that this doctrine may be shown to favour, rather than to destroy scepticism" (*AQ,* p. 388).

Shelley's subsequent statements on the problem of identity appear, like Reid's, together with his concept of signs; but as Shelley has transformed the implications of Reid's sign theory, so he reverses entirely Reid's argument on personal identity. Significantly, Shelley does so not by returning to Hume's formulation, nor by rehearsing any arguments from Drummond: instead, he leaves *skepsis* where Reid and his followers wanted certainty; where Reid had put common sense for a dogma, Shelley leaves questions unanswered; where Reid expressed genuine fright at the "abyss of scepticism" (*Inquiry*, p. 103), Shelley comments, "What wonder if we grow dizzy to look down the dark abyss of—how little we know" (*On Life*, R&P, p. 478).

Reid had proceeded from his discussion of natural signs to an argument about the existence of external bodies and then to an argument about the existence of personal identities or minds; Shelley recapitulates that movement, reversing Reid's dogmatic conclusions at each point. Signs signify not external objects, as for Reid, but rather other thoughts; rather than inform us to a point of dogmatic certainty that external objects exist, such a sign theory leads Shelley to the statement that the "difference is merely nominal between those two classes of thought which are vulgarly distinguished by the names of ideas and of external objects" (*On Life*, R&P, p. 477). And Shelley similarly offers a skeptical refusal to assent to Reid's dogmatism on identity and individual minds:

> Pursuing the same thread of reasoning, the existence of distinct individual minds . . . is likewise found to be a delusion. The words *I, you, they*, are not signs of any actual difference subsisting between the assemblage of thoughts thus indicated, but are merely marks employed to denote the different modifications of the one mind (*On Life*, R&P, pp. 477–78).

As I have already shown, Shelley is not expressing solipsism but rather describing the personal pronouns as "grammatical devices invented simply for arrangement"; he asserts (in the dogmatic sense) nothing whatsoever, nor (in contrast to Hume) does he deny.

For Reid, the class of natural signs that discloses the existence of personal identity (of one's own mind) is the same as that which discloses the existence of solid external bodies (material objects); and this class of signs "is the foundation of common sense" (*Inquiry*, p. 122). Later, Reid's account of this common sense leads him to deal with the concept of facticity: he cites Frances Hutcheson, whose theory of the moral sense offered a kind of ethical *katalepsis* whereby moral judgments are not only arrived at by reasoning but also, in the case of universal moral truths, clearly, distinctly, and naturally perceived. As Reid cites him, all of the senses, whether external or internal, have been represented by philosophers as the means of furnishing our minds with ideas, without including any kind of judgment. Dr. Hutcheson defines a sense to be a determination of the mind to receive any idea from the presence of an object independent on our will.[117]

In *On Life,* Shelley does with facticity exactly what he does with the theory of signs. He adopts the commonsense formulation but to transform it, intellectualizing the terms and placing both the act of the mind and the object of thought within the epistemological circle, not in a putative externality of objects: "Thoughts and feelings arise, with or without our will" (R&P, p. 475). In moral as well as physical knowledge, the perceiver and perceived are enclosed in mental space: "The object of the forms according to which human society is administered is the happiness of the individuals composing the communities which they regard." Moral law, like physical sensation, is a mental phenomenon: "The human being . . . is . . . pre-eminently an imaginative being. His own mind is his law; his own mind is all things to him" (*Treatise on Morals,* Tokoo, pp. 24, 21–22; I&P, 7:72, 65). For Shelley, in contrast to Hutcheson and Reid, facticity—an idea's independence of our volition—does not imply that the idea exists external to perception.

Earlier, Joseph Priestley had engaged with Reid in debate on the mind–matter problem: Priestley sought to overcome the mind–matter dualism, as Shelley was later to do, but their methods are opposite to one another. Where Shelley and the intellectual system of Drummond would overcome the distinction between mind and matter by the principle that "nothing exists but as it is perceived" (*On Life,* R&P, p. 476), Priestley unifies thought and thing by making them both things: "What we call mind, or the principle of perception and thought, is not a substance distinct from the body, but the result of corporeal organization."[118] Here Priestley is in accord with Holbach and the French materialists: mind or soul "is only the body itself considered relatively with some of its functions, or with those faculties of which its nature and its peculiar organization renders it susceptible."[119] As Reid's citation from Priestley makes clear, an important impulse behind this dogmatic materialism is the urge for certainty, for absolute truth beyond the relativity of perception:

By this term ["sense"] philosophers in general have hitherto denominated those faculties in consequence of which we are liable
to *feelings* relative to *ourselves* only, and from which they have
not pretended to draw any conclusions concerning the *nature
of things;* whereas truth is a thing not relative, but *absolute,*
and real.[120]

Drummond makes use of arguments from relativity, pointing out,
"If external things exist at all, they cannot exist with opposite and
contradictory properties"; he points to "the various and contradictory sensations of men, who will all with equal justness of reasoning
trace their own feelings to them"; and he concludes, "How infinite,
then, must be the differences of opinion concerning these positive
properties in bodies!" (*AQ,* p. 106). As Montaigne had done, Drummond produces examples from travelers and "savage nations" (p. 103)
to illustrate variety of tastes, perceptions, and judgments. He applies
the trope of relativity to the case of one individual's perceptions: "The
man coming out of the warm bath could never agree with him quit-
ting the cold, about the temperature of the air" (p. 104). He shows
that from such a variety of basic perception must follow a variety of
opinion and judgment in more complex matters; where the dogmatic
materialism of Priestley flies from relativity to absolute truth, Drummond is (like Shelley after him) still comfortable in the "dark abyss of
how little we know." Drummond narrates the "total dissolution of
Dr. Priestley's material world" (p. 396).

Arguments from relativity had long been part of skeptical tradition, as Gisela Striker has shown.[121] They appear in Plato's *Theaetetus*
and in the fragments from Democritus: "We know nothing in reality," says Democritus, in a statement to which Shelley alludes in *On
Life,* "for truth lies in an abyss."[122] And Democritus uses precisely the
topical arguments from relativity to clarify his negative claim:

Sweet exists by convention, bitter by convention, colour by
convention. . . . We know nothing accurately in reality, but
[only] as it changes according to the bodily condition, and the
constitution of those things that flow upon [the body] and im-
pinge upon it (*Ancilla,* p. 93).

These arguments from relativity, personal and cultural, are formalized and codified for skeptical tradition in the ten tropes of Aenesidemus (*PH*, I,36–163; DL, IX,79–88).

Shelley rehearses the general argument repeatedly. In the *Treatise on Morals,* relativity becomes a moral problem and not only an epistemological crux (see, e.g., Tokoo, p. 28; I&P, 7:81–82). Here again, Shelley is following the pattern of Reid's argument, but to reverse Reid's values. For Reid, the epistemological value of common sense leads directly to a moral and political agenda. He quotes Pope's "Epistle to the Earl of Burlington" ("Good sense . . . is the gift of heaven") and comments:

> This inward light or sense is given by heaven to different persons in different degrees. There is a certain degree of it which is necessary to our being subjects of law and government, capable of managing our own affairs, and answerable for our conduct towards others: this is called common sense, because it is common to all men with whom we can transact business, or call to account for their conduct (*Essays on the Intellectual Powers,* p. 422).

Not only does Reid link his epistemological criterion, common sense, with the criterion of consensus, but he also invests it with social, political, and economic values. His emphasis on the "different degrees" of this value that belong to "different persons" implies a class distinction, especially as it is immediately coupled with the demands of "law and government." "The laws of all civilized nations distinguish those who have this gift of heaven, from those who have it not. The last may have rights which ought not to be violated, but, having no understanding in themselves to direct their actions, the laws appoint them to be guided by the understanding of others" (p. 422).

The economic definition of these class lines is obvious. While some are to be excluded from freedom of action, because they lack this "inward light or sense," Reid defines the class of persons who should guide and govern (who possess the inward light) in strictly economic terms: "Common sense is that degree of judgment which is common to men with whom we can converse and transact business" (p. 421).

What at first appeared to be an abstract problem of epistemology

74

has thus become pressingly practical. Reid's criterion of certainty includes an indication of who "is a competent judge" of questions in dispute, in language that recalls the elitism of the Stoic Sage. Despite Reid's verbal repetition of the commonality of good sense, he limits access to it in narrowly legalistic ways: "When it is made a question whether a man has this natural gift or not, a judge or a jury, upon a short conversation with him, can, for the most part, determine the question with great assurance" (p. 422).

The commonsense philosophy thus masks authoritarianism under an apparent democratization of judgment. Beginning with language that recalls the Cartesian criterion of clear and distinct ideas (and, behind Descartes, the Stoic *katalepsis*), Reid moves quickly from epistemology to a model of law enforcement:

All knowledge, and all science, must be built upon principles that are self-evident; and of such principles every man who has common sense is a competent judge, when he conceives them distinctly. Hence it is, that disputes very often terminate in an appeal to common sense.

While the parties agree in the first principles on which their arguments are grounded, there is room for reasoning; but when one denies what to the other appears too evident to need or to admit of proof, reasoning seems to be at an end; an appeal is made to common sense, and each party is left to enjoy his own opinion.

There seems to be no remedy for this, nor any way left to discuss such appeals, unless the decisions of common sense can be brought into a code in which all reasonable men shall acquiesce. This, indeed, if it be possible, would be very desirable (*Essays on the Intellectual Powers*, p. 422).

The variety of opinion and judgment that Drummond points out as a condition of the intellectual life is for Reid a malady requiring remedy. Reid calls for a uniform code, to be defined and enforced by men of business and by judges and juries. Conspicuously, Shelley follows Drummond, linking the epistemological dispute over the criterion to ethical and political problems, but producing a libertarian ethos to oppose the uniform code that Reid advocates:

If we would see the truth of things, they must be stripped of this fallacious appearance of uniformity. In truth, no one action has, when considered in its whole extent, an essential resemblance with any other. Each individual composing the vast multitude . . . has a peculiar frame of mind which, whilst the features of the great mass of his actions remain uniform, impresses the minuter lineaments with its peculiar hues (*Treatise on Morals*, Tokoo, p. 28; I&P, 7:81–82).

Shelley, like Drummond, discerns that the criterion of conventional assent cloaks political conservatism and religious orthodoxy. Where Reid enjoins his readers to observe and revere a consensus defined as agreement among the classes already empowered in law and government, Shelley articulates a libertarianism based upon the skeptical arguments of variety, relativity, and multiplicity of points of view. Where Reid would bring his readers under the authority of a uniform code, Shelley "bids them cast aside the chains of custom and blind faith," as did Jesus Christ and "all reformers" in Shelley's eyes (*Essay on Christianity*, I&P, 6:243).

Like his apparently theological writings, Shelley's epistemological essays thus take a precisely political context, as Scrivener, among others, has noticed;[123] the popular democratic reform movements that are the nominal subject of *A Proposal for Putting Reform to the Vote* and *A Philosophical View of Reform* also lie behind the *Essay on Christianity* and the *Treatise on Morals*, including the portion conventionally called *Speculations on Metaphysics*. Shelley's deconstruction of conventional certainties amounts to an application of the same radical skepticism that shows itself in these political contexts:

The system of society as it exists at present must be overthrown from the foundations with all its superstructure of maxims & of forms before we shall find anything but dissapointment [sic] in our intercourse with any but a few select spirits (*Letters*, 2:191).

Shelley does not insist that political institutions and practice cause philosophical positions; nor does he argue, in reverse, that such abstract conceptualizations as Reid's or Drummond's can cause particular political structures or acts. The dialectical interplay of these levels of discourse is one major feature of Shelley's *Philosophical View of Re-*

form, as I shall be arguing subsequently. The skeptical paradigm of metaphysical analysis involves, in Shelley as in the history of skepticism, a questioning of authority, an undermining of dogma, an overthrow of antecedent conceptual structures. In Shelley's political world, with the growing pressures and vitality of movements for reform and social revolution, it is the case that these paradigmatic forms of the skeptical dialectic arise from the political and economic conflicts that Shelley observed so keenly; at the same time, those metaphysical speculations and critiques are invested with concrete historical applications and forms. For Shelley as for Democritus, "speech is the shadow of action" (*Ancilla,* p. 105).

2

SHELLEY AND
HISTORICAL
DIALECTIC

SHELLEY, MARX, AND CULTURAL CONTEXT

Shelley's political philosophy is connected systematically with his writing on metaphysical problems. In both cases, he elaborates a structure of thought that not only unifies his own works but also suggests that the nominally different topics—e.g., contemporary politics, poetic theory, the history of religion, and the mind-body problem—submit to the same dialectical methods of analysis. Specifically, four principles from skeptical tradition that are important in Shelley's metaphysical writing also become structural features of his political prose: these features are the epistemological circle, facticity, nominalization, and the constructive power of imagination, expressed even in "delusion" that can develop "the whole powers" of humanity.

Shelley states in many places the connectedness of the different manifestations of culture—political, economic, philosophical, religious, and aesthetic. That ideological linkage of cultural forms is part of the burden of the *Defence of Poetry,* and it is affirmed as well in *A Philosophical View of Reform* and in what Marilyn Butler has recently taken as an epigraph for her study of Romantic ideology—the statement in the preface to *Prometheus Unbound:* "Poets, not otherwise than philosophers, painters, sculptors, and musicians, are in one sense the creators and in another the creations of their age" (R&P, p. 135). One sense of the word "ideology" involves the structure of thought and correlative action that unifies these levels of human enterprise.

Another of Shelley's expressions of the ideological linkages makes clear the dual point. It is a thought structure that unifies the diversity of cultural endeavor, but this thought structure is anchored firmly and practically in social and historical life and circumstance:

79

For all the inventive arts maintain, as it were, a sympathetic connection between each other, being no more than various expressions of one internal power, modified by different circumstances,
either of an individual, or of society (I&P, 7:223).

It is an inexorable reciprocity whereby artistic and philosophical
work is a product of social and historical forces, while society and the
conditions of history are themselves products of the prolific human
mind, which is to be considered not only as an individual thing but
rather as a collective.

Shelley's skeptical methods connect his epistemological arguments
(*On Life, Treatise on Morals*) with a philosophy of action (*A Philosophical View of Reform*). Cameron has called *A Philosophical View of
Reform* "the most advanced work of political theory of the age," and
it is that largely because of the dialectical method of analysis that
Scrivener has pointed out in the essay.[1] This unification of metaphysical and political theory, by way of a dialectical method, is usually ascribed to Marxism, and Shelley's political thought has been
compared with that of Marx and Engels.[2] What follows in this chapter is an attempt to show three things. First, Shelley's political writing
shares with some central texts of Marx and Engels an emphasis on
methodological unification of contexts. That is, the limited topical
reference of essays—to a proposed reform of the franchise, or to
Athenian drama, or to Malthus—should not distract us from the essential project, the elaboration of a dialectical method for the analysis
of theory and practice in all forms of human life. Second, the methodological features that most closely associate Shelley's work with that of
Marx and Engels belong to the skeptical tradition that they share. Finally, those points at which Shelley's political philosophy differs most
from Marxism are exactly those cruxes at which Marxism itself contradicts its own skeptical methodological foundations.

Marx's mastery of classical philosophy, including the Hellenistic
skeptics, is amply documented. His dissertation (presented to the
University of Jena in 1841) was a comparison of the philosophical systems of Democritus and Epicurus. In the preface to this work, Marx
expresses his more comprehensive interest in the Hellenistic philosophies: "This treatise should be considered as only the preliminary to a
larger work in which I will describe in detail the cycle of Epicurean,
Stoic, and Sceptic philosophies in their relationship to the whole of

Greek speculation."[3] That Marx's familiarity with the texts of Hellenistic skepticism remained fresh much later in his career is suggested by the fact that in *Capital,* he cites Sextus Empiricus, author of the most extended ancient compilation of skeptical arguments.

These factual records do not show that Marx perceived his own arguments as an extension of the classical skeptical paradigms or that he wished for his own arguments to be understood in that way. Together with a formal analysis of Marx's arguments, these facts might show that Marx's arguments *are* an extension of skeptical paradigms, but Marx may have judged it likely that the recognition of this fact might work to his polemical disadvantage. Roy Edgley has aptly summarized the way in which Marx represents himself, in relation to skepticism:

The philosophical alternative to total skepticism is always some ontology, metaphysics, or epistemology. The non-philosophical alternative with its acknowledged basis in material reality itself is science. For science, knowledge of reality is possible, but no idea, however deeply embedded within the conceptual framework, is totally beyond question.[4]

Three things about this Marxist self-definition should be pointed out. First, the defensiveness of this claim to a "non-philosophical alternative" is obvious, when that claim comes to rest on another about reality itself. Any claim about reality itself is ontological in the broad sense of that word, and the establishment of such a claim is a precisely philosophical project.

Second, if every possible idea is questionable, then, though "knowledge of reality" may be possible, no criterion is available within cognitive apparatus to discern which idea is knowledge of reality and which is illusion. Skeptics (Hellenistic, Renaissance, and modern) routinely point out this fact, and there is nothing in Marx, Engels, or Edgley to overcome this critical point.

Finally, Marx and Marxism typically argue that no idea is beyond question, and the philosophical method consistent with that persistent presence of doubt is skepticism. For a variety of political and rhetorical reasons—predominantly, I shall argue, to mask the presence of dogmas that he would prefer not to have to defend—Marx pretends otherwise. My point at the outset of this three-way comparison of Shelley, Marx, and classical skepticism is threefold: Marx's knowledge of classical skeptical dialectic is factually demonstrable; critical and dubitative procedures are common to Marx and classical skeptical dialectic; and a claim of a "basis in material reality itself" rests upon an ontological dogma, a concept of what reality-in-itself is. This dogma is incompatible with the critical and dubitative arguments of Marxism. Shelley's arguments are free of the inconsistency that, after him, was to trouble Marxist theory.

The first substantial point of comparison between Shelley and Marx is a constant contextualization of cultural products, including philosophical systems: it is a point of dialectical method, common to Shelley and Marx, that works of philosophy and art arise within social and natural environments and that these products engage in relations of reciprocal conditioning with their environments. This principle, in turn, leads to a conceptual linkage: political, economic, philosophical, and artistic products participate equally in the larger conditioning context.

What is probably Marx's most famous statement of the connection of literary, philosophical, and political products and forms is a passage in his preface to *A Contribution to the Critique of Political Economy:* from the economic structure of society "rise legal and political superstructures," and to these in turn correspond "definite forms of social consciousness." What Marx calls ideological forms are the "legal, political, religious, or aesthetic" forms in which human beings become conscious of fundamentally economic conflicts.[5] Though these two central concepts, superstructure and ideology, are by no means simple, clear, or consistently applied in Marx or in Marxism, one feature of the preface to *A Contribution* remains fairly consistent in Marxist thought: these concepts link the apparently disparate areas of material and intellectual conditions and activities, though these linkages are often expressed in contradictory ways. As Louis Althusser expresses this principle of connection, "Marx has shown that all social formations constitute an 'organic totality' which comprises three essential 'levels': the economy, politics and ideology or the forms of social consciousness."[6] Raymond Williams points out that "the force of Marx's original criticism had been mainly directed against the *separation* of 'areas' of thought and activity."[7]

Just as explicitly, Shelley repeatedly links the social and political environment with such intellectual products as poetry, philosophy, and religion: conflicts "waged under the names of religion . . . have seldom been any more [than] the popular and visible symbols which express the degree of power in some shape or other asserted by one party" (*A Philosophical View of Reform,* I&P, 7:6). At the time of the Reformation, in England, "the exposition of a certain portion of religious imposture drew with it an enquiry into political imposture and was attended with an extraordinary exertion of the energies of intellectual power" (7:7). Poetry and philosophy—for example the works of Shakespeare and Bacon—"were at once the effects of the new spirit in men's minds, and the causes of its more complete developement" (7:7). The conditions of civilization—including literature, art, theology, and law—are, Shelley says, correlative with political events. It will be necessary to examine in some detail the different concepts of unification that appear in Shelley and Marx—the different formulations of the relatedness of material, social, and intellectual activities—but on this general procedural assumption they agree: forms of consciousness and products of intellectual exertion are historically correlative with political and economic structures, and the two nominally distinguished areas of activity respond to one another and manifest a coherent ideological structure. As Edward Aveling and Eleanor Marx argued in 1888, "Every word that [Shelley] has written against religious superstition and the despotism of individual rulers may be read as against economic superstition and the despotism of class."[8] Ideological analysis, Shelley's or Marx's, approaches the correlative structures of thought and action as a unity.

Aveling and Eleanor Marx also focus on class theory in Shelley's political philosophy. Behind their exposition lies this sentence from Karl Marx:

The real difference between Byron and Shelley is this: those who understand and love them rejoice that Byron died at thirty-six, because if he had lived he would have become a reactionary *bourgeois;* they grieve that Shelley died at twenty-nine, because he was essentially a revolutionist and he would always have been one of the advanced guard of socialism.[9]

Cameron also points out Shelley's class consciousness, in his comparison of Shelley and Marx. Two things, says Cameron, "caused Marx to believe that Shelley would have become a socialist": his "sense of identification with the working people" and his "understanding of the exploitation of labor." [10] Cameron also observes aptly that for Shelley as for Marx, "the whole hideous system of human exploitation and oppression was supported by the ruling class and its State," and he notices that the oppression of women is part of this exploitative and class-based structure. As Aveling and Marx put the point, "The woman is to the man as the producing class is to the possessing. . . . And this Shelley understood not only in its application to the most unfortunate of women, but in its application to every woman." [11]

Some points of comparison have a specifically political range of reference, as Cameron observes: Shelley's identification with working people, the institutionalized oppression of women, the exploitation of labor, and the oppressive efficacy of the ruling class in Regency England. Aveling and Eleanor Marx also raise issues pertinent to the formal dimensions of Shelley's intellectual system:

> To the younger Shelley *l'infame* of Voltaire's *ecrasez l'infame* was to a great extent, as with Voltaire wholly, the priesthood. And the empire that he antagonised was at first that of kingship and that of personal tyranny. But even in his attacks on these he simultaneously assails the superstitious belief in the capitalistic system and the empire of class. As time goes on, with increasing distinctness, he makes assault upon these, the most recent and most dangerous foes of humanity. . . . he scarcely ever fails to link with [priest, king, and statesman] the basis on which they all rest. [12]

What is missing, therefore, from a checklist of political issues on which Shelley's essays agree with Marxism is this structural element of Shelley's thought. Often interpretations of Shelley are in fact arguments about what his arguments are about: for example, a claim that *A Philosophical View of Reform* advocates a moderate or radical reform in the voting system for parliamentary representation. Shelley's prose often takes an occasional (specifically political) reference, but a way of thinking is often more to the point than such local reference. The relevant way of thinking characteristically involves a skeptical dialectic that seeks to overthrow claims to authority. This dialectic operates to undermine such claims equally when they pertain to authority in philosophical knowledge and when they pertain rather to political power. An opponent of the skeptical dialectic, the subject of critical argument, is shown to be no authority, or at least the authority is challenged and rendered dubious.

One way in which Shelley's thinking undermines the authority of dogma—political or otherwise—is to place each issue within a transitory and experiential framework. Because forms and products of intellectual work are linked to their specific historical occasions, no solution or form of a human problem has permanent authority. Ethical and political questions submit themselves to criteria of a purely experiential and utilitarian kind; Shelley criticizes the reification of absolutes, including political hierarchies and institutional solutions (e.g., the settlement of the Revolution of 1688). Shelley analyzes the origination of Catholicism, for example, as a historically specific instance of such a reification: "Names borrowed from the life and opinions of Jesus Christ were employed as symbols of domination & imposture; & a system of liberty & equality for such was the system preached by that great Reformer, was perverted to support oppression."[13] Shelley had first written "to cement oppression" and then changed his language to "support oppression." The originally ethical and revolutionary system of Jesus Christ was appropriated by a ruling class, as a means of consolidating power; furthermore, this appropriation for exploitative purposes involved a solidification ("cementing") of an ideological form (Christ's system of doctrines).

Shelley's analysis of a wide range of political and economic problems is based on a theory of class interest that is as explicit as his demystification of the "imposture" of early Catholicism. He explains that a conflict has arisen in England between the producing classes (workers) and the profiting classes (owners of capital). He shows how, historically, the number of politically excluded persons (i.e., the working class, excluded from the franchise) has increased in proportion to the numbers in the empowered classes that enjoy franchise. In Shelley's analysis this schematization by class does not represent a bare fact of economic distribution but rather an ideological dispersal: those who argue against reform of the franchise "derive for the most part great advantage and convenience from the continuance of these abuses" (7:21). Shelley does not apply the principle of interestedness in a mechanical manner—"It is not alleged that every person whose interest is directly or indirectly concerned in the maintaining things as they are, is therefore necessarily interested"—but rather he treats interest as a class phenomenon. Public credit, for example, is analyzed according to the principles of class interest: "This device is one of those execrable contrivances of misrule which overbalance the materials of common advantage produced by the progress of civilization, and increase the number of those who are idle to those who work, while it increases, through the factitious wants of those indolent, privileged persons, the quantity of work to be done" (7:25).

In this way, class theory serves for Shelley to distribute the principle of interest according to political and economic distinctions. He avoids specifically the stronger claim, that institutions and their rationales are causally determined solely by economic interest and that in the case of each individual person, attitudes and beliefs are thereby so determined. Instead, he offers what (in *Sceptical Essays*) Bertrand Russell was to offer as a principle for the analysis of beliefs—this is motivism, or the general premise that where attitudes and beliefs differ from group to group, or from person to person, the interests of the group or person are involved in the determination of the belief or attitude.[14] This principle derives from older skeptical tradition, where cultural and personal relativity—the principle that opinions, institutions, and customs are time- and place-specific—had been a commonplace since the fourth century B.C. What Shelley adds to the common topic of cultural and individual relativity is an interpretation according to economic class.

Shelley's linkage of the economic class distinction with intellectual and aesthetic production gives his class theory great explanatory power: "We owe, among other causes, the exact condition belonging to [our own] intellectual existence to the generous disdain of submission which burned in the bosoms of men who filled a distant generation and inhabited another land" (7:6). That distant generation was Dante's, and the other land was Italy: "Florence long balanced, divided, and weakened the strength of the Empire and the Popedom. To this cause, if to anything, was due the undisputed superiority of Italy in literature and the arts over all its contemporary nations" (7:5).

The nature of ideological analysis, however, insistently binds the intellectual to the political and economic, in a process of mutual transformation that continues ceaselessly over history: "The great writers of our own age are, we have reason to suppose, the companions and forerunners of some unimagined change in our social condition or the opinions which cement it" (preface to *Prometheus Unbound,* R&P, p. 134). Shelley's rhetoric is skillfully ambiguous: the makers of intellectual products (poems) are said to accompany or to precede a change; and this change, too, is said to be institutional or ideational. Shelley connects these ranges of reference and associates A, the phenomena of mind, with B, material and social conditions. But he does so without a dogmatic assertion of a linear causality: he does not insist that A causes B, or the reverse. He suggests either interpretation, and he sometimes suggests both, but the burden of his argument is the unification of those fields of action and analysis.

A Philosophical View of Reform makes it clear that this linkage of what is ideational with what is material and social is a conception that belongs not to self-conscious analytical discourse alone but in fact to that which is given in experience. Institutions, Shelley argues, are overlaid with opinions, and these, solidified into dogma, serve to conceal and to support a system of class exploitation:

The name and office of king is merely the mask of this power [i.e., the power of the rich], and is a kind of stalking-horse used to conceal these 'catchers of men,' whilst they lay their nets. Monarchy is only the string which ties the robber's bundle. Though less contumelious and abhorrent from the dignity of human nature than an absolute monarchy, an oligarchy [of the rich] exacts more of suffering from the people because it reigns both by the opinion generated by imposture, and the force which that opinion places within its grasp (7:25).

That the ruling class rules by ideational structures that serve class interest, as well as by material and institutional means, is a formulation of ideological theory. "Legal and political superstructures," to use Marx's phrase, both of which have economic bases, correspond with forms of consciousness that (as Shelley says) "support" or "cement" those social, political, and economic structures.

Shelley assimilates this form of interpretation with a historical analysis. At the time of the Reformation, for example, what was at issue was more than religious doctrine or even hierarchy: "The poor rose against their natural enemies, the rich" (7:6). The paradigm of class conflict recurs recognizably across history, in different national settings: the rising of the Protestant poor was a phenomenon having features in common with the uprisings, for example, of the West Indian plantations, though those phenomena were not identical. This interpretation of history is dialectical in a number of senses, and one of them—bearing most directly on the theory of classes—is that these great changes in social condition (or in opinion, or in both) arise from a contest of classes whose interests conflict; what emerges is historical progress: "The result, though partial and imperfect, is perhaps the most animating that the philanthropist can contemplate in the history of man" (7:6).

On this issue of perfectibility—i.e., the working assumption that no state of understanding is permanent, perfect, absolute, or final—Cameron makes an important claim that the remainder of this chapter will investigate: "Although [Shelley] saw historical evolution, he did not perceive that the basic factor was social and that human thinking was derivative; rather he neutrally depicted both in interaction."[15] It is clear that Shelley did not dogmatize about the precise form of interaction between material or social conditions and intellectual activities or products; it is, further, clear that Shelley did insist on the interaction of the two, not a linear and one-directional relationship. What is not clear, however, and what requires more rigorous analysis is a set of problems raised by the first part of Cameron's claim. What does it mean to say that the "basic factor was social"? If a model of causation is implied, then what conception of cause is relevant? One of those, perhaps, that Hume attacked? If, instead, determination is implied, rather than causation, then which of several available senses of "determine" is relevant? These questions are important for several reasons: Shelley's thought is not merely described by Cameron's assertion, it is evaluated; the judgments involved rest on concepts that require analysis. Further, it often happens in writing on Marxism (as opposed to Marx) that two sets of purposes are confused: an account of a Marxist conception (such as the priority of the social determining factor and the derivative nature of thought) can be an exposition, referring to a text or set of texts; or it can be an instance of advocacy, referring to social determinism and human thinking. What follows, in an alignment of Shelley's thought with what is said in certain documents by Marx and Engels, is expository in that sense rather than polemical; that is, the statements and concepts asserted are the immediate objects of analysis; their value and utility in human relations existing outside scholarship and letters are judgments that can rest, subsequently, on the outcome of that analysis.

Cameron's judgment, based in part on the most massive compilation of information about Shelley in political context that has ever been assembled, involves two related sets of assumptions. First,

> Marx's social views were integrated with a scientific materialism that had practice as its basic criterion of truth, viewing mind as an emanation from matter, and perceiving reality as essentially developmental in response to inherent contradictions. Shelley . . . became a philosophical sceptic, leaving open the possibility of the primacy and uniqueness of mind.[16]

The second assumption is contained in the claim that Shelley "did not perceive" certain things that Marx (and Marxists) allegedly did and do perceive. To test those claims will involve analyzing some central texts and concepts from Marxist theory and then juxtaposing those concepts with what is stated and implied in Shelley's political prose. Again, the resulting judgments can be expected to be analytical in character, according to the interpretive project that takes the concepts of Marx and Shelley for its subject; the kind of judgment that turns from that interpretive project to the making of truth claims about the world external to the texts and concepts will wait.[17]

THE DIALECTICS OF SKEPTICISM AND MARXISM

Marxist philosophy is one form of skepticism. That is, the Marxist theory of knowledge arises from recognizably skeptical premises and procedures, and that philosophy of knowledge is put forward in texts whose argumentative occasions also exhibit the traditional skeptical features of debate and dialectical critique. Judgments about the extent to which Shelley's philosophical thinking resembles Marxism, or anticipates Marxism, require more, however, than a recognition of such a generic resemblance. A judgment, for example, that Shelley's thinking falls just short of Marxist thought because Shelley failed to recognize certain truths is a judgment that presupposes the truth of those truths. Since Marxist texts articulate criteria for testing such truth claims, it will be useful to clarify those criteria; these are the principles of a Marxist philosophy of knowledge. Those criteria can be then applied to the set of claims that Shelley shares with Marx and Engels, and to a set of claims that he does not make but Marx and Engels do make. Skepticism, in its classical expressions, provides the methodological framework within which both Shelley and Marx-Engels construct their critical philosophies, but differences among them are as important as that general set of resemblances.

Two central statements of the Marxist philosophy of knowledge are Engels's *Herr Eugen Dühring's Revolution in Science (Anti-Dühring)* and *Ludwig Feuerbach and the End of Classical German Philosophy.* Like classical texts of skepticism, each of these works arises in the context of a debate against a particular dogmatist and a particular dogmatism. Dühring had made claims for the eternal validity of certain absolute truths in a sequence of books that Engels undertakes to criticize. Ten years later, Engels takes up another context of argument, defined by Hegel's dialectical philosophy and then the work of the young Hegelians, especially Ludwig Feuerbach. In both cases, Engels uses the critical and negative stance implied in his rhetorical occasion. As Shelley says, the skeptical argumentation produces a kind of negative truth, clearing intellectual space of certain dogmatic errors.

Engels quotes directly one of Dühring's more general claims:

> The special truth out of which, in the course of evolution, the more complete moral consciousness and . . . conscience are built up . . . may claim a validity and range similar to the concepts and applications of mathematics. *Pure truths are absolutely immutable* . . . so that it is altogether a stupidity to think that the validity of knowledge is something that can be affected by time and changes in reality.[18]

These claims for the absoluteness of truths are what Engels sets out to attack. The issues involve three closely related claims: first, that there are such things as absolutely immutable truths; second, that the concepts of mathematics belong to this set of truths; and third, that moral truths can also claim such an absolutely immutable validity, on the analogy of mathematical concepts. Engels challenges all three claims, and he focuses on the skeptical arguments from relativity as the crux of the issue. He cites Dühring's claim that "moral principles stand 'above history and above the present difference in national character-istics'" (p. 95), and he cites Dühring's explicit attack on skeptical methods that argue otherwise: "In the sphere of morals, the denial of general principles clutches at the geographical and historical variety of customs and principles," says Dühring. The ideology of skepticism goes "beyond the recognition of the real validity and actual efficacy of concordant moral instincts." This *"mordant scepticism,* which is not only directed against particular false doctrines but against mankind's capacity to develop conscious morality, resolves itself ultimately into a real Nothing" (quoted in *Anti-Dühring,* p. 95).

Engels attacks "all these pompous phrases . . . about final and ulti-mate truths [and about] the certainty of knowledge" (p. 95). He does so by reproducing the ancient arguments for relativity. Just as Dioge-nes Laertius had presented those arguments (DL, IX,79–88) and as Sextus Empiricus had elaborated them (*PH,* I,36–163), Engels treats relativity in two forms—individual or personal variability (first) and cultural and historical variety (second).

Engels's argument with Dühring is thus much like Drummond's critique of Descartes: as Drummond pointed out, the dogmatist's cer-tainty belongs to the mind of the dogmatist; "How is the individual to assert, that one clear perception is more certain than another?" (*AQ,* p. 152). This is the problem of the epistemological circle, which Engels reproduces: "As for the sovereign validity of the knowledge in each individual's mind, we all know that there can be no talk of such a thing." Like Shelley, Engels then politicizes this epistemological problem: "Eternal truths" are incompatible with "the conditions of human life, social relationships, forms of law and the state" (*Anti-Dühring,* p. 99).

First, Engels challenges Dühring's claim that there are such things as absolutely immutable truths. He does so by means of the first kind of argument from relativity, i.e., individual or personal variability of perception and understanding:

> Herr Dühring himself declares that consciousness, and therefore also thought and knowledge, of necessity can only become manifest in a number of individual beings. . . . But as for the sovereign validity of the knowledge in each individual's mind, we all know that there can be no talk of such a thing, and that all previous experience shows that without exception such knowl-

edge always contains much more that is capable of being improved upon than that which cannot be improved upon or is correct (pp. 96–97).

Then, Engels criticizes Dühring's claim that the concepts of mathematics belong to the supposed set of immutable truths. Here, he avoids the strongest form of argument—which would be the negative claim that no such mathematical truths do or can exist. Instead, he undermines the claim for the certainty of truth supposedly belonging to mathematical concepts. He admits that there are final truths in mathematics (e.g., twice two makes four). But the qualification with which Engels follows that admission is strong enough to refute effectively claims (like Dühring's) to possess such truths:

But very far from all their results have this validity. With the introduction of variable magnitudes and the extension of their variability to the infinitely small and infinitely large, mathematics, in other respects so strictly moral, fell from grace; it ate of the tree of knowledge, which opened up to it a career of most colossal achievements, but at the same time a path of error. The virgin state of absolute and irrefutable certainty of everything mathematical was gone forever; mathematics entered the realm of controversy, and we have reached the point where most people differentiate and integrate not because they understand what they are doing but from pure faith, because up to now it has always come out right (p. 98).

Engels's argument is clear and systematic, but it is worth summarizing, to point out its similarities with the patterns of argument that Engels shares with virtually every other philosophical skeptic making use of the traditional forms of skeptical argument. For Engels, the trope of individual relativity refutes Dühring's first claim, that there are such things as absolutely immutable truths. The second claim, that the concepts of mathematics belong to this set of immutable truths, depends upon a criterion that does not exist. Since some truths are falsehoods, then we can admit that there may be—even maintain that there are—final truths; but we would need a criterion to distinguish true truths from false ones, and no such criterion is available to us, as the record of human fallibility, even in mathematics and the exact sciences, demonstrates.

The third claim of Dühring's—that moral truths can also claim absolute validity, on the analogy of mathematical concepts—has already been shown to be untenable: without the second claim, there is no demonstration of the third claim. But Engels produces yet another refutation, this time applying the larger skeptical argument from relativity, involving cultural and historical variety:

> But eternal truths are in an even worse plight in the . . . historical group of sciences . . . the conditions of human life, social relationships, forms of law and the state, with their ideal superstructure of philosophy, religion, art, etc. . . . . In social history . . . the repetition of conditions is the exception and not the rule (p. 99).

This variety among social conditions has deleterious effects on the immutability of truths: "Knowledge is here essentially relative, inasmuch as it is limited to the perception of relationships and consequences of certain social and state forms which exist only at a particular epoch and among particular people and are of their very nature transitory" (p. 100).

For Engels, this epistemological constraint has therefore a negative dimension: "Anyone . . . who sets on this field to hunt down final and ultimate truths, truths which are pure and absolutely immutable, will bring home but little" (p. 100). But the same principle, of inescapable cultural relativity, has also a positive implication: the contradiction between human thought, conceived as absolute, and the actuality of human beings, limited in their knowledge, "can only be solved in the infinite progressions . . . of generations of mankind" (p. 97). This notion of perfectibility rests paradoxically on the heuristic assumption that perfection is unattainable; that is, precisely because any given act of thought, or system of thought, is necessarily limited in its truth content, it follows that each such act or system will have successors, allowing for a progression apparently without end.

Such a notion of perfectibility is also central to the argument of William Godwin's *Political Justice,* a book that Shelley praises and from which he draws during all of his adult life.[19] Thus, Godwin asserts that "man is perfectible," but he explains that proposition in terms that assert perfection to be unattainable:

By perfectible, it is not meant that he is capable of being brought to perfection [but rather that mankind have] the faculty of being continually made better and receiving perpetual improvement. . . . The term perfectible, thus explained, not only does not imply the capacity of being brought to perfection, but stands in express opposition to it.[20]

Engels's notion of "infinite progressions" is comparable to Godwin's "perpetual improvement." The skeptical trope of relativity (including the inescapably historical flux of social forms) proscribes final or ultimate truths and systems.

Shelley's arguments, however, lie somewhere between Godwin and Engels:[21] all three writers share a concept of perfectibility as an unending process of displacement of truths by other truths. This perpetual displacement is determined by the fact that all truths are imperfect. But Godwin could be said ultimately to depoliticize the process, insisting in *Political Justice* and also in later works that political revolution is no solution but rather another evil; the renovations that Godwin advocates are educational, ideational, and at root individualized: "Individuality is of the very essence of intellectual excellence."[22] Shelley and Engels, in contrast, accept political solutions and actually produce political advocacy. In *A Philosophical View of Reform* as in the prefaces to *Prometheus Unbound* and *Hellas,* Shelley encourages, commends, and advocates specific political revolutions.

A related set of issues also locates Shelley between Godwin and Engels: for Godwin, the relativity of knowledge encases all intellectual development within an individualistic framework; hence his hostility to collective action, to institutions, and to cooperative forms of social action. Shelley, in contrast, writes of "the fervid awakening of the public mind" (preface to *Prometheus Unbound,* R&P, p. 134). Shelley assimilates intellectual structures and their variety to collective social structures, as Marx and Engels were to do, rather than, as Godwin suggests, merely psychological parameters: "The great writers of our own age are, we have reason to suppose, the companions and forerunners of some unimagined change in our social condition

94

or the opinions which cement it. The cloud of mind is discharging its *collected* lightning" (my italics).

Godwin also affirms the connectedness of political and intellectual structures, but without Shelley's sophisticated sense of reciprocal or dialectical efficacy; says Godwin, "Are not the governments of modern Europe accountable for the slowness and inconstancy of its literary efforts, and the unworthy selfishness that characterizes its inhabitants?" (1:5). Shelley's sense of writers as "companions and forerunners of . . . change in our social condition" re-engages intellectual work with political efficacy. For Shelley, the gap between fallible knowledge claims (anchored in human individuality) and political institutions not only should be but can be and is overcome: "The equilibrium between institutions and opinions is now restoring, or is about to be restored" (preface to *Prometheus Unbound,* R&P, p. 134).

Political Justice is unremittingly hostile to such forms of collectivity, insisting instead that oppression and the overcoming of oppression are mental and psychological (i.e., individualistic) matters. At the opposite extreme, Engels puts a stronger claim for the social dimension of thought than Shelley does. But these distinctions among the three thinkers are largely political rather than epistemic: the three writers share the traditional skeptical arguments from relativity, inescapable uncertainty, hostility to dogma, and consequent unending revisionism. Perfection (finality) being unattainable, progress (or at least change) is and should be perpetual.

Accordingly, even the most abstract principles are, by Shelley and Engels, placed within particular limiting contexts:

> The result of the labours of the political philosophers has been the establishment of the principle of utility as the substance, and liberty and equality as the forms according to which the concerns of human life ought to be administered. [These forms are related to] many new theories, more or less perfect, but all superior to the mass of evil which they would supplant (*A Philosophical View of Reform,* 7:10).

Engels expresses that same point about those same values:

> The idea of equality . . . is itself a historical product, the creation of which required definite historical conditions which in

turn themselves presuppose a long previous development (*Anti-Dühring*, p. 118).

Marx, too, complains that the idea of equality "already possesses the fixity of a popular prejudice" (quoted in *Anti-Dühring*, p. 118). For Marx, Engels, and Shelley, this idea—like all ideas—is "anything but an eternal truth."

For these thinkers, though not for Godwin, even such relative truths are valid within their limited and limiting contexts and therefore worth struggle and enactment in what Marx came to call praxis. One example that Shelley produces concerns the doctrines of the Christian missionaries working in India during Shelley's lifetime. These doctrines were already unacceptable in the European context, but in their application in the missionary activities in India—a different cultural setting characterized by a different degree of progress and a different set of reigning superstitions—the promulgation of these false doctrines still has beneficial effects (*A Philosophical View of Reform*, 7:17).

Beyond the content of particular doctrines, however, Engels deals with the form of dogmatic reasoning as well. He points out the inadequacy of polar opposites in any doctrinal formulation (p. 101). The structure of an antithesis (for example the relation of the polar opposites, truth and error) becomes itself relative, in a process whereby the content of the propositions shifts while the structure of the polarity is preserved. When an assertion that was true comes to be recognized as false, then the antithesis remains although truth has become falsehood. The polarity of the oppositions, Engels observes, is an inadequate structure for reasoning, because of the relativity of the propositions' truth content. Truth content changes over time.

In fact, Engels argues, virtually any object of knowledge (any subject of a proposition) changes over time; it is not only statements that vary historically and culturally but also the referents of statements. Defending an earlier position of Marx's, Engels says that this fact of change is the reason that reality itself is contradictory:

So long as we consider things as static and lifeless, each one by itself, alongside of and after each other, it is true that we do not run up against any contradictions in them. . . . But the position is quite different as soon as we consider things in their motion, their change, their life, their reciprocal influence on one another. Then we immediately become involved in contradictions (*Anti-Dühring*, p. 132).

This topic of mutability, with its implied challenge to knowledge claims, is another mode of skeptical argument as old as ancient Pyrrhonism. Diogenes, for example, explains it as the fourth of ten structural modes whereby the ancient skeptics argued: this mode is "due to differences of condition and to changes in general." Owing to the constancy of change, it is not only assertions about perceptions and appearances but actually the perceptions themselves that are rendered dubious: "The impressions received thus appear to vary according to the nature of the conditions" (DL, IX,82).

Like the relativity of knowledge claims, this topic of mutability applies both to individual perceptions and experience and also to the larger cultural contexts that vary similarly. The topic of variability can be constructed in several different modes: "The *first* mode relates to the differences between living creatures. . . . The *second* mode has reference to the natures and idiosyncracies of men"; but another application of the same principle "is derived from customs, laws, belief in myths, compacts between nations and dogmatic assumptions" (DL, IX,79–83). For Diogenes, Engels, and Shelley, these structures are social and cultural: thus Engels argues that morality, religion, and political systems, together with the rationales that underlie such structures, vary constantly and specifically over history. And Shelley, in the *Defence,* treats mythologies, religions, and shared bodies of dogma as social rather than personal phenomena. In the same sentence he insists on their historical relativity:

When change and time shall have added one more superstition to the mass of those which have arisen and decayed upon the earth, commentators will be learnedly employed in elucidating the religion of ancestral Europe only not utterly forgotten because it will have been stamped with the eternity of genius (R&P, p. 499).

Shelley here ascribes the mythic systems of Dante's and Milton's Christianity to historically specific circumstances. The value, vitality, and even the nature of those systems are culturally relative. To read

Shelley's word "eternity" as an attribute of Dante, Milton, or their poetic and ideological products would be to misunderstand his statement utterly: it is the process of ideological construction (the formation of mythic systems by genius and the codification of such systems in poetic products) that is, Shelley says, eternal. The ideological products are relative, and so are their truth content and social efficacy. And on this general point, his claim is compatible with Diogenes' and Engels's.

An important difference arises, however. Engels concludes his refutation of Dühring's claims for eternal moral truths with what is more than a summary; he offers in fact a new dogma:

> We therefore [owing to arguments of historical and cultural relativity] reject every attempt to impose on us any moral dogma whatsoever as an eternal, ultimate and forever immutable law. . . . We maintain on the contrary that all former moral theories are the product, in the last analysis, of the economic stage which society had reached at that particular epoch (*Anti-Dühring*, p. 105).

Here Engels introduces a qualification of his skepticism. Given what he has just said about the unending relativity of knowledge, we might question how any analysis could be the last analysis. In the case of the mathematical sciences, Engels had also introduced a qualification: some few truths, he said, do have the kind of final and absolute validity that Dühring had claimed. Here, in the moral context (or, more broadly, in the social and historical context), he arrives at a dogmatic claim for economic determinism. The nature of that claim is complex, however, as Engels's term "product" is susceptible of several definitions, and the whole set of issues involved in determinism is also involved here (as the expositions below will demonstrate). But it is clear already that Engels's pattern of argument is recognizable: he uses a skeptical methodology, including topical arguments from classical skeptical tradition, but arrives finally at a dogmatic claim whose assertion may be incompatible with the methodological constraints that he has just articulated.

That pattern is not unique to *Anti-Dühring* or to Engels or to Marxism: Leibniz's introductory statement about Locke, in his *Essays on the Human Understanding,* is exemplary, as Albert William Levi has said:

The logical factor does indeed attest the desire to "prevent authority from prevailing against reason" and to emphasize that "it is chiefly for truth's sake" that we are all laboring. . . ." But philosophical controversies are always *dated* controversies with an anchorage in history and the context of social institutions.[23]

Producing eventually a "truth," a doctrine, Leibniz retreats at last from the skeptical imperative; and that collapse back into a dogma (which his own method has resisted) is visible in Engels, as well, when economic determinism is reified as cause, and culture is rendered as effect.

The essential issue is as simple as that summary suggests, but its presentation is enormously complex. The argument, for example, is presented at several different times by Engels alone, and by Marx, and often texts disagree with one another. Again in *Ludwig Feuerbach and the End of Classical German Philosophy*, Engels articulates the skeptical method, this time in a treatment of Hegel's dialectical philosophy:

It once for all dealt the deathblow to the finality of all products of human thought and action. Truth, the cognition of which is the business of philosophy, was in the hands of Hegel no longer an aggregate of finished dogmatic statements. . . . Truth lay now in the process of cognition itself.[24]

Engels goes on with what can serve as a summary of one of the hallmarks of skeptical tradition:

This dialectical philosophy dissolves all conceptions of final, absolute truth and of absolute states of humanity corresponding to it. For it (dialectical philosophy) nothing is final, absolute, sacred (*Ludwig Feuerbach*, p. 199).

Again Engels assimilates the topics of mutability and relativity: skeptical dialectic "reveals the transitory character of everything and in everything; nothing can endure before it except the uninterrupted process of becoming and passing away" (pp. 199–200).

Those principles—transitoriness, and the relativity of truth and value—are exactly the structural features of Shelley's assessments of social and political phenomena in *A Philosophical View of Reform*. For example, he describes characteristics of Germany's "rapidly maturing revolution" in such terms:

the enthusiasm, however distorted, of their religious sentiments; the flexibility and comprehensiveness of their language which is a many-sided mirror of every changing thought, their severe, bold and liberal spirit of criticism, their subtle and deep philosophy however erroneous and illogical mingling fervid intuitions into truth with obscure error (for the period of just distinction is yet to come) and their taste and power in the plastic arts (7:15).

All of these characteristics of the revolutionary social and political setting and populace are intellectual, relative, and limited. Such constraints on intellectual work and products are what Engels describes, and so is an open-ended structure of interpretation: "And what holds good for the realm of philosophical knowledge holds good also for that of every other kind of knowledge, and also for practical action" (*Ludwig Feuerbach*, p. 199). As he had done in *Anti-Dühring*, Engels applies the paradigm of variability to existences, and not only to statements about existence: "Just as knowledge is unable to reach a complete conclusion in a perfect, ideal condition of humanity, so is history unable to do so" (p. 199).

That linkage of philosophical propositions to historical and political circumstances is exactly what Shelley constructs in *A Philosophical View of Reform;* for example, he writes of French philosophy of the period immediately prior to the Revolution:

Considered as philosophers their error seems to have consisted chiefly of a limitedness of view; they told the truth, but not the whole truth. This might have arisen from the terrible sufferings of their countrymen inviting them rather to apply a portion of what had already been discovered to their immediate relief (7:9).

Admitting its error and its limited view, Shelley nonetheless finds much to value in this French philosophy: "It conducted to inferences at war with the dreadful oppressions under which the country groaned"; what is more, the "new philosophy," whose truth content, Shelley says, is limited and which is affected by "error," has the kind of negative dialectical value that Shelley elsewhere says belongs to other forms of skepticism: this philosophy "made familiar to mankind the fals[e]hood of their religious mediators and political oppressors" (7:9).

Both Shelley and Engels, then, link philosophical projects and propositions to historical conditions in which they arise and in which they have effects. For both Shelley and Engels, the truth content of any knowledge claim is not absolute; the total of available human experience fails to indicate that a human being can determine which, if any, assertions have absolute and eternal validity. And the limitations that apply to knowledge claims (limitations involving variability and mutability) apply also to perception and experience itself. Nonetheless, relative goods are operative within historically specific occasions.

Accordingly, Engels articulates a theory of progress that acknowledges the value of systems, even while denying their "so-called absolute truth": "all successive historical systems are only transitory stages in the endless course of development of human society." To say that does not, however, nullify the systems or their worth and importance: "Each stage is necessary, and therefore justified for the time and conditions to which it owes its origin" (*Ludwig Feuerbach*, p. 199). And Shelley makes just that point; celebrating the progress of reform in the eighteenth century and especially in the instance of the American Revolution, Shelley says that "many new theories, more or less perfect, but all superior to the mass of evil which they would supplant, have been given to the world" (7:10).

What Shelley says of the Constitution of the United States is an application of this same appreciation of relativity (perfectibility in the sense of a heuristic assumption that perfection is not attained or attainable): the law whereby the Constitution is amendable is, Shelley says, commendable because the framers of the Constitution acknowledge thereby the limited truth or good of their product:

Every other set of men who have assumed the office of legislation, and framing institutions for future ages, with far less right to such assumption than the founders of the American Republic assumed that their work was the wisest and the best that could possibly have been produced: these illustrious men looked upon the past history of their species and saw that it was the history of his mistakes, and his sufferings arising from his mistakes (7:11–12).

This is the contrast that Engels makes, in *Anti-Dühring,* between the "pompous phrases . . . about final and ultimate truths" that he finds in Dühring and the recognition that "without exception such knowledge always contains much more that is capable of being improved upon than that which cannot be improved upon or is correct" (*Anti-Dühring,* pp. 96–97). In contrast to such pompous dogmatists as those prior legislators who instituted their own variety of wisdom for eternity, the American legislators, Shelley says, "observed the superiority of their own work to all the works which had preceded it, and they judged it probable that other political institutions would be discovered bearing the same relation to those which they had established which they bear to those which have preceded them" (7:12). The epistemological constraints of the relativity argument thus manifest themselves in concretely political form: "They provided therefore for the application of these contingent discoveries to the social state" (7:12). Both the contingency and the relational validity of the concepts underlying the social state belong also, concretely and immediately, to the social institution itself. Like Engels in *Anti-Dühring* and like Marx in his *Economic and Philosophical Manuscripts,* Shelley links the theoretical property (relativity of knowledge) to a political manifestation, arguing that the contradictions implied by the transitoriness of truth belong equally to existence and to assertions about existence.[25]

MARX, ENGELS, HEGEL, AND THE ABSOLUTE IDEA

Engels points out that these principles of transitoriness and relativity (belonging to assertions and also to the subjects of assertions) "are a necessary conclusion from [the] method" of dialectic, and that Hegel formalized that method. Thus Hegel "emphasized that . . . eternal truth is nothing but the logical, or the historical, process itself." But Hegel "nevertheless finds himself compelled to supply this process with an end." That end (*Ausgang*) is "the Absolute Idea." This terminus of history and of reasoning, Engels says, amounts to a point of dogma; and "the whole dogmatic content of the Hegelian system is declared to be absolute truth, in contradiction to his dialectical method, which dissolves all dogmatism" (*Ludwig Feuerbach,* pp. 200–201). Dialectic, including Hegelian dialectic, "leaves alone 'absolute truth,' which is unattainable along this path[;] . . . instead one pursues attainable relative truths . . . and the summation of their results by means of dialectical thinking" (p. 202). The dogmatic end—Hegel's Absolute Idea—is doctrinally incompatible with the dialectical method by which it is reached.

Engels's critique is more rigorously skeptical than Hegel's philosophy. The charge is that Hegel evades the constraints of his own premises and method. Earlier, Godwin had formulated the skeptical stance toward the end, outcome, or product of reasoning in terms wholly compatible with Engels's later essay: "Godwin admits that certain 'resting-places for the mind' are permissible," to quote Scrivener's apt summary, "as long as we realize that these points of stasis, these theoretical conclusions, are only tentative, liable to be overthrown by later enquiry and further revision."[26]

Like Godwin, Shelley discredits the truth content of his own formulations, claiming contextual efficacy but no more (*A Philosophical View of Reform*, 7:46–47). "One of the most unquestionable characteristics of the human mind, has appeared to be its progressive nature," says Godwin. In the pursuit of knowledge "we should never stand still[;] . . . everything most interesting to the general welfare . . . should be in a state of change." Like every skeptic since Pyrrho, Godwin opposes vigorously any "institution tending to give permanence to certain systems and opinions."[27] For Shelley, the monarchy and aristocracy are such reifications of opinion, tyrannously maintained as permanent institutions; for Engels, Hegel's Absolute Idea, offered as a terminus of philosophical inquiry, is just such an unwarrantable reification in metaphysics.

But again a difference arises between Shelley and each of those other dialectical thinkers: in contrast to Godwin, Shelley advocates explicitly the active political displacement of that tyrannous structure with another political structure; such a political advocacy is inimical to Godwin. In contrast to both earlier thinkers, Engels "maintain[s] on the contrary that all former moral theories are the product, in the last analysis, of the economic stage which society had reached at that particular epoch" (*Anti-Dühring*, p. 105). Here a problem of reflexive application arises: the central argument of *Ludwig Feuerbach and the End of Classical German Philosophy* is that Hegel's dialectical philosophy does not pass the test of a reflexive application of its own dialectical procedure. Putting a conceptual end to his argument, Hegel offers a philosophical assertion that is not true of itself. It is a question

whether Engels's "last analysis" is exactly similar: dialectical philosophy "once for all dealt the deathblow to the finality of all products of
human thought and action"; there can be therefore no last analysis.
"This dialectical philosophy dissolves all conceptions of final, absolute truth"; how things, thoughts, persons, and the world really are is
not determinable. It is a question whether that epistemic constraint is
compatible with evidently dogmatic claims by Marx and Engels themselves, of which the following is only one example: "The social structure and the state are continually evolving out of the life process of
definite individuals, but of individuals not as they may appear in their
own or other people's imagination, but as they really are, i.e., as they
are effective, produce materially, and are active under definite material limits, presuppositions, and conditions independent of their
will."[28]

That sentence from *The German Ideology* culminates in an assertion
of no more than facticity, a principle wholly compatible with the
most rigorous skepticism, as the previous chapter of this book has
shown. Terms and concepts in that sentence require a great deal of
definition—a whole library of it. "Social structure," "life process,"
and "material limits" are phrases that could be naming a number of
different things, and the epistemological status of the sentence will
vary depending upon whether, for example, the "social structure" is
an institutional or ideational affair, or whether "material" means
"natural" or "efficacious." Similarly, what is probably the most famous sentence in all ideological theory may or may not mean anything, depending on which of many definitions is assigned to key
terms: "Life is not determined by consciousness," say Marx and Engels, "but consciousness by life" (*The German Ideology*, p. 247). Possible meanings of "determine" (e.g., "limit," "condition," "control,"
"cause") affect decisively the meaning of that statement and therefore
its epistemological status (as dogma, nonsense, factual description, or
relative truth). Much of what follows in this chapter is devoted to
analyzing these problematic constructions, but my point here is a
simpler one: it is by no means self-evident whether the apparently
dogmatic claims of Engels and of Marx-Engels are compatible with
their own epistemological principles (and especially the relativity of
knowledge). I do not affirm that it is the case, but I point out that it is
possible to suggest that Engels and Marx-Engels recapitulate precisely the dogmatic process with which Engels charges Hegel. Such a

charge could be put simply in these terms: they walk into an argument with skepticism, but they walk out with a dogma.

Shelley does not do that.

Three central concepts in Marxist philosophy embrace most of the theoretical problems that distinguish Shelley and the classical skeptical paradigm from such a philosophy. These concepts are ideology, superstructure, and determine. The similarities of Shelley with Marx-Engels are methodological, and they appear at the outset; the discrepancies are doctrinal and appear rather after some fairly rigorous and difficult analysis of concepts. That whole library of exposition that I have said is needed for the problematic issues in Marxist theory does, in fact, exist, and I shall be summarizing some of its contents because the exposition and evaluation of skeptical dialectic, including Shelley's, is already, as a matter of interpretive history, linked to those problems. The charge that Shelley failed to perceive certain truths must stand or fall with the ontological status of those truths. That ontological status can only be determined epistemologically, by the analysis of concepts and their relations. The polemical character of what follows arises from that fact: paraphrase of Shelley's texts will not suffice, nor will paraphrase of the Marx-Engels texts, because such a paraphrase will necessarily rest on a particular understanding of those key terms, those central concepts, and the relations among them. The truth value of statements by Shelley, Marx, Engels, or any interpreter is wholly a matter of the meaning of terms, and in the case of those three crucial terms and concepts—ideology, superstructure, and determine—no consensus that is even conversationally adequate exists.

The issues are rendered difficult when contradictions appear in centrally important Marx-Engels texts. But to define the contradictions is to clarify the relevant issues. For example, in *Ludwig Feuerbach and the End of Classical German Philosophy,* Engels writes that a "revolutionary character" is "the only absolute dialectical philosophy admits" (p. 200). It is questionable whether dialectical philosophy can admit any absolute, including that one, according to definitions that Engels himself offers; but beyond that question lie other claims, in the same essay and elsewhere, that at least appear to be offered as absolutes. To use Engels's words against his own argument: if Engels's claims *are* offered as absolutes, then "the whole dogmatic content of the [Marx-Engels] system is . . . in contradiction to [their own] dialectical method, which dissolves all dogmatism" (p. 201). For example, Engels says that "science . . . mounts from lower to ever higher levels of knowledge" (p. 199). The question that I would raise, here, is not whether science does in fact do so but rather what sort of assertion is it that claims that such a development is forever the case? Again, human history is said to exhibit an "endless ascendancy from the lower to the higher" (p. 200); Shelley posits a succession of systems and conditions, and Godwin posits a ceaseless change among them, but Engels is here claiming more: he is claiming a teleology. That teleology does not inhere in, or follow from, the dialectical method that dramatizes succession merely; it is a value-laden assertion imposed upon that dialectical succession.

Its status, as contradictory or heuristic, depends on the kind of assertion that we take it to be. If we take Engels to be describing a factual state of affairs—observing reportorially that all human history does and must, in fact, exhibit such an ascendancy—then the claim can be tested by checking the evidence. We would compare the facts against the description and see whether they agree.

If, alternatively, the statement is to be taken as an evaluative assertion—as a bestowal of approval on the progress, whatever it is, that has in fact taken place—then no truth test whatever is applicable. The truth value of the claim is moot: it reports an attitude and not an extensional object or event.

Such a problem does not arise in Shelley's prose when he distinguishes (A) moral from (B) factual truth (*A Philosophical View of Reform*, 7:42). The report of a claim belonging to class A is a report of affect, impulse, preference, and volition; a report of class B refers to what occurs "without our will" (*On Life*, R&P, p. 475). "That equality in possessions which Jesus Christ so passionately taught is a moral rather than political truth" (*A Philosophical View of Reform*, 7:42). The "unbending realities of actual life" involve political truths (7:43). A "moderate reform, that is a suffrage whose qualification should be the possession of a certain small property," is a principle in which "all reformers ought to acquiesce" (7:46). This statement of Shelley's is a claim of kind (class B). It is susceptible of truth tests, because it submits itself to the constraints of facticity and because it claims predictive power, since Shelley is prepared to describe what such a reform would and would not accomplish. In contrast, "the omnipotence of the mind of man, the equality of human beings, and the duty of internal purity" (I quote from a fragment on the doctrines of Jesus Christ—see

I&P, 7:145) are truths of class A. There are important relationships between these two kinds of discourse (Shelley says in the *Essay on Christianity* that A must precede B), but Shelley preserves the distinction between them.

The following assertion, from Marx and Engels, is more problematic:

[1.] We set out from real, active men, and on the basis of their real life process we demonstrate the development of the ideological reflexes and echoes of this life process (*The German Ideology*, p. 247).

If that is an assertion of kind B, then according to criteria offered by Marx and Engels, it is testable:

[2.] The phantoms formed in the human brain are also, necessarily, sublimates of their material life process, which is empirically verifiable and bound to material premises (*The German Ideology*, p. 247).

Claim 2, indicating that some things are "empirically verifiable," may thereby furnish a criterion with which to test the truth value of claim 1. Alternatively, claim 1 could be an assertion of kind A, voicing an attitude or an aspiration toward action rather than a description of it.

Another sentence from the same argument is yet more ambiguous. The claim that follows may be a judgment of kind A, or it may be a description of "empirically verifiable" fact, or it may be a third kind of assertion, an ontological dogma.

[3.] Men, developing their material production and their material intercourse, alter, along with this, their real existence, their thinking, and the products of their thinking (*The German Ideology*, p. 247).

If this statement records a wish, its truth value is moot. If, instead, we take 2 as a criterion of empirical verifiability, whereby 1 and 3 can be tested, then simple observation will suffice, and no philosophical examination is necessary. The truth value of the claim is to be determined just as, for example, we would check to see what was the color of a neighbor's elephant. If, alternatively, more is claimed, and the argument contained in 3 rests upon a doctrine of what is real—distinguishing "material intercourse" as a reality from what 2 calls "phantoms formed in the human brain," which are illusions—then, simply checking the facts will not suffice to test the claim. The statements would depend upon an ontological doctrine, which would then be liable to a skeptical critique of the kind already performed by Marx and Engels in their account of Hegel. Their critique would undermine their dogma.

Unfortunately, the context of the Marx-Engels argument offers no clue about which sort of statement 3 is: it might be a judgment of kind A, or it might be an empirically verifiable statement of fact, or it might be an ontological dogma. Whether it is to be believed, enjoyed, tested, used, or obeyed is impossible to determine.

DIALECTIC AND NEGATIVE DOGMA

Dialectical philosophy is in fact often liable to the charge of self-contradictory dogmatism, when "dogmatism" is taken in the classical sense—as an assertion of the nonevident. The skeptics of the New Academy (Arcesilaus and Carneades, chiefly) were thus sometimes charged with a negative dogma, as if they had asserted as a matter of belief or knowledge that truth was unknowable. Such an assertion would be dogma, because it claims knowledge of that which is (by definition included within the statement) unknowable. Instead, the arguments of Arcesilaus and Carneades go no further in this connection than this: a criterion whereby we might distinguish false from true perceptions is not available; whether some perceptions and assertions are or are not true is a different question. Again, in the dialectical philosophy of the Marxist variety, the same possible charge arises. One form of apparent dogmatism results from the structure of the polar antithesis, to which dialectical arguments are typically prone. As Engels argues, the bipolar opposition of terms is a structure of reasoning, possessing no truth value and even, possibly, being essentially false.

Shelley's criticism of the thought-thing dichotomy can serve as an example: he denies (in the *Treatise on Morals*) that an essential distinction exists between external objects and internal thoughts; but he continues to use that vocabulary of distinction, in ways that could be said to vitiate the truth value of his statements. Similarly, Shelley denies (in *On Life*) that the personal pronouns ("I," "you," "they") denote any actual difference among the referents of the terms. But he continues, obviously, to use those nonreferential words in ways that deprive many statements of even ostensible truth value. One's own usages are not exempt from the constraints that one accepts as universal.

What have appeared thus to be outright contradictions and dogma are common in the discourse of Marxism. For example, a famous sentence of Engels's (from a letter to Franz Mehring) says that "ideology is a process accomplished by the so-called thinker consciously . . . but with a false consciousness. The real motive forces impelling him remain unknown to him."[29] Appearing in a context that involves thought in a very general sense, this distinction between false and true has led to paraphrases like this one, from Antonio Labriola: an "ideological envelope" encloses "human works": this "envelope" is an "impediment" to "the clear and complete vision of the real things."[30] The distinction between consciousness, which is "false," and the status of Engels's knowledge claim is not clear. Similarly, Labriola posits a falsification from which his own sentence is in no way exempt. Whether Engels's formulation is self-contradictory will depend on how his terms are to be understood, and a multitude of incompatible definitions of the word "ideology" have been proposed. But the simpler point that I wish to emphasize here is that like Shelley with the thought-thing dichotomy, or like the skeptics of the New Academy who appeared to claim that truth is unknowable, the dichotomy of consciousness and reality that is embedded in the sentences from Engels and Labriola looks like a dogmatism.

Such a dogmatism would be self-contradictory because in it the constraint of the epistemological circle (the "ideological envelope") would clash with the universality and even the extensionality claimed for the "truth" of the statement. The term "ideology" is a frequent locus for such dogmatism: Terry Eagleton, for example, follows such earlier Marxists as Engels and Labriola when he predicates realities apart from ideologies.[31] But ideology is not the only problem in which the issue arises, for the Marxist writers or for Shelley. For example, Shelley writes defensively in *On Life:* "I confess that I am one of those who am unable to refuse my assent to the conclusions of those philosophers, who assert that nothing exists but as it is perceived" (R&P,

p. 476). The apologetic tone of that remark arises from the fact that his own skeptical methods entail a suspension of belief and assent.[32] Shelley had read in Cicero's *Academica* of the skeptical avoidance of assent to propositions that are negative or positive (*Ac.*, II, 104). The skeptical suspension of belief and assent arises in large part from the fact that belief contradicts the claim made by its own assertion. The epistemological circle (or ideological envelope) does not allow us to know anything outside it. Therefore assent to a proposition whose terms do claim reference external to such a circle—as real things are external to false consciousness—is contradictory.

One way to analyze the problem posed by Shelley's statement of assent is to recognize it as a nonself-applicable proposition. That is, if the speaker of that sentence ("Nothing exists but as it is perceived") is telling the truth, then he or she is limited in knowledge to his or her own perceptions. But since the sentence claims knowledge (though of a negative sort) about what is true external to his or her perception, that sentence is not true. A nonself-applicable proposition is one that if true, is not true.[33]

The problem of self-applicability is a bit more complex in the case of moral and political claims, but not much. For example, Fredric Jameson begins a substantial argument about politics and interpretation with this injunction: "Always historicize!"[34] Because that statement is an imperative rather than a description of fact, it may seem to be protected against the charge of self-referential absurdity. That is, the statement asks to be universalized ("always") and also to be relativized ("historicize"). There seems to be a contradiction here. But the truth value (as opposed to wisdom or goodness or utility) of a pure injunction is moot; it pretends to be useful or desirable, not true.

But as usually happens, this injunction (genuinely representative of Marxist thinking) does rest on an assertion of truth. As Jameson says, the statement "Always historicize" is "the one absolute and we may even say 'transhistorical' imperative of all dialectical thought." I refer not to the contradiction between "historicize" and "transhistorical" but rather to the fact that the statement will not work as a subject of its own predicate. That is, if we historicize the statement "Always historicize," we will not always historicize. Similarly, if the truth content of the larger statement, which contains the word "transhistorical," is that "reality is historically relative," then the statement "Reality is historically relative" is historically relative. If it is true, it is not true but rather relative. If it is false, it may be true.

Exactly the same situation is found with Engels's claims for the relativity of knowledge: to say that "nothing is universally or absolutely true" is to say that "'Nothing is universally or absolutely true' is not universally or absolutely true." To offer such a statement as a claim of knowledge will not work, because its truth requires its falsehood. To reason in that way would be absurdity.

Shelley is in some instances culpable of that absurdity, but in the course of his brief life he learns how to overcome it, in ways more effective than simply adding an apologetic tone to a negatively dogmatic statement. For example, he does present the statement "Nothing exists but as it is perceived" as an independent sentence unattached to a qualifier (in *On Life*, R&P, p. 477), and the sentences that surround this one do not qualify the claim. That sentence is exactly the kind of nonself-applicable proposition that Engels and Jameson also make. It is not only false by its own terms but it also is meaningless. To say that "nothing exists but as it is perceived" is to commit oneself to an assertion belied by one's assertion: "'Nothing exists but as it is perceived' exists but as it is perceived." The logic demanded by Shelley's statement makes Shelley's statement false or meaningless.

But Shelley does three things that not only overcome the absurdity; they also empower his philosophy of action with (not validity but) viability, not dogmatic truth but efficacy. The values that he proposes for his political discourse are defined not by abstract standards of veridicality but rather by utility, by the beneficial impact of that discourse within the parameters of human experience. And he does so without committing himself to absurdity.

First, he presents his assertion as a description of his cognition rather than as a description of the world. The assertion "I confess that I am one of those who am unable to refuse my assent" is about his inability to refuse his assent, as I have already suggested; it is not about the proposition to which he says he assents. It is about his cognitive event, and no more. The same advantage (the avoidance of the dogmatic absurdity of self-contradiction) is available when it is others' cognitions that are reported. Thus Shelley does not say that the conclusions of Drummond's intellectual system are true but rather that "the most discriminating intellects have been able to discover no train of thoughts in the process of reasoning, which does not conduct" to those conclusions.

A second method of avoiding the absurdity of self-contradiction appears at the last instance in his career when Shelley makes such an assertion about existence. He adds a qualifier whereby, though his statement is about existence rather than the cognition of existence, it is nonetheless logically applicable to itself: "All things exist as they are perceived: at least in relation to the percipient" (*Defence of Poetry*, R&P, p. 505). Applied to itself, that version of the claim produces a logically coherent proposition: "'All things exist as they are perceived: at least in relation to the percipient' exists as it is perceived, at least in relation to the percipient." Similarly, the existence of other beings and of a power that is to perception what a cause is to an effect is not a certainty but a "conjecture[,] a persuasion, or a conviction" conditioned by "the various disposition of each" percipient (Tokoo, p. 19; I&P, 7:59). That claim is not falsified by self-application; the stronger claims of negative dogma and of the historical relativity of knowledge are, in contrast, rendered untrue by their own logic. By means of qualifiers, Shelley solves that problem, though he is still able to talk of existence, and not merely prescriptively about the rules for doing so.

A third method of avoiding contradiction is more complex and general. The paradox of nonself-applicability reveals this problem: we need a way to make and to use statements such that language can offer and require something other than truth as a product. Shelley responds to this problem by distinguishing forms of discourse. Moral claims are not metaphysical claims. But "it is presumptuous" (it is dogmatic) to assert "a distinction between the moral and the material universe" (I&P, 7:62). It would, however, be convenient to use such a distinction. Absurd or otherwise, metaphysical discussion admits of no essential distinction between those thoughts or things. But then Shelley makes an observation that frees him to assert such distinctions without contradicting himself and without subjecting himself to a criterion of truth: "Important distinctions of various degrees of force indeed, are to be established between [thoughts and things] if [they were,] as they may be[,] subjects of ethical or economical discussion" (Tokoo, p. 20; I&P, 7:60). That is, the same assertion that is false if it is offered as metaphysical can be nonetheless valuable when it is offered in another way—in ethical or economic discussion. Some statements include in their cognitive content an assertion of their own truth. Others, including Shelley's economic and ethical statements, do not even assert that they are themselves true but rather propose other criteria for their own evaluation.

To summarize: Shelley overcomes the kind of self-contradiction to which dialectical philosophy is liable, in three ways: 1. Some of his assertions have only intensional reference and do not pretend to report more than cognitive events. 2. Some of his assertions include in their predicates qualifiers that allow assertions about existence only as assertions, without contradiction. 3. Some of his discourse does not pretend to truth but rather to utility. The problem of the criterion of truth—the oldest crux in skeptical dialectic—has not been overcome in the entire history of philosophy, as Shelley recognizes; consequently, it would be highly advantageous if we could find a form of discourse that did not depend on our finding such a criterion. Ethical and economic discourse (broadly, political discourse) is such a form.

The advantages of Shelley's solutions are considerable: their importance is especially apparent when his solutions are compared with the contradictions that remain as flaws in some other forms of dialectical philosophy. What follows, in the final sections of this chapter, is an analysis of three crucial concepts from the dialectical philosophy of historical materialism: ideology, superstructure, and determinism. These concepts will serve as points of comparison between Shelley's political thought and other forms of dialectic. The primary purpose of that comparison is to clarify the nature of Shelley's political assertions in *A Philosophical View of Reform,* but a secondary purpose is the argument that Shelley's political philosophy is not deficient, as the materialist claim of Cameron with which this chapter began would suggest; rather, Shelley's more rigorous skepticism frees his specific claims as well as his conceptual framework from vitiating absurdities that persist in the more narrowly materialist forms of Marxist dialectic. A third argument in what follows is this one: the advantages of Shelley's political philosophy consist largely in those elements of method in which he is closer to the classical paradigms of skeptical tradition than are Marx and Engels in their subsequent applications of the skeptical method.

X IS Y, UNLESS IT IS NOT

One general problem afflicting ideological theory is summarized by Neil McInnes: when one affirms that knowledge is limited to partial ideologies—an argument of Karl Mannheim, for example, and of György Lukács—one has implicitly claimed some sort of knowledge about the whole of history into which all partial ideologies fit; the alleged partiality assumes and asserts a whole, even while it prohibits or denies access to knowledge of that whole.[35]

Another form of self-contradiction, however, afflicts the kind of ideological theory of, for example, Engels and (after him) Lenin: this theory affirms a "total concept of ideology."[36] According to this concept, it is not this or that idea that is specific to one time and one place, and therefore only relatively true; it is the total of the elements making up any available worldview that is thus limited. All knowledge is accordingly relative, except (and the exception is not explained thoroughly) a small number of propositions that are affirmed to be absolutely true. For Engels and Lenin, these absolute truths include some propositions from mathematics and logic and Marxist theory (which thus exempts itself from itself, according to one possible critique).

More recently, Louis Althusser's definitions are so broad as to exclude nothing: no thoughts or knowledge and not even his own argument. Whatever is said elsewhere about science being different from ideology or potentially exempt from ideological illusions and falsehoods, the following statements by Althusser leave no basis at all for any such exclusion. First, "an ideology is a system (with its own logic and rigour) of representations (images, myths, ideas, or concepts, depending on the case) endowed with an historical existence and role within a given society"; "So ideology is as such an organic part of every social totality." Enthused by his own impulse for inclusiveness, Althusser allows the definition to swell: "Human societies secrete ideology as the very element and atmosphere indispensable to their historical respiration and life. Only an ideological world outlook could have imagined societies *without ideology*"; "historical materialism cannot conceive that even a communist society could ever do without ideology"; ideology "is a structure essential to the historical life of societies," more far-reaching than consciousness. The "'lived' relation between men and the world, including History (in political ac-

tion or inaction) passes through ideology, or better, *is ideology itself*."
Althusser seeks to acknowledge the absurdity implied in the reflexive application of his claim: by his own definition, his own claim is an
ideological illusion. Beyond that absurdity, however, lies a profound
uselessness of the definition: that which excludes nothing can name
nothing. It can be said without exaggeration, therefore, that Althusser is here talking of nothing at all.[37]

Where Shelley uses three methods of avoiding self-contradiction,
Marxist forms of dialectic also seek to protect themselves against
counterarguments, but in a different way: briefly, Marxist theory
makes itself a self-confirming system by means of an open-ended production of subsidiary hypotheses. When enough of these supplementary assertions are invented and produced, then any self-confirming
system can be made compatible with any conceivable fact or its
opposite.

Historically, this kind of critique is associated with Karl Popper. "It
became clear to me," Popper reports retrospectively, "that what made
a theory, or a statement, scientific was its power to rule out, or exclude, the occurrence of some possible events—to prohibit, or forbid,
the occurrence of these events: *the more a theory forbids, the more it tells
us.*" Popper associates this criterion with the interplay of dogmatic
and critical kinds of thinking:

> If somebody proposed a scientific theory he should answer, as
> Einstein did, the question: "Under what conditions would I ad-
> mit that my theory is untenable?" In other words, what con-
> ceivable facts would I accept as refutations, or falsifications, of
> my theory?
>
> I had been shocked by the fact that the Marxists (whose cen-
> tral claim was that they were social scientists) and the psycho-
> analysts of all schools were able to interpret any conceivable
> event as a verification of their theories.

Popper's critique is thorough and particular, and his summary is
worth quoting in full:

> As I pointed out in my *Open Society,* one may regard Marx's the-
> ory as refuted by the course of events during the Russian Revo-
> lution. According to Marx the revolutionary changes start at the

bottom, as it were: means of production change first, then social conditions of production, then political power, and ultimately ideological beliefs, which change last. But in the Russian Revolution the political power changed first, and then the ideology (Dictatorship plus Electrification) began to change social conditions and the means of production from the top. The reinterpretation of Marx's theory to evade this falsification immunized it against further attacks, transforming it into the vulgar-Marxist (or socioanalytic) theory which tells us that the "economic motive" and the class struggle pervade social life.[38]

Of course Popper's criterion of falsifiability is itself subject to criticism, and though it is useful in discriminating informative from redundant propositions, it cannot be considered absolute. For example, if the criterion of falsifiability is stated as a claim—i.e., that no theory is tenable except that which meets the test of falsifiability—then this claim is not itself falsifiable. But it is a critical tool with which dogmas of all kinds can be approached in telling ways, and two systems of dogma—Marxism and psychoanalysis—have served Popper well as examples.

One procedure by which these systems of dogma (like others) can seek to immunize themselves against refutation is a simple technique of producing additional hypotheses, as I have said. When a fact or event contradicts a claim, produce an additional hypothesis that will so adjust the reference of the claim that the fact or event no longer contradicts it. For example, redefine Marx's theory of revolution in such a way that the fact that the Russian Revolution occurred in a society dominated by agrarian economy no longer refutes it; or, to use Popper's example, redefine Marx's theory so that revolutionary change that begins in political form no longer contradicts the theory. A question arises, in such a case, about what point it is at which such an adjusted and adjustable theory ceases to mean anything at all.

Among others, Sidney Hook and Martin Seliger have illustrated ways in which Marx and subsequent Marxists have produced additional hypotheses to preserve a claim in the face of its inconsistency with the facts.[39] The purposes of this chapter do not warrant an analysis of all the enormously complex issues involved in those charges, but only one set of them.

That set involves the assertion that both ideology and superstructure (in any of several senses in which those terms can be used) are determined by another thing, or set of things, or force, or set of forces, or activity, or set of activities. It is sometimes said in Marxist theory that ideology and superstructure are determined by an economic base; a weaker form of the same general claim is that ideology and superstructure are materially determined, where "materially" can mean any of several things. Marxist theory characteristically affirms one or the other of those statements of determinism, often qualified in any of several ways. Shelley's political philosophy does not rest on such a statement. The preceding section of this chapter has shown that the character of political discourse, in Shelley's sense, is insusceptible of veridical criteria, and that point of theory accounts for his avoidance of such truth claims; but if any one of the possible statements of ideological and superstructural determinism is true, and can be shown to be true, then Shelley's reticence is a deficiency, as Cameron alleges.

Here again is Cameron's formulation of the problem: "Although [Shelley] saw historical evolution, he did not perceive that the basic factor was social and that human thinking was derivative; rather he neutrally depicted both in interaction." Behind that admirably clear sentence lies an ambiguous passage from *The German Ideology:*

> The production of ideas, of conceptions, of consciousness is at first directly interwoven with the material activity and the material intercourse of men. . . . Conceiving, thinking, the mental intercourse of men appear at this stage as the direct efflux of their material behavior. The same applies to mental production as expressed in the language of the politics, laws, morality, religion, metaphysics of a people.[40]

Part of the ambiguity involves what "first" means, and "at this stage": what is asserted may be simple chronological priority, or it may be some kind of logical priority pertaining to analysis rather than temporal sequence. But whatever is meant is also, apparently, what Cameron means by "basic"—conceiving and thinking are derivative of another element, or an "efflux" of it, and that of which they are an efflux is said to be material, which in most Marxist discourse includes what is social. The theory expressed in *The German Ideology* "explains the formation of ideas from material [or social] practice" (p. 258).

But it sometimes happens that it is manifestly not the case that an idea or act of thinking is the effect of an immediate material act or thing, but that instead material activity is affected by thoughts and conceptions. Therefore, Marx and Engels say that there is a "reciprocal reaction" of "material production" and "the whole mass of different theoretical products and forms of consciousness, religion, philosophy, ethics, etc." (pp. 257–58). What makes that formulation confusing— and what has produced dozens of volumes of definition, explanation, and disputation—is the fact that a linear relation of priority is different from and essentially incompatible with a reciprocal relation of interaction.

Cameron correctly points out that Shelley portrays an interaction of ideational and social elements in human experience. So do Marx and Engels, apparently, but they also then return to an allegedly overarching priority of the material and social base. When the strongest form of the claim of priority conflicts with facts that manifestly contradict it, the theory protects itself by producing the subsidiary hypothesis of a reciprocal relation. The cognitive content of the claim depends on definitions that I shall be summarizing below, but what I wish to emphasize here is the structural feature of the argument; it is an illustration of a self-confirming system.

The problem is not unique to *The German Ideology*. Terry Eagleton, for example, says of ideology that "it consists of a definite, historically relative structure of perception which underpins the power of a particular class."[41] But it sometimes happens that certain elements in the structure of perception belonging to the ruling class manifestly do not accord with the maintenance of that class's power. Therefore, to protect the theory, a subsidiary hypothesis is produced: "an ideology is never a simple reflection of a ruling class's ideas," though "ideology" has just been defined as a structure of perception specific to the ruling class; "on the contrary, it is always a complex phenomenon, which may incorporate conflicting, even contradictory, views of the world."[42]

What is a "definite . . . structure of perception" is said to be definite until it manifestly is not, whereupon it is said that it "may" include "conflicting, even contradictory views." What is a (single) worldview is only said to be that until it is manifestly not a (single) worldview, whereupon it is redefined as something else that includes many worldviews.

A flexibility that allows a term to carry whatever definition occasion warrants is in fact a strategy of theoretical self-protection. One continues to make assertions that pretend to be about an existing state of extensional reality, but in such a way that no conceivable state of affairs will falsify the assertion. The advantage of such a procedure is obvious; its disadvantages include a failure to mean anything. I refer, here, not to the criterion of falsifiability, applied by Karl Popper, Sidney Hook, and others, but rather to a dearth of cognitive content that results from an undifferentiated plethora of coverage. For example, if I were to say that "everything visible in the world is red in color, unless it is not," I have in fact said nothing at all.

Similarly, if I were to say that something (social, material, economic, or otherwise) acts and is, prior to something else (conceptual, intellectual, emotive, or institutional), I have made an assertion whose truth content (should it be found to have any) would be definite. But if I were to say that something acts and is, prior to something else, unless it is otherwise, I have said nothing at all. Historical struggles (x) can certainly involve embedded ideas (y); but to affirm dogmatically, as Engels does, that x produces or generates or causes y, and then to affirm, as Engels also does, that y may after all produce, generate, or cause x, is to end by affirming nothing.[43]

My observations concern the structure of these assertions, and not yet the specific meanings of the terms within them. What is meant by "ideology" or "determine" is not at issue in the point that I want to make here, which concerns rather the question of whether anything can be said, or is in fact said, by an assertion having that structure. The priority or reciprocity of base and superstructure is a problem to which I will be returning, after some definitions. It is worthwhile, however, to recognize first this structural principle: a statement that "x is y" has positive referential content, whether intensional or extensional; a statement that "x is y, unless it is otherwise," has none. Some formulations of the base-superstructure relationship take that latter form.

IDEOLOGY, SUPERSTRUCTURE, AND DETERMINISM

Shelley's clearest statement of the base-superstructure relationship appears, like Marx's similar statements, in the context of a revolutionary argument: "The system of society as it exists at present must be over-thrown from the foundations with all its superstructure of maxims & of forms" (*Letters*, 2:191). The implied relationship between a no-tional "superstructure" and its "foundations" is described in those same terms by Marx:

> Upon the several forms of property, upon the social conditions of existence, a whole superstructure is reared of various and pe-culiarly shaped feelings, illusions, habits of thought and con-ceptions of life. The whole class produces and shapes these out of its material foundation and out of the corresponding social conditions.[44]

Shelley's statement, however, indicates that this superstructure is not only notional ("maxims") but also institutional ("forms"), and so too does Marx, in a definition that involves the term "ideology":

> The sum total of [the] relations of production constitutes . . . the real foundation, on which rise legal and political superstructures and to which correspond definite forms of social consciousness.[45]

What Marx calls "ideological forms" are "legal, political, religious, aesthetic, or philosophic" (p. 44).

Sometimes Shelley expresses the relationship between the material foundations of society and the superstructure in a way that implies that the foundations determine the superstructure: according to Ave-ling and Eleanor Marx, Shelley "understood that men and peoples were the result of their ancestry and of the environment" (p. 10), and as evidence they produce a sentence from the letter to Leigh Hunt in which Shelley writes of "the system of society" and its "superstruc-ture": "It is," Shelley says, "less the character of the individual than the situation in which he is placed which determines him to be honest or dishonest" (*Letters*, 2:191). Similarly, the theory expressed in *The German Ideology* "explains the formation of ideas from material prac-tice" (p. 258), as I have indicated above.

But for Shelley and also for Marx-Engels, the relationship between the ideological superstructure and the material or social base (founda-tion) becomes more complex: "There is an interaction of all these ele-ments," says Engels.[46] Comparably, in *A Philosophical View of Reform*

Shelley says that the different levels of material and intellectual reality or experience are linked: "systems of faith" are built upon "popular mistakes," and they are immediately related to a "superstructure of political and religious tyranny" (I&P, 7:8); but Shelley avoids asserting a direct unilinear causal relationship.

For Engels, "economic [conditions] are ultimately decisive" in the formation of "philosophic theories, religious views, and their further development into systems of dogmas" (letter to Bloch, p. 398). So too for Shelley, "the condition" of those "from whose labour the materials of life are wrought" involves religious superstition and dogma (*A Philosophical View of Reform*, 7:30). But for Engels, these ideological forms "also exercise their influence upon the course of the historical struggles"; and for Shelley the development of moral and metaphysical systems is connected reciprocally with conditions of national prosperity (7:52).

Thus, statements of one-directional determinism (e.g., material base determines the ideological superstructure) are balanced, by both Shelley and Marx-Engels, against statements of a reciprocal relationship. Says Shelley, "Poets, not otherwise than philosophers, painters, sculptors and musicians, are in one sense the creators and in another the creations of their age" (preface to *Prometheus Unbound*, R&P, p. 135). Marx and Engels say exactly the same thing: "Circumstances make men just as much as men make circumstances" (*The German Ideology*, p. 258).

This issue is central to E. P. Thompson's sustained and forceful critique of Althusser's theory, which is (Thompson argues) rather a new form of dogmatic idealism than a genuinely dialectical philosophy. Althusser, says Thompson, "falsifies the 'dialogue' with empirical evidence inherent in knowledge-production, and in Marx's own practice, and thereby falls continually into modes of thought designated in the Marxist tradition as 'idealist'."[47] Thompson's summary of the relevant formulation is worth citing especially because he avoids philosophical technicalities, writing as a historian rather than as a philosopher:

If we are to employ the (difficult) notion that social being determines social consciousness, how are we to suppose that this is so? It will surely not be supposed that 'being' is here, as gross materiality from which all ideality has been abstracted, and that 'consciousness' (as abstract ideality) is there? For we cannot conceive of any form of social being independently of its organising concepts and expectations, nor could social being reproduce itself for a day without thought. What we mean is that changes take place within social being, which give rise to changed *experience;* and this experience is *determining,* in the sense that it exerts pressures upon existent social consciousness, proposes new questions, and affords much of the material which the more elaborated intellectual exercises are about (p. 8).

This argument for reciprocity between being and consciousness, like that which Shelley asserts between human beings and their historical age, is active and constant, to such an extent that it overcomes the absolute authority of the dichotomy altogether; the two are evidently inextricable in the phenomenal facts of life:

> Consciousness, whether as unself-conscious culture, or as myth, or as science, or law, or articulated ideology, thrusts back into being in its turn: as being is thought so thought also is lived— people may, within limits, *live* the social or sexual expectations which are imposed upon them by dominant conceptual categories (p. 9).

As I have argued above, either of these claims (for one-directional determinism or for a reciprocal relationship) can have a specific cognitive content, which will depend on the definitions of those terms, and many such definitions have been offered, as I shall illustrate below.[48] When the claim is organized in a particular form (x is y, unless it is not), nothing is said, no matter what the definitions, but other forms of the assertion (x is y, or x and y function reciprocally) are free of that absurdity. What follows, therefore, is a summary of the definitions of x and y that have been most important historically. The meanings of Shelley's statements depend on the definitions of the terms, and so does the relationship of his political thought to that of Marx-Engels and to other ideological theories.

A. Superstructure

Three senses of the word "superstructure" appear in ideological theory; usages of the word become more complex when it appears in the phrase "ideological superstructure," as I shall be illustrating below, but all three senses of the word alone are explained concisely in Marx's preface to *A Contribution to the Critique of Political Economy:*

1. Superstructure is the set of "legal and political" institutions of a society.

2. Superstructure is a set of "definite forms of social consciousness" that correspond to those legal and political institutions. In *The Eighteenth Brumaire of Louis Bonaparte,* this definition is presented alone: there, "feelings, illusions, habits of thought and conceptions of life" are said to be superstructural, while "corresponding social conditions" belong with the material "foundation."

3. Superstructure is a set of "forms in which men become conscious of [fundamentally economic] conflict and fight it out."[49]

Sense 1 is institutional; sense 2 is notional; sense 3 involves action and practice rather than a special substance or entity.

Any of these senses of the term can participate in a meaningful statement. Similarly, the whole list can be implied meaningfully: something could be predicated of 1, 2, and 3 collectively. But the concept can be emptied of meaning by more contradictory sets of statements. For example, "social conditions" that include "property relations" (preface to *A Contribution,* p. 44) are said to be superstructural in the preface to *A Contribution,* but they are said to be basic in the *Eighteenth Brumaire.* If they are both, or either, then the distinction of superstructure and base loses its meaning and lacks explanatory usefulness.

B. Ideology

Far more complex is the problem of defining "ideology." That word appears first in philosophical discourse in the work of French sensationalist philosophers—Condillac, Cabanis, Helvétius, and Destutt de Tracy.[50] Assuming that sensory data are the basis of all knowledge, the French Ideologues articulate a simple materialistic empiricism that Shelley characterizes in *On Life* as "a seducing system to young and superficial minds"; Shelley says that he "was discontented with such a view of things as it afforded" (R&P, p. 476). Shelley's own concepts are subsequently less mechanistic and more dialectical.

Among concepts of ideology in dialectical philosophy, immense variety exists. The prevalent notions, however, can be roughly divided into four kinds. Two are negative, entailing falsehood as part of the definition—what is ideological, according to the first two senses of the term, is necessarily false. Two other definitions are positive, implying no necessary judgment on the truth value of what is ideological; a particular idea can be both ideological and true, according to these definitions.

Whereas the three alternative definitions of superstructure may be contradictory, but are not necessarily so, these four alternative concepts of ideology are wholly incompatible with one another. To list them is to summarize the history of debates within ideological theory.

1. Perhaps the most limited and specific definition of ideology is the concept of inversion, explained in *The German Ideology:* "Men are the producers of their conceptions, ideas, etc.," but it sometimes happens that people forget this fact; when persons mistake ideas that they have themselves produced for objectively existing powers, an inversion has taken place. This inversion is the first definition of ideology:

> If in all ideology men and their circumstances appear upside down, as in a *camera obscura,* this phenomenon arises just as much from their historical life process as the inversion of objects on the retina does from their physical life process (p. 247).

Ideology is a "consolidation of what we ourselves produce into an objective power above us" (p. 254), when those products are ideas. What Marx and Engels call the "German Ideology" is the illusion that ideas determine practice; in fact, they argue, material and social practice produces and determines ideas. As Jorge Larrain emphasizes, this concept of ideology is negative (implying illusion, distortion, or falsehood of an idea), but it is a specific kind of falsehood that is implied: only the illusion of inversion deserves, according to this account, to be called ideology.[51]

2. A second concept of ideology, also negative in that the definition implies falsehood, is far more inclusive. This is the notion of false consciousness, and its locus in the Marx-Engels corpus is a statement by Engels from a letter to Franz Mehring:

> Ideology is a process accomplished by the so-called thinker consciously, it is true, but with a false consciousness. The real mo-

tive forces impelling him remain unknown to him; otherwise it simply would not be an ideological process.[52]

This concept of false consciousness is the definition of ideology offered by such Marxists as Althusser, Pierre Macherey, and Eagleton. It is also the version endorsed recently by Jerome J. McGann, who takes his definition from Althusser: "Ideology is 'false consciousness,' or (more particularly) the system of structures and concrete apparatuses which generate and maintain an 'imaginary representation of the real world.'"[53] This is Franz Jakubowski's sense of the term: "Ideology means, first of all, a false consciousness which is not in accord with reality," so that all consciousness is false consciousness.[54]

As Martin Seliger has explained, ideology in this sense is simply distorted thought; for Marx and Engels, all thought is dependent on economic and social conditions, and this limitation on thought imposes distortions.[55] But it is simply not true that, as McGann says, this is the concept of ideology maintained and used by "virtually all English, West European, and American Marxist thinkers." Larrain argues, in fact, that the concept is dogmatic and incoherent: such a definition, says Larrain, "on the one hand would affirm the universal precariousness of knowledge, and on the other, it would exclude itself from the general rule without any justification."[56]

In *Toward a Rational Society*, Jürgen Habermas offers an example of a total conception of ideology, illustrating along the way how such a concept acquires sufficient flexibility that it can be made to encompass any phenomena whatsoever. Habermas argues that Marx's specific argument on ideology "can no longer be applied as it stands to advanced capitalist society." Instead, what Habermas calls a "technocratic intention," i.e., a system of "purposive-rational action," "serves as an ideology for the new politics." The Marxian category of ideology "can no longer be employed"; "this new form of [technocratic] legitimation has cast off the old shape of *ideology*"; "Technocratic consciousness is . . . 'less ideological'" because it "is not an 'illusion' in Freud's sense"; but nonetheless Habermas calls it "the new ideology." To schematize the argument: *x* is not *y;* but with that fact acknowledged, let us call it *y* nevertheless.[57] That this concept of ideology is an incoherent dogma is also the argument of Seliger; Larrain, rejecting it for the same reasons, prefers sense I—ideology as inversion, a more precise concept. Seliger, alternatively, seems to abandon the concept altogether.

Labriola's metaphor of the ideological envelope is another expression of ideology 2. But as both Larrain and Seliger would argue, that envelope encloses Labriola's argument, too, by definition. One way out of the dilemma is the creation of a distinction between ideology 2 and superstructure 2. If "ideology" implies distortion (false consciousness), and the ideological superstructure (as in *Anti-Dühring*, chapter 9) encompasses all social consciousness, then all the ideas in a society—including Marx's, Labriola's, McGann's, and mine—are false.[58] This claim is negative dogmatism. But if we posit an ideational superstructure (superstructure 2) that includes both ideological (false) and nonideological (true) forms of consciousness, the problem can be overcome.

In this sense, ideology 2 is still false consciousness, but it is not, like superstructure 2, inclusive. To make it inclusive again, as the original concept of superstructure 2 was inclusive, dialectical thinkers have had to divest the concept of ideology of its negative implications, producing ideology 3, to which I now turn.

3. Positive conceptions of ideology identify that term's meaning with superstructure 2, as it is defined in the preface to *A Contribution to the Critique of Political Economy* and *Anti-Dühring*. One version of the positive concept is Lenin's: "ideology" refers to the political consciousness of various classes; an opposition can be marked between, especially, the ideologies of the bourgeois and socialist-proletariat classes, without implying that both are always false.[59] According to Daniel Bell, ideology is "an interpretative system of political ideas embodying and concretizing the more abstract values of a polity (or social movement)."[60] This is the concept of ideology expressed by A. A. Trew, and following Trew, David Aers, Jonathan Cook, and David Punter, in their studies of English Romantic literature: ideology is "a system of concepts and images which are a way of seeing and grasping things, and of interpreting what is seen or heard or read . . . [and of locating] the phenomena we perceive in a network of causality, a given interpretative and evaluative framework."[61]

In contrast to ideology 1, this sense of the term is unrelated to the notion of error-by-inversion. In contrast to ideology 2, the term limits the ideas to be called ideological, not by requiring the falsehood of those ideas but rather by identifying them with class membership (political, economic, or social). A simple extrapolation leads to yet another definition of ideology, the last that I shall be considering.

4. A positive total concept is possible: that is, just as ideology 2 is inclusive of all false consciousness, so too a total concept can be constructed without the negative judgment. This version is constructed by Karl Mannheim, who glides almost imperceptibly from ideology 3 to ideology 4:

> Here we refer to the ideology of an age or of a concrete historico-social group, e.g. of a class, when we are concerned with the characteristics and composition of the total structure of the mind of this group.[62]

In contrast to what Mannheim calls "particular ideologies" ("specific assertions which may be regarded as concealments, falsifications, or lies without attacking the integrity of the total mental structure of the asserting subject" [p. 266]), the concept of total ideology can swell to include everything that is thought in a particular society. This totality is affirmed to be limited by group membership, or class consciousness, or national distinction, or cultural determinants. But in contrast to ideology 3, this sense of the term does not imply necessarily a discrimination among classes within a society; without any judgment on the truth value of ideas, this positive total concept can subsume all ideas, bourgeois, socialist, or otherwise, that are possible within a national or cultural setting.[63]

C. Determine

Marx and Engels consistently involve their statements about ideology with a statement of social determinism. No definition of the concept ideology is free, in the Marx-Engels corpus, from some claim about the determination of ideology by something else. Just as superstructure implies base, so ideology implies determination. But alternative senses of the word "determine" affect statements that "base determines superstructure" or that "social relations determine ideology." Cameron's complaint that Shelley "fails to distinguish basic from derivative elements" in the relationship of consciousness and social reality is a charge that rests on the principle of social determination of ideas. But more senses than one of "determine" appear even within Shelley's work, and yet more appear in the critical discussion of the Shelleyan concepts. And so it may be helpful here to separate the different operative definitions of that key word.

1. In the weakest sense, "determine" means "condition." A clear usage in this sense is Marx's statement in the preface to *A Contribution to the Critique of Political Economy*, "Social existence determines . . . consciousness," but that claim is said to mean no more than this: "The mode of production in material life determines the general character of the social, political, and spiritual processes of life" (p. 43).

In fact, Larrain uses "conditions" rather than "determines" in a translation of that sentence.[64] An interaction of terms can be denoted by "determine" in this weak sense: "x determines y" will mean that x and y affect each other, or affect the form or appearance or efficacy of one another. Labriola and Georgy Plekhanov, among others, argue for a sense of "determine" that will allow for the efficacy of y as well as x in the statement "x determines y." In such a case, Marx's claim in the preface to *A Contribution* (that modes of production in material life determine social, political, and intellectual processes) is entirely compatible with Engels's retraction, formulated late in Engels's life: "The *ultimately* determining element in history is the production and reproduction of real life. More than this neither Marx nor I has ever asserted. . . . The economic situation is the basis, but the various elements of the superstructure [in senses 1, 2, and 3] also exercise their influence upon the course of the historical struggles."[65] What Engels means by "ultimately" is unclear, but the statement of mutual influence suggests plainly enough a sense of "determine" as "condition" or "affect," reciprocally or otherwise.

2. Another sense of "determine" is stronger, limiting more narrowly the relationship between x and y in the statement "x determines y." This second sense of the word is equivalent to the sense of the word "limit": to determine is to establish limits of possibility, as the kind or number of bricks available limits the sort of bungalow that I can construct. The materials, in such an instance, do not merely interact with the product but positively allow and prohibit certain outcomes. I might make a round dwelling, in the shape of an igloo, or a miniature replica of St. Paul's; but given a certain number of bricks, I am not going to make a bungalow the size of St. Paul's, nor a structure as pellucid as the Crystal Palace.

This is the sense of "determine" that Marx uses when he describes the relationship of the base and superstructure in the *Eighteenth Brumaire:* a "superstructure" rises upon "the social conditions of existence"; this "superstructure" (here used in sense 2) is created and formed out of the "material foundations" and "social relations" of an entire class. Like the bungalow and the bricks, the superstructure is limited in the possibilities of its form and content by the materials of which it is made.

This is the sense of "determine" that Marx uses again in *Capital:* the economic structure is said to be

> the direct relation of the owners of the conditions of production to the direct producers—a relation always naturally corresponding to a definite stage in the development of the methods of labour and thereby its social productivity—which reveals the innermost secret, the hidden base of the entire social structure.[66]

The materials of the production of life correspond to features of the social arrangement of life, and to these in turn correspond certain cognitive and attitudinal ranges. Shelley uses the word in that sense when he says that "it is less the character of the individual than the situation in which he is placed that determines him to be honest or dishonest (*Letters,* 2:563). He says more, that is, than merely that the individual's trait of honesty interacts with the individual's circumstances, or that the individual's honesty is affected by the individual's circumstances; he makes the stronger claim that the circumstances impose limits on the individual's traits. Given certain conditions, the trait of honesty will be positively proscribed, or rendered unavailable or unlikely. The range of possibilities for y is circumscribed by the nature of x. Where determine 1 puts the two related terms in a position of mutual or reciprocal efficacy, determine 2 affirms instead that x draws a circumference around the possibilities for y.

3. In the history of dialectical philosophy and polemic, determine 1 slides easily into determine 2, and under pressure of argument or political struggle an even stronger sense is sometimes sought. That is, not all dialectical thinkers remain content for long with a form of assertion as undogmatic as those provided by determine 1 and 2. To borrow words from Raymond Williams, "the analytic categories, as so often in idealist thought, have, almost unnoticed, become substan-

tive descriptions, which then take habitual priority."[67] Williams points out that "in practice determination is never only the setting of limits; it is also the exertion of pressures" (p. 87); but he also observes that a danger arises, "of falling back into a new passive and objectivist model" (p. 86).

Larrain explains the solidification of "determine" that sometimes occurs and which amounts to a regression to predialectical concepts of causation: "The determination of the superstructures [any and all senses] by the base necessarily becomes an external mode of causation, whereby a dead economic objectivity is assumed to be able to produce specific forms of consciousness."[68] Thus, for proponents of some narrowly economic doctrines of determinism, the assertion has become "*x* causes *y*," and the interpretive and analytical response to the claim must be an account of the concept of causation.

A discussion of Shelley's most sustained political argument, *A Philosophical View of Reform,* will follow in the next section of this book, and that discussion will make use of the interpretive classifications that have been set down here. But the importance of such analytical work, in the interpretation of Shelley's thought or in arguments about Romantic ideology, or in ideological theory generally, can be made clear quickly even here. Some statements—by Shelley, about Shelley, or about ideological theory at large—mean entirely different things, depending on the choice of definition. To illustrate that point, I will apply, simply and briefly, the foregoing machinery to some highly problematic statements. The first such problem is the most general, concerning the theory of ideology. Then, I will turn to a statement about the Romantic ideology, whose meaning deserves both clarification and emphasis. Finally, I will look at some statements by and about Shelley. In each of these cases, assignment of definition should clarify claims and descriptions in important ways.

One general argument that has been made with some frequency is this one: economic structure determines ideology, but ideology at the same time can dominate in the economic structure.[69] When Althusser, Nicos Poulantzas, and Etienne Balibar make that argument, they do so on a particular understanding of its key terms, and that rigor is essential for the meaning of the statement. Their sense of "ideology" is what I have called sense 2, the total conception of false consciousness; their sense of "determine" is what I have called sense 2, "limit." As a result, their claim is this: the economic structure sets limits on the kinds of illusions that people have; those illusions play a dominant part in the way that people conduct their practical affairs. This claim is coherent.

Alternatively, it becomes an incoherent dogmatism when another, equally common definition of "determine" is substituted. Were we to take "determine" in sense 3, as some distinguished dialecticians have done, we would arrive at absolute nonsense. The claim would then be this one: economic structure causes illusions, which have caused the economic structure. The absurdity inheres in the sense of the terms.

But the same formulation works in yet another sense in Shelley's philosophical prose. The *Essay on Christianity,* for example, describes the ideational content of religion as ideology 1: "Mankind . . . have not failed to attribute to the universal cause a character analogous with their own. The image of this invisible mysterious being is more or less excellent . . . in proportion to the perfectness of the mind on which it is impressed" (I&P, 6:238). This phenomenon is what Marx-Engels call the German Ideology: what is constructed by the human mind is (by inversion) rendered as an object above and beyond the human mind. This putative object—in religious terms, a paternal monarch—is an "illusion" (Marx-Engels), "the idle dreams of the visionary, or the pernicious representations of impostors" (Shelley). The same phenomenon is portrayed in *The Revolt of Islam:*

> Some moon-struck sophist stood
> Watching the shade from his own soul upthrown
> Fill Heaven and darken Earth, and in such mood
> The Form he saw and worshipped was his own (8:6).[70]

Shelley does not use the word "ideology" but rather the concept of ideology 1. He does not use the word because, in his time and place, it denoted a concept of the French Ideologues—a concept of material mechanism and an epistemology of material sensationalism. In its place, Shelley puts a critique and an alternative explanation of the formation of ideas and ideational structures. Ideology 1, the Marx-Engels inversion, works well as a designation of this concept, which is recurrent in Shelley's prose as well as his poems.

As the general argument from Althusser, Poulantzas, and Balibar indicates, "ideology" is normally coupled with some sense of "determine," and here again Shelley agrees. It is hardly an exaggeration to

say that Shelley's prose is devoted to an argument for the social determination of ideas, but this fact will become apparent only when the
right sense of "determine" is applied. The argument from Althusser,
Poulantzas, and Balibar—that economic structure determines ideology, which can be dominant in the economic structure—works as an
exposition of some of Shelley's statements as well, but in a different
sense of the terms. Putting ideology 1 for their ideology 2, such an
exposition produces this understanding: economic structure (including classes of "men to whom birth had allotted possessions") gives
rise to inversions that solidify as "political or religious institution."
The ideology 1, inversion, affects then the entire society: "Men from
whom these things [possessions, wealth, control of the economic
structure] were withheld by their condition" perpetuate and reproduce the ideological inversion that is, at bottom, an illusion designed
to support the ruling class (6:251). What arises in subjectivity ("the
idle dreams of the visionary") is employed as a stratagem ("the pernicious representations of impostors"), solidified as a false objectivity
("paternal Monarch") that supports the institutions of political and
economic power (these "usurpers . . . assumed the dominion of the
world power").[71]

For Shelley, then, in the *Essay on Christianity,* the Marxist argument
of Althusser, Poulantzas, and Balibar works perfectly though in a different sense from theirs: the economic structure, imposing fixed social relations, establishes parameters within which particular illusions
are created and promulgated; these illusions play a politically effective
role in the maintenance and increase of the institutions of power, and
these are class-based. But Shelley's version is more finely tuned than
the more recent versions, which would put a stronger sense on "determine" or a more total concept for "ideology."

This same method of interpretation works equally well when we
turn from arguments about ideological theory generally to arguments
about Romantic ideology in particular. For example, McGann bases
his study of Romantic ideology on this version of the concept: "All
ideological phenomena, including poetry, are produced and reproduced within some concrete historical apparatus."[72] What is asserted
by Althusser and here endorsed by McGann is determine 2: "Poetry is
written, and read, within the determinate limits of specific social
structures." Shelley shares with McGann that sense of "determine":

"national and religious predilections" limit ideological phenomena, including poetry (*Essay on Christianity,* I&P, 6:243). If these predilections are notional, Shelley also makes it clear that "social forms modelled upon" such notional systems (superstructure 2) impose precisely the same kinds of limits on ideological phenomena (*A Philosophical View of Reform,* I&P, 7:18).

Shelley avoids the Althusserian negative dogma that all consciousness (with one or two exceptions) is false consciousness, a dogma that McGann seems to endorse.[73] Shelley's statement that society must be overthrown from the foundations, with all its superstructure of notions and institutions, comes close to McGann's formulation of the pernicious falsehoods of both false consciousness and the "concrete apparatuses which generate" it. But McGann is using ideology 2, a total conception, which commits him with Althusser to the negative dogma. Shelley limits particular statements to the concept of inversion, ideology 1, so that the argument is more precisely what McGann says of the German Ideology: "The illusion is that a critique of ideology can be launched from, and grounded in, conceptual space."[74] Both Shelley and McGann insist that pressures of historical facticity limit (determine 2) critical constructions: "We are not the creators of our own origin and existence, we are not the arbiters of every notion of our own complicated nature; we are not the masters of our own imaginations and moods of mental being" (*Essay on Christianity,* I&P, 6:231). Historically specific conditions exert pressure on the construction of thought systems (superstructure 2), though these pressures need not be said to cause those thought structures. McGann's critical imperative, therefore, and Shelley's are the same:

This is why the past and its works should be studied by a critical mind in the full range of their pastness—in their differences and their alienations (both contemporary and historical). To foster such a view of past works of art can only serve to increase our admiration for their special achievements and our sympathy for what they created within the limits which constrained them—as it were, for their grace under pressure (McGann, p. 2).

It is of no small moment to the success even of a true cause that the judges who are to determine on its merits should be free from those national and religious predilections which render the multitude both deaf and blind (*Essay on Christianity,* I&P, 6: 242–43).

In *A Philosophical View of Reform* and again in the *Defence,* Shelley uses such a method, considering the thought systems of Christianity and the French Ideologues, for example, in their (removed) historical contexts, and this technique of contextualization arises from the skeptical trope of relativity. Coupled with the second sense of "determine," as "limit," and with the concept of contextual pressure, this method enables Shelley to say that, for example, religion is a tool of political oppression, and political oppression is a manifestation of an economic base. (That is, economic structures determine superstructure 1, and superstructure 1 in turn determines superstructure 2.) McGann claims no more, until he extrapolates from ideology 1 to ideology 2; but that negative dogmatism is not shared with Shelley, and it is not necessary for the argument that either McGann or Shelley makes.

The method that works for the Romantic ideology works also for the Shelleyan ideology. Thus, when Aveling and Eleanor Marx describe that Shelleyan ideology, their statement is both true and false, depending entirely upon the choice of a sense for the terms: Shelley, they say, "understood that men and people were the result of their ancestry and of their environment." The sense of "determine" that is implied by "result" seems to be sense 3, "cause"; and Shelley says no such thing. "Cause," he says, "is only a word expressing a certain state of the human mind with regard to the manner in which two thoughts are apprehended to be related to each other" (*On Life,* R&P, p. 478). In contrast, the strongest sense of "determine," the sense that appears to operate in Aveling-Marx, asserts more than the constant conjunction of concepts: determine 3 asserts extensional veridicality for a one-directional relationship, as we have seen. Shelley, like Hume or Drummond or the ancient skeptics whose arguments on causation are summarized in the tropes of Aenesidemus, rejects that dogma altogether. If, alternatively, we were to substitute the sense of determine 1, then the Aveling-Marx claim will be entirely consistent with the facts of Shelley's philosophical statements.

The association of ideational and cultural entities with historical development and conditions is a commonplace in Shelley's prose, and this sense of "determination" is simply the weakest version of the Marxist formula: political, economic, and ideological (notional) "levels interpenetrate with each other at all points. We distinguish the levels for purposes of analysis."[75] Constant conjunction (Aenesidemus, Hume, Drummond, Shelley) is not equal to the conventional concept of cause, because that concept reifies a one-directional relationship in extensional space; for Shelley and his skeptical predecessors, the notion is conceptual and analytic, not objective and hypostatic. It is a form of inversion, in fact, whereby determine 1—constant conjunction—is solidified into determine 3—cause.

Whether the Aveling–Marx statement about Shelley and the determination of ideas is accurate, therefore, depends not upon what they say, nor upon what Shelley says, but rather upon the more problematic and interpretive act that *we* perform: the assignment of a sense to the descriptive terms. But as Marx insists in *Capital,* there is nothing dialectical about determine 3. If we follow some Marxists in reifying the constant conjunction of base and superstructure into a one-directional relationship of causation, we are in fact regressing to the ideology of the French material mechanists. What is dialectical about the Marxist concept is precisely the extent to which x and y are conjoined in a reciprocal relationship, or at least in an inextricable association; the flattening of this conceptual system into a linear equation of causality is a reinstitution of those modes of thought that Marx had sought to overcome.[76]

When we return, therefore, to the charge by Cameron that Shelley "did not perceive that the basic factor was social," we can analyze that charge more precisely. Shelley "did not perceive . . . that human thinking was derivative; rather he neutrally depicted both in interaction." I have already shown that both Shelley (in *A Philosophical View of Reform*) and Engels (in the letter to Bloch) depict such an interaction, and Cameron also admits that "Shelley's emphasis upon interactions in this regard, even though he fails to distinguish basic from derivative elements, is insightful and dialectical. So, too, is his emphasis on the interactive nature of the power structures of society."[77] The only point at issue between Cameron and Shelley, therefore, is the reservation about what is basic and what is derivative. But Cameron's formulation, I would argue, is not only not Shelleyan; it is not Marxist. It is dogmatic. Insisting upon determine 3, Cameron locks his argument within a mechanistic determinism, a French Ideology that both Marx and Shelley attack. This predialectical notion of causation is only momentarily obscured by clothing it in language of "ultimate" or "basic" determinants, or postponing the dogmatism to a last analysis; these dodges do not alter or improve the dogma. Admitting the interactive character of base and superstructure, Engels (in the letter to Bloch) does then retreat to determine 3, as I have said; characterizing human reality as a process of interacting elements, Engels (like Cameron) then backs up and, without evident justification, asserts a point of truth outside that interaction: the base, then, is "ultimately decisive" (Engels) or "primary" (Cameron).

Moreover, the epistemic character of this maneuver is made (perhaps unwittingly) conspicuous in Cameron's construction of Marx:

Marx's social views were integrated with a scientific materialism that had practice as its basic criterion of truth, viewing mind as an emanation from matter, and perceiving reality as essentially developmental in response to its inherent contradictions. Shelley . . . became a philosophical sceptic, leaving open the possibility of the primacy and uniqueness of mind.[78]

According to Shelley, Marx, Engels, and every skeptic in the history of philosophy, a "basic criterion of truth" is not available. The assertion of such a criterion is dogmatism, against which dialectic—Marx's, Shelley's, Erasmus', Cicero's, Carneades'—arrays its arguments. Other dogmatisms embedded in Cameron's passage betray the power of that central dogmatic premise: for instance, the dualism of mind and matter, which Cameron actually endorses in the first sentence of that passage, is a mechanistic dogmatism. Marxist philosophy meets that doctrine with the concept of determine 1, the conjunction or interpenetration of levels of experience and practice; this flexible conception avoids a reification of cause. Material reality includes social reality, and social phenomena include what is mental (superstructure in senses 1 and 2). Notional and institutional contents of ideology 2 and their "material foundation" can be separated only analytically. To reify those conceptual categories into a material cause and a mental effect is to perpetrate an inversion, as Marx (in *The German Ideology*) and Raymond Williams (in *Marxism and Literature*) argue so forcibly. As Larrain complains, "The determination of the superstructures by the base . . . becomes an external mode of causation, whereby a dead economic objectivity is assumed to be able to produce specific forms of consciousness." Shelley repudiates that notion of causation when (as in the French Ideology) it becomes an ontological dogma. It does not help Cameron's claim to introduce a reciprocal efficacy of the superstructure upon the base, so long as an "ultimate" or "primary" efficacy of the base is posited outside or before that reciprocity. There is no ultimate position outside the interpenetrations of history.

One exposition of Marx's historical materialism is by G. A. Cohen, who observes that "knowledge and belief are particularly important for the enjoyment and exercise of *collective* power," which is exactly what Shelley says in the last stanza of the *Mask of Anarchy*. "If all the slaves acted in unison, they would overwhelm their masters," says Cohen;

> But it does not follow that they have much (or any) collective power over their masters since even if each knows that, acting together, they could prevail, each is insufficiently confident that rebellious action on his part would be supported by others.[79]

Cohen offers an epistemic sense of power for the interpretation of Marx's social thought, and that is exactly what Shelley offers as well— the concept of power is an analytical and conceptual tool, not an objectified, externally existent thing: by "power" and "cause," "we mean to express no real being, but only to class under those terms a certain series of co-existing phenomena" (*On a Future State*, I&P, 6:208).

My point in contrasting Cameron and Cohen is twofold: Cameron solidifies power and cause into allegedly real being, anterior to the dialectical process of history, which is interactive.[80] Cohen shows that Marx does not do that but instead renders power as epistemic and knowledge as essentially and always interactive with the material foundations of reality. Second, I mean to emphasize that Shelley's positions are not dogmatic like the French Ideologues' and like Cameron's; they are dialectical and analytic, like Cohen's in this respect, and like Marx's as Cohen portrays them.

The entire dispute, however, can be recast with a flick of the wrist: if we take Cameron to be urging a sense of determine 2 rather than the dogmatism of determine 3, then there is no point at issue between him and Shelley at all; Shelley does argue for the social determination of ideas, as my account of *A Philosophical View of Reform* should demonstrate below. Cameron might be said, in such a case, merely to overlook the exact concurrence of his claims with Shelley's.

But such a charge would be an unjustifiable presumption: his work demonstrates that he does know exactly what Shelley's arguments state and imply. The presumption that there is no essential conflict, therefore, is untenable. What remains is a point of ideological disagreement—ideology 1 against ideology 2, and determine 2 against determine 3. Cameron is entirely correct in what he says about Shelley, but Shelley confronts such a mechanistic determinism with an ideological critique. His alleged failure to perceive ultimate causation is a positive and dialectical accomplishment. The charge of failure rests upon an untenable criterion of truth. As Cameron himself has suggested, the dialectics of skepticism exclude a dogmatism of causation. Rightly, Cameron credits Shelley with an avoidance of that dogmatism. But it is my claim that Shelley's skeptical stance is consistent with the dialectical thought of Marx, and it is here—and only here—that my argument diverges from Cameron's.

A negative argument, however—insisting chiefly on what Shelley does *not* say—is hardly enough to warrant a political argument of the scale of *A Philosophical View of Reform*. What I shall be arguing, in the discussion of that essay that follows, is twofold: Shelley's concepts of superstructure (1, 2, and 3) and of determination (1 and 2) enable him to make important and valuable statements, without the kinds of contradiction to which less careful forms of dialectic are liable. Second (but simultaneously) I shall be showing how the kind of discourse that Shelley constructs, aiming not at veridicality but rather at utility, has practical and political advantages and not only epistemological ones. The constraints that he admits in the logic of his arguments, including his metaphysical arguments, have powerful applications in the conditions of human living.

3

SHELLEY'S
PHILOSOPHICAL PROSE

POLITICS AND SHELLEY'S PHILOSOPHICAL PROJECT

Shelley's prose brings together those two traditions and methods, skeptical philosophy and ideological theory. The complex and expansive spectrum that those traditions delineate is a conceptual field on which Shelley's philosophical project can be located, and its location is precisely at the conjunction of those two bodies and methods of thought, one epistemological and abstract, the other politically concrete. These purposes and forms of discourse had been implicated in one another before, as in the case of the epistemological arguments over the criterion: the authority of absolute truth had been historically invested in institutional systems of authority; to challenge one was to threaten the other. Skeptical methods of philosophical inquiry threaten to overthrow claims of authority generally, and this tendency (in Drummond and Shelley), more than any particular position or set of positions regarding church or state, charges Shelley's discourse with polemical vitality.

Among Shelley's immediate sources, Godwin (for example) had come to argue that any reigning social and political order "insinuates itself into our personal dispositions, and insensibly communicates its own spirit to our private transactions" (*Political Justice*, 1:5):

Were not the inhabitants of ancient Greece and Rome indebted in some degree to their political liberties for their excellence in art, and the illustrious theatre they occupy in the moral history of mankind? Are not the governments of modern Europe accountable for the slowness and inconstancy of its literary efforts, and the unworthy selfishness that characterises its inhabitants? Is it not owing to the governments of the East, that that part of the world can scarcely be said to have made any progress in intellect or science? (*Political Justice*, 1:4–5).

A political order not only manifests an ideology or way of knowing; it also constitutes and engenders such a structure of thought and feeling. Morality (concerned with individuals) and political science (concerned with collectivities) are inextricably involved, by the same logic that makes skeptical epistemology into a radically political method.

Shelley's rhetoric regularly treats the linkage of ideational forms with social forms as a feature of experience and not merely as a feature of discourse; dialectic, as Engels was to insist, belongs to life and to things and not merely to propositions about them. The epistemological circle in which Shelley encloses his metaphysical assertions implies an experiential circle enclosing his philosophy of action, in moral (personal) and political (collective) frames.

Three principles from the foregoing chapters can serve as theoretical premises for the following analyses of Shelley's statements. First, to relativize criteria of truth and forms of thought—in abstract metaphysical discourse or in politicized ideological analysis—is to challenge the reigning order. Second, in Shelley's discourse, including his political prose, this skeptical critique concerned with structures of thinking is always more to the point than any particular political issue or set of positions. Shelley's polemic concerns conceptual frames; a reform of the franchise, or national debt, or a publisher imprisoned for sedition, only and always exemplifies such frames. Finally, the topical typologies for discourse are impertinent; metaphysics is morality, which is political philosophy; the circumference drawn by the first (that is, the epistemological circle) encloses them all.

Whether or not Shelley's fragmentary *Speculations on Metaphysics* and *Speculations on Morals* were designed to form one larger treatise,[1] these essays are linked by a coherent conceptual development. Shelley begins with a critique of knowledge and constructs imperatives for ethical action. This project was begun in 1817, by Cameron's best estimate, and the final extant portions were probably composed in 1821.[2] Midway between these dates, when Shelley perceives that the English "people are nearly in a state of insurrection" (*Letters*, 2:149), he indicates that he will direct his philosophical project toward the immediate political crisis. In the following month he supposes, as he says to Leigh Hunt, that "we shall soon have to fight in England" (*Letters*, 2:167), a country that, he says, "has arrived, like the nations which surround it, at a crisis in its destiny" (*A Philosophical View of Reform*, I&P, 7:19). Under this conjunctural pressure, Shelley composes *A Philosophical View of Reform*, a political treatise that, with its dialectical analysis of history, joins his "intellectual system" with an immediate political program.

The massacre of demonstrators at Manchester on August 16, 1819 (the so-called Peterloo Massacre), was a massive instance of the kind of unrest, oppression, and violent governmental reaction that was becoming widespread; only four months later, the radical reformers Arthur Thistlewood and James Watson organized another meeting that turned into a riot, and in February Thistlewood and four others were hanged.[3] These riots, executions, and massacres manifested an economic crisis: the post-war depression had impoverished the largest class of the population through unemployment and inflation, while it simultaneously enriched a small class of owners and capital investors. A related political conflict involved a series of movements for reform of the suffrage: industrial cities including Birmingham, Manchester, Sheffield, and Leeds, whose populations had grown rapidly, had no parliamentary representation at all,[4] and the system of suffrage elsewhere was so limited (by class) and corrupt (by borough-mongering) that movements, demonstrations, and even the bloody riots increased to the scale of a national emergency.

Shelley's essay addressing this national crisis differs from virtually every comparable tract of its time and place. Like Jeremy Bentham's *Plan of Parliamentary Reform*, the speeches of Robert Owen, and Thomas Jonathan Wooler's periodical *The Black Dwarf*, Shelley's polemic offers a program of immediate action, but unlike those other works, Shelley's essay places that program within a coherent theory of history and a comprehensive philosophical context. This political argument, with all its practical urgency, is a part of "the intellectual system," and not again until Marx's *Eighteenth Brumaire of Louis Bonaparte* is a conjunctural crisis in its historical specificity placed so solidly within a theoretical context of historical dialectic.

Behind the *Philosophical View of Reform* lie seven years of directly political writing, beginning with the *Address to the Irish People*, which Shelley had composed in January of 1812 (*Letters*, 1:233). Here, as a young man of nineteen, Shelley expresses some of the principles from Godwin's *Political Justice*, from which his more mature political philosophy will depart but whose dialectical character nonetheless forms an important starting point for Shelley. Godwin had written that "the characters of men originate in their external circumstance" (that sentence is in fact the title of a chapter from *Political Justice*), and in the *Address to the Irish People* Shelley says that "political institution has even the greatest influence on the human character" (I&P, 5:237). The "despotic power" of "Kings, Princes, Dukes, Lords, or Ministers" will "destroy" the "good dispositions" among a national population (5:218). From the start, therefore, Shelley recognizes the connection of political and ideational levels of reality, though his earliest formulations of that connection merely repeat the Godwinian solutions, which are (as I have said in the preceding chapter) hardly dialectical at all: the progress of national reform "is founded on the reform of private men, and without individual amendment it is vain and foolish to expect the amendment of a state or government" (5:236). The educational solution is thus essentially individualistic, though the efficacy of institutions in forming character has also been affirmed: "You can in no measure more effectually forward the cause of reform than by employing your leisure time in reasoning, or the cultivation of your minds" (5:224), says Shelley to the "Irish people" whose appalling poverty, under conditions of economic depression and political disenfranchisement, made them "one mass of animated filth," as Shelley says in a letter to Godwin (*Letters,* 1:268).[5]

Four elements of Shelley's thinking at this period stay with him throughout his life. One of them is related to the efficacy of circumstances in determining thought and belief (and I use "determine" in the sense of "condition"). This is the principle of facticity, the independence of a thought or perception from volition. In *The Necessity of Atheism* Shelley had denied that "belief is an act of volition" (5:205), simply repeating what he had read in Hume ("belief consists . . . in something, that depends not on the will").[6] The idea reappears in the Irish political pamphlet: "We cannot believe just what we like"; "How little power a man has over his belief. . . . he cannot believe what he does not think true" (5:221–22). Joined to the efficacy of institutions in conditioning knowledge and belief, this epistemological claim becomes a political principle, although in 1812 it is still joined to the individualistic educational solution from Godwin.

A second principle that Shelley retains all his life is a simple form of social-contract theory: "The benefit of the governed is the origin and meaning of government" (5:227). This principle is later to be substantially reinterpreted, because it suggests here a theory of voluntary and fundamentally individual-based determination that gives way, in

A Philosophical View of Reform, to a more complex recognition of re-ciprocal determination. But what Shelley preserves from this earlier theory is the logical sense of "origin," rather than the use of the term as descriptive of history. That is, the final cause of government is the benefit of the governed, when government is analyzed for a justifica-tion; the more dogmatic claim that government does in fact originate historically according to this kind of deliberation is an illusion that Shelley gives up before composing the *Philosophical View of Reform.*

A closely related principle that also remains with Shelley is a form of moral utilitarianism. When the social-contract theory is stated in moral terms, it becomes a slightly different kind of claim, whereby standards of right and wrong inhere not in absolute criteria but rather within the historically specific occasions of human experience and, more narrowly still, within the limits of human awareness: "The good-ness of a Government consists in the happiness of the Governed" (5: 228). Obviously this statement is a paraphrase of the social-contract theory that I have just quoted, but it is a paraphrase with a difference: to put "happiness" for "benefit" is to affirm by implication the essen-tially subjective or at least experiential nature of "benefit."

The *Address to the Irish People* is thus an early example of Shelley's politicizing the skeptical premise of the epistemological limit. Mind always encloses what is known; the object of knowledge is ideational. Accordingly, awareness (human experience) encloses the object of po-litical action as well; the circle that, in the metaphysical essays that I cited earlier, appears abstractly epistemological is here engaged in the definition of political right: the object in both senses is enclosed within the circumference of human awareness, and so too, therefore, are cri-teria for judging.

Finally, among the principles of the *Address to the Irish People* that reappear in Shelley's later work, there is an analysis of political in-stitution, power, and right according to economic class: "The rich command, and the poor obey, and . . . money is only a kind of sign, which shews, that according to government the rich man has a right to command the poor man, or rather that the poor man . . . is forced to work for the rich man, which amounts to the same thing" (5: 235–36). This way of thinking is also deepened, extended, and re-fined in the later work, but it is still recognizable there: "The oligarchy of party . . . under colour of administering the executive power lodged in the king, represented in truth the interests of the rich" (*A*

Philosophical View of Reform, 7:24), and "the name and office of king is merely the mask of this power" (7:25).

A companion piece to the *Address to the Irish People* is the *Proposals for an Association of Philanthropists,* which appeared in March of 1812. This time Shelley addresses a narrower audience of already educated "philanthropists," and while he rehearses some of the general positions articulated in the earlier document, he adds one argument here that is more narrowly philosophical and that has a direct bearing on perhaps the most complicated problem raised in *A Philosophical View of Reform:* that is the problem of causation, analyzed epistemologically but relevant within a practical and political discussion.

In the *Proposals* Shelley restates the dialectical relation of facticity and volition ("Man cannot make occasions, but he may seize those that offer" [5:253]); he produces a version of social-contract theory ("Government . . . is a delegation for the purpose of securing [rights] to others" [5:260]). What is new in this essay is a discussion of philosophical literature: "I do not deny that the Revolution of France was occasioned by the literary labors of the Encyclopedists" (5:264), and he names some of those French Ideologues, including Condorcet, whose mechanistic sense of determinism I have discussed in the preceding chapter. Here Shelley says, "When we see two events together, in certain cases, we speak of one as the cause, the other the effect." As I argued earlier, Shelley assigns these French philosophers the concept of determine 3, the mechanistic notion of causation. But already in 1812, Shelley disavows that dogmatism, preferring the skeptical critique of the concept of causation that he had read in Hume and that replaces the dogmatic conception with the weaker and more phenomenal observation of a constant conjunction of ideas: "We have no other idea of cause and effect, but that which arises from necessary connection [i.e., facticity]" (5:264). This epistemological argument has an application in the interpretation of political events: "It is therefore, still doubtful whether D'Alembert, Boulanger, Condorcet, and other celebrated characters, were the causes of the overthrow of the ancient monarchy of France" (5:264).

In the terms used in the preceding analysis, Shelley says that it is doubtful whether an ideational superstructure can cause legal and political institutions. He does not deny the efficacy of literary and philosophical structures to condition legal and political institutions, but he does not assert a one-directional determination of any kind. This kind of *epochē* (suspension of judgment) is especially impressive in the Irish pamphlets because Shelley is here as dogmatic, in the philosophical sense, as he was ever to be, and yet he stops short of this particular dogmatism, the assertion of cause. He also explains specifically the relevance of the skeptical critique of cause to the question of determination in political and historical dialectic.

It is worthwhile, however, to illustrate the kind of dogmatism that does appear in the Irish pamphlets but that disappears from the later philosophical work. In the *Proposals for an Association of Philanthropists,* Shelley says, "The laws of [mankind's] moral as of his physical nature are immutable, as is everything of nature" (5:262). This claim of "immutable" laws of nature and morality is a blunt and simplified restatement of a dogma from the blunt and simplified philosophy of the French writers whom he names in the same essay, and more particularly of Baron d'Holbach, whose *Système de la Nature* he quotes again, repeatedly and approvingly, in the notes to *Queen Mab*. But in the subsequent document in which he commends the intellectual system of Sir William Drummond's *Academical Questions,* he says specifically that he outgrew the "violent dogmatism" of the popular dualism and also the simple mechanistic determinism of the French philosopher.

I would argue that the appearance of this retraction in *On Life* is significantly located—it appears in the same notebook as the draft of *A Philosophical View of Reform*. Reiman makes the stronger claim that the essay *On Life* "grew directly from an early passage in his *Philosophical View of Reform*" (R&P, p. 474). The point that I would emphasize is that the dogmatism expressed in the earlier political prose disappears as Shelley joins his skeptical method of thinking (*On Life*) with his political argument (*A Philosophical View of Reform*). The dialectical avoidance of the claim that "*x* causes *y*" appears already in 1812; subsequently Shelley presses his skeptical methods to purge his arguments (metaphysical and political) of other dogmas as well.

While Shelley was in Ireland, Daniel Isaac Eaton was put on trial for publishing part of Paine's *Age of Reason* (March 6, 1812). Exactly one month later, Shelley returned to Wales, and then, on May 15, Lord Ellenborough brought Eaton's trial to an end by sentencing the publisher to confinement in the pillory and to one year and six months in prison. Swiftly—by June 11, at least—Shelley responded to these events by composing *A Letter to Lord Ellenborough*.[7] I emphasize the specificity of the concrete occasion and the directness and immediacy of Shelley's response because these facts make all the more impressive the theoretical level to which Shelley raises the issues and the arguments.

As he says in his letter to Godwin, announcing the composition of the *Letter to Lord Ellenborough,* he does not mean to suggest that the "poor bookseller has any characteristics in common with Socrates or Jesus Christ," but "still the spirit which pillories & imprisons him, is the same which brought them to an untimely end" (*Letters,* 1:307–8). His remark is similar to Drummond's in *Academical Questions:* "The spirit of dogmatism is still the same, though it speak by other oracles" (p. 3). The issues of Shelley's attack and defense are not atheism and Christianity, or blasphemy and orthodoxy: they are more precisely skepticism and dogmatism, as the *Letter* itself makes plain.

Specifically, Shelley ascribes the punishment of Eaton, an unjust sentence in his view, to a particular variety of dogmatism—ideology considered as the thought structure of a particular class in power: "What but antiquated precedents, gathered from times of priestly and tyrannical domination, can be adduced in palliation of an outrage so insulting to humanity and justice?" (5:283). According to Shelley, the crime of Eaton the publisher or Paine the author was not the expression of a doctrine, heinous or otherwise. It was rather a skeptical procedure: "He has questioned established opinions"; the "crime" is not blasphemy or treason, but *skepsis,* "the crime of inquiry" (5:284). Thus the conflict at issue in the court and in Shelley's polemical response is not the conflict of Christianity and atheism; it is the conflict of dogmatism and skepticism, as Shelley had already insisted in his letter to Godwin on the subject. He writes in the *Letter to Lord Ellenborough* in terms that could have been used by Sextus, or by Cicero, or by Drummond—except that their application in the specific rhetorical occasion is precise: "Implicit faith [dogmatism] and fearless inquiry [*skepsis*] have in all ages been irreconcileable enemies. Unrestrained philosophy has in every age opposed itself to the reveries of credulity and fanaticism" (5:284).

Accordingly, Shelley's defense of Eaton and Paine is not a defense of any particular assertion or position that they maintain. It is rather a justification of a method—inquiry, dialectic, and debate. "That which is false will ultimately be controverted by its own falsehood" (5:284). The opponent of *skepsis* is not a doctrine; it is the mind-set that *wants* a doctrine: "Even now the lash that drove Descartes and Voltaire from their native country, the chains which bound Galileo, the flames which burned Vanini, again resound" (5:285–86).

Every one of those thinkers named in that last sentence was notable (notorious) for playing a part in the history of skepticism. Lucilio Vanini was "a part of the movement to break with the dogmas of scholasticism and the authority of Aristotle."[8] He was arrested in November 1618, convicted of atheism, and sentenced to execution; his tongue was cut out and he was then strangled at the stake. As Shelley implies, his crime, like that of Eaton and Paine, was in fact a skeptical method and not an atheistic doctrine: Vanini's *Amphitheatrum Aeternae Providentiae Divino-Magicum* (1615) is a series of arguments against atheists, but like Shelley's *Refutation of Deism* and like the other skeptical dialogues on religion that I have mentioned in the first chapter of this book, Vanini's method of argument is "largely ironical, and cannot be taken as expounding his real views."[9] In a book published in the following year, Vanini admits exactly that about his own arguments in the *Amphitheatrum*.[10] Furthermore, Vanini's running title, *Dialogi,* calls attention to his genre of skeptical theological debate.[11]

A charge commonly brought against Shelley at this point is that his professions of *skepsis* are an excuse for his atheism. His arguments for freedom of inquiry are sometimes said to be mere pretense, cloaking his negative and dogmatic belief in atheistic materialism. I would argue that such a charge is facile: it is a plain ad hominem. It is also false, because the love of dogma is what Shelley attacks and not what he endorses, even implicitly. And the logic of his argument would remain, whatever we wish to say about the life of the man or his alleged motives at this time of his life. And that logic is the same element of the classical skeptical paradigm that is used in Godwin's *Political Justice,* for example in the argument about the heuristic and tentative character of "resting-places" for the mind. It is also the kind of argument that appears again in John Stuart Mill's essay *On Liberty,* where Mill argues (like Shelley) that the constancy of critical discourse encourages intellectual progress. It is an argument that cannot be overcome or reasonably dismissed by a charge of disingenuousness. Further, it persists, though refined, in Shelley's own subsequent work.

The occasion and even the date of Shelley's essay *On the Punishment of Death* are far more difficult to determine than the occasion and date of the *Letter to Lord Ellenborough,* but this essay begins with a statement of a political purpose that is almost as specific: "The first law which it becomes a Reformer to propose and support, at the approach of a period of great political change, is the abolition of the punishment of death" (6:185). But to consider Shelley's essay philosophically is to discover here what has already been shown in the *Proposals for an Association:* an anchoring of the immediate political purpose in a conceptual framework. Like Hume and Drummond, Shelley employs a critical method against a metaphysical dogmatism.

Like Godwin, Shelley argues "that revenge, retaliation, atonement, [and] expiation" do not deserve "a place in any enlightened system of political life." The reason he offers is again utilitarian: "They are the chief sources of a prodigious class of miseries" (6:185).[12] But Shelley adds a set of arguments drawn from skeptical tradition, involving the immediately political issue with a metaphysical critique. As Cicero had done in the *Academica,* Shelley argues that it is wiser to withhold assent concerning matters that are nonevident:[13] "Whether death is good or evil, a punishment or a reward, or whether it be wholly indifferent, no man can take upon himself to assert" (6:185). This was the *skepsis* that Byron recorded in his journal at about the same time: "Is there anything beyond?—*who* knows? *He* that can't tell. Who tells that there *is?* He who don't know."[14] Within three weeks of making that remark, Byron links that problem of uncertainty to an elementary atomism: "Why I came here—I know not—where I shall go it is useless to enquire—in the midst of myriads of the living & the dead worlds—stars—systems—infinity—why should I be anxious about an atom?"[15]

Like Byron's, Shelley's statements on the problem of immortality apply *akatalepsia*—a lack of certainty. Both writers also advocate *epochē,* a suspension of judgment. But Shelley's analysis goes much further, first by placing the entire problem in an immediately political framework and then by specifying a formally skeptical approach to its solution. Both Shelley and Byron mention the doctrine of material atomism as an alternative to dogmas of immortality, but Shelley's treatment is far more critical. First, he produces the conventional argument of universal consensus: "That that within us which thinks and feels, continues to think and feel after the dissolution of the body" is the conventional doctrine of immortality. It does not, Shelley says, warrant belief; it is opinion, *doxa,* not an evident fact. But this doctrine has "been the almost universal opinion of mankind." Shelley reports what response has been made to this case by every skeptic since Pyrrho, including David Hume: "The accurate philosophy of what I may be permitted to term the modern Academy . . . renders probable [*pithanon,* persuasive] the affirmative of a proposition, the negative of which it is so difficult to conceive" (6:185). But the Academic philosophy takes this stance of provisional probability as an alternative to a knowledge claim: the analysis of *to pithanon* does not respect truth but works in the opposite way, "by showing the prodigious depth and extent of our ignorance respecting the causes and nature of sensation." What we do not know constrains us to intensional assertions— some propositions are more "difficult to conceive" than others. The extensional veridicality of the proposition (i.e., the independent existence of a definite object to which the proposition points) is not affirmed; in fact, the logic of the critique positively rules out such an affirmation.

At this juncture in the argument, Byron turns, in the letter to Annabella Milbanke, to material atomism as a hypothesis that is an alternative to the popular dogma of the immortality of the soul. But Shelley shows that this hypothesis is untenable for exactly the same reason: "popular arguments against" the immortality of the soul are "derived from what is called the atomic system" (6:185). This is the material mechanism of the French Ideologues, arising in part from the atomic philosophy of Lucretius and in part from eighteenth-century science. This philosophy rests upon a conception of necessity that is simply another form of determination in its strongest sense, or causation. These arguments "are proved to be applicable only to the relation which one object bears to another, as apprehended by the mind, and not to existence itself" (6:185–86). Statements of cause refer to the facticity of an association of perceptions. The proponents of French materialism had claimed extensionality for their reference, but Shelley points out that their statements have no such thing. The advantages of his version of the causal claim (treating it as purely intensional) are considerable: "Every student may refer to the testimonials which he bears within himself to ascertain the authorities upon which any assertion rests," as Shelley says in the *Treatise* (7:63).

At the same time that Shelley moves the argument into the conceptual space of intensional reference ("cause" names a perceptual relationship, not an external actuality), he also moves it outward into political imperative and polemic. It is precisely the criterion of utility that achieves this linkage: as the criterion of right in political action is the happiness of the governed, the end of political action is itself experiential and phenomenal. The authority of deity is said by the orthodox to transcend human experience, and the materiality of cause and effect is said by the French Ideologues to transcend human awareness; for Shelley (as for Hume and Drummond), neither authority nor efficacy transcends those limits. Instead, human experience is a circle that includes such authority and efficacy. The epistemological circle (in metaphysics) is parallel with an experiential circle (in politics). Shelley argues for the wrongness of punishment by death just as Godwin does: its effects in the educational, ethical, and political impacts that it has upon the observing multitude are pernicious.

The connection between Shelley's metaphysical criticism and his philosophy of action can thus be summarized in this way:

1. A criterion is not available to warrant the truth content of knowledge claims. Thoughts and perceptions are immediately evident; their causes are not. The reference of metaphysical assertions is intensional, concerning concepts and not external objects or independent verities. This constraint is what I have called the epistemological circle.

2. The object of political action and institution is the happiness of the persons who make up the political community. This object (happiness) is experiential. This constraint is what I have called the experiential circle.

From 1 and 2 follows this conclusion:

3. The epistemological circle that constrains metaphysical assertions (1) is precisely parallel with the experiential circle that constrains political right (2).

Shelley's skeptical system is not only compatible with a radical political activism; the terms of that system virtually demand it.

Shelley works out the paradigm that I have just summarized in several places, including the *Essay on the Punishment of Death*, its first explicit elaboration in his work. Its fullest exposition, however, is in the *Treatise on Morals*. For the sake of a heuristic device, I propose that we adopt for a moment the following schematization (whether it be true or false) of that work. The fragment known as the *Speculations on Metaphysics* presents the arguments for 1. The fragment known as *Speculations on Morals* presents the arguments for 2. A *Philosophical*

View of Reform, written midway through the composition of those fragments, presents the arguments for 3. Further, the conclusion expressed in 3 is already implied in the conjunction of the *Speculations on Metaphysics* with the *Speculations on Morals.*

The following synopsis is intended to clarify and to flesh out that schematization.

1. "It is an axiom in mental philosophy, that we can think of nothing which we have not perceived" (Tokoo, p. 19; I&P, 7:59). This axiom puts an epistemological circle around our assertions. "Metaphysics" is a word that names "an inquiry into the phenomena of mind" (7:62). Discourse is possible without extensional veridicality because "we are ourselves then depositories of the evidence of the subject which we consider." This system of intensional reference does not imply solipsism or inhibit political analysis and action for two reasons. First, the distinction between internal and external objects of assertion and action is nominal, "an affair of words" (Tokoo, p. 22; I&P, 7:65). Second, such a distinction can be valuable in ethical and economic discourse, which is "altogether distinct" from metaphysical discourse (Tokoo, p. 20; I&P, 7:60). One form of discourse offers imperatives for volition; the other offers descriptions of notional or extensional fact.

2. The enclosure of knowledge claims within an epistemological circle is precisely paralleled by the enclosure of political injunctions within an experiential circle. "The object of the forms according to which human society is administered is the happiness of the individuals composing the communities which they regard" (Tokoo, p. 24; I&P, 7:72). As no extended object in external space can be known to cause an idea in 1, so too here no externally sanctioned criterion of right transcends human experience. Within the experiential and phenomenal moments of awareness, right and wrong of political action work themselves out, as qualities of the only given that is available—experience.

3. It follows that the "condition belonging to [our own] intellectual existence" is correlative with political conditions of liberty and tyranny (I&P, 7:6). The concept of determination 1 (condition) links economic prosperity, political freedom, and the ideational superstructure. These levels of experience and analysis are at once the causes and effects of one another. "Cause" and "effect" name a conjunction of

ideas and not a one-directional relationship of efficacy ("We know no more of cause and effect than a constant conjunction of events" [*Defence,* R&P, p. 489]).

I should emphasize that this schematization is designed to show how Shelley thought, rather than what he thought in a narrowly topical sense; it is a conceptual structure, a form for interpretation, rather than a sequence of concrete instances. Further, there is some evidence to suggest that the prose fragments belong together in one treatise with the joint aim that I have summarized, but there is also dispute about the matter, and I want my own claim to rest not on the textual question (which is perhaps indeterminable) but rather on the conceptual design. That design, as I have tried to show, invades even Shelley's essays on particular political events (the trial of Eaton) and specific legal-political questions (punishment by death), as well as his openly philosophical essays, and the incipient forms of that structure are to be found as early in his writing as 1812, though they flower into full expression in the *Philosophical View of Reform* in 1819.

IMAGINATION AND MORALS

That structure of conception also appears in the later essay *A Defence of Poetry,* where it is embedded in a different argumentative context, this one a debate with Peacock about the value and importance of poetry in the modern intellectual setting. One element of Shelley's argument is precisely a moral claim stated first in the *Treatise.* "The great instrument of moral good is the imagination" (*Defence,* R&P, p. 488). "Poetry enlarges the circumference of the imagination"; therefore "Poetry strengthens that faculty which is the organ of the moral nature of man." This argument treats poetry as an instance of a larger phenomenon; the comprehensive issue is the relationship between imagination and morality. Poetry is offered in that paragraph from the *Defence* as only one example of the more general phenomenon treated in the earlier essay. There, Shelley writes, "The imagination acquires by exercise a habit as it were of perceiving and abhorring evil however remote from the immediate sphere of sensations with which that individual mind is conversant" (Tokoo, p. 23; I&P, 7:75). This exercise is what strengthens, in that way, "the organ of the moral nature of man": i.e., the imagination. Moral good (virtue) is said actually to inhere in the exercise of that faculty: "The only distinction between the selfish man and the virtuous man, is that the imagination of the former is confined within a narrow limit, while that of the latter embraces a comprehensive circumference."

Given the reciprocal efficacy of social relations and mental phenomena, the actualities of political institutions play an important part in the enhancement of this intrapsychic faculty: "The inhabitant of a highly civilized community will more acutely sympathize with the sufferings and enjoyments of others than the inhabitant of a society of a less degree of civilization" (Tokoo, p. 23; I&P, 7:75).

As Dawson has suggested, Shelley's argument on the linkage of imagination and morals is comparable to William Hazlitt's arguments in his *Essay on the Principles of Human Action.*[16] But Shelley's argument goes farther than Hazlitt's demonstration of the fact that disinterestedness is possible. Shelley uses the three-part structure that I have outlined above to show that the mental phenomena that we call existence (life "which includes all" [*On Life*, R&P, p. 475]) align themselves with the structure of the moral claim. Right and wrong are definable as they are because of a metaphysical (factual) structure that Shelley articulates. That is, "should"-statements are based upon the structure of "is"-statements. It is not the possibility of virtuous action but rather the nature of virtuous action that follows from the intellectual system, and this claim is more than Hazlitt makes. Second, as a point of historical record, the context of both Shelley's argument and Hazlitt's should be deepened and extended beyond the dialogue of these two writers. The linkage of imagination with morals that both Shelley and Hazlitt articulate is a matter of skeptical tradition, appearing in Hume's *Treatise of Human Nature* and, among the Academic skeptics, in the speeches of Carneades.

Hazlitt's argument, like Shelley's, uses the concept of an epistemological limit that encloses motives within ideational space. But Hazlitt uses this argument only to show what motivates right action and not to produce a definition of what a right action would be, or how one might determine which action would be right.

All voluntary action, that is all action proceeding from a will, or effort of the mind to produce a certain event must relate to the future, or to those things, the existence of which is problematical, undetermined, and therefore capable of being affected by the means made use of, with a view to their production, or the contrary. But that which is future, which does not yet exist can excite no interest in itself, nor act upon the mind in any way but by means of the imagination. The direct primary motive, or impulse which determines the mind to the volition of any thing must therefore in all cases depend on the *idea* of that thing as conceived of by the imagination, and on the idea solely.[17]

Shelley's epistemological constraint, the observation that perception is a form of thought, acknowledges no ontological distinction between perceptions immediately present (physical sensations) and ideas of memory or imagination. Hazlitt's argument that motives can and even must originate in the ideational elements of thought accords with that principle. Both Shelley and Hazlitt thus treat imagination as a more efficacious factor in human action than would, for example, a material mechanist. But Shelley's epistemological principle (1) is parallel with a practical morality (2) that produces a definition of right as an epistemological circle that "embraces a comprehensive circumference" in contrast to the "narrow limit" that confines the motives of a selfish person. Hazlitt's argument concerns the mechanism of motivation; Shelley's concerns the definition of moral right and wrong.

All the essential elements of Shelley's argument—the concept and metaphor of the expanding circle of sympathy, the broad view of utility as the ethical end of action, and the definition of moral right (as well as its motivating mechanism)—are, as a matter of documentary record, features of older skeptical arguments, as I have said. Perhaps the earliest formal expression of them is the second address of Carneades in the Roman Forum; Cicero records the substance of the moral argument presented there (*De Finibus,* xxiii), and he quotes from the speech (*De Re Publica,* III,7ff.). It is in summarizing Carneades' argument that Mary Mills Patrick shows the relevance of the circle concept to the general claims:

Of all the different forms of wisdom, the highest is the native active sense of justice. This begins in a narrow circle, gradually extends until it includes fellow countrymen, later, other nations, and, finally, the whole human race.[18]

Shelley had read and admired the philosophical dialogues of Cicero before composing the *Treatise,* but he also found the arguments presented again, in English works belonging to "what I may term the modern Academy"—i.e., British skepticism of the eighteenth and nineteenth centuries, and especially the books of Hume and Drummond. Hume associates imagination with sympathy, as Shelley subsequently does in the *Treatise* and in the *Defence:*

Sympathy is not always limited to the present moment, but . . . we often feel by communication the pains and pleasures of others, which are not in being, and which we only anticipate by the force of imagination.[19]

It follows that, as Shelley says, "the great secret of morals is Love; or a going out of our own nature, and an identification of ourselves with the beautiful which exists in thought, action, or person, not our own" (R&P, p. 487). "For this reason," says Hume, "pity or a sympathy with pain produces love, and that because it interests us in the fortunes of others."[20]

This explanation of the mechanism of motives is linked, by a broad application of the utilitarian principle, to the skeptical critiques of metaphysics: it is "varieties in the state of the soul" which "occasion the happiness or misery of human existence" (Drummond, *Academical Questions,* p. 16). These phenomenal states impel or "occasion" (N.B.: not cause action: "Passion rouses us from indolence, and urges us on to enterprise" [Drummond, *Academical Questions,* p. 16]). Again, the mechanism of ethical action and also the object of ethical action are enclosed within the experiential circle.

An expansion occurs when the ethical principles become political imperatives, which they do for the ancients, for Hume, and for Shelley alike. In his copy of Diogenes Laertius, Shelley had marked with evident approval certain passages at about the same time that he composed the *Essay on the Punishment of Death.* Among those passages was this statement, expanding the circumference of the ethical circle: "The only true commonwealth was [according to the earlier Diogenes] that which is as wide as the universe."[21] Hume agrees: a human being, he says, "has the most ardent desire of society, and is fitted for it by the most advantages." It follows that ethical issues and imperatives rapidly become political imperatives: "We can form no wish, which has not a reference to society."[22]

What Shelley might have read in Hazlitt's *Essay on the Principles of Human Action,* therefore, or what he might have heard from Hazlitt in conversation at Leigh Hunt's house, was one version of a more comprehensive argument that he had already encountered in Diogenes, Cicero, and Hume. This older version in fact offers Shelley more than what he might have found in Hazlitt: a concept of justice that moves from the "narrow limit" of an individual consciousness to the "comprehensive circumference" of a society. This movement is recapitulated in the progress from the 1812 pamphlets, with their confusion of public problems and private solutions, to *A Philosophical View of Reform,* with its thoroughly dialectical conception of history and human life. It is to that essay, therefore, as to a conceptual culmination, that I now turn.

SHELLEY AND REFORM

To place Shelley's *Philosophical View of Reform* in its historical context is to unfold a series of circumstances that help to move Shelley in that intellectual direction that I have schematized in the preceding section. The theoretical demands and conditions of skeptical argument move Shelley's reasoning away from the abstractions of metaphysics toward a union of purely intellectual concerns with imperatives for immediate political action. What I have called the particular argumentative occasion—the set of historical circumstances within which a paradigmatic argument repeats itself—applies pressures on the argument that shape its substance, and the conjuncture of theoretical imperatives with political events is especially important in the case of this essay. The constant conjunction of the material foundations of social life with the intellectual superstructure, or with the literary and philosophical products of an age, is both the subject of Shelley's essay and the interpretive model best suited for its analysis.

Some of the proposals that Shelley presents in the *Philosophical*

View of Reform are those he had presented earlier, in *A Proposal for Putting Reform to the Vote*. In January of 1817, Shelley was developing a friendship with Leigh Hunt, editor of the *Examiner;* on January 19, Hunt published Shelley's "Hymn to Intellectual Beauty" in the *Examiner,* putting beneath the poem (in the same column, on the same page) the following statement:

Reform
A select Meeting of Independent Gentlemen, friends of economy, public order, and reform, dined on Friday at the Freemasons' Tavern. Their object was to take into consideration the present most alarming state of the country, and the daily increasing pressure on all descriptions of his Majesty's subjects, and to endeavour to promote an union and co-operation between the great leading landed interests of the country and the other classes of the community, for the attainment of a reduction in the present enormous and unconstitutional military establishment—in the wasteful expenditure of the public money—and a constitutional Reform in the Commons House of Parliament.[23]

That syllabus for the meeting is a checklist of particular topics that Shelley treats in the specific proposals for immediate action in the later *Philosophical View*. Here, in January of 1817, he could not and did not overlook the fact that his own verses on Intellectual Beauty were appearing in a context (literally on the page) of the political problems.

In the following month, Shelley composes *A Proposal for Putting Reform to the Vote*. On February 16, Hunt publishes in the *Examiner* Keats's sonnet "To Kosciusko," praising the Polish patriot who was a hero among British liberals. On the same page as Keats's sonnet appears an article about a reported "attempt upon the life of his Royal Highness" the Prince Regent (*Examiner* for February 16, 1817, p. 107). In the following week, Hunt publishes Keats's sonnet "After dark vapors have oppress'd our plains," reporting on the same page that "four State Prisoners in the Tower are confined in different parts of that fortress" (*Examiner* for February 23, 1817, p. 124). In every issue of the *Examiner* during this period, Hunt prints reports and polemical arguments for the friends of constitutional reform.

On March 2, Hunt reports a "Meeting of the Friends of Public

Order, Retrenchment, and Reform," at which speakers included Sir Francis Burdett, a supporter of parliamentary reform with whom Shelley corresponded; Douglas Kinnaird, Byron's friend and his literary and business agent; and John Philpot Curran, a reformer whom Shelley had met while he was in Ireland composing and distributing his *Address to the Irish People* and *Proposals for an Association of Philanthropists*. Among them, these speakers articulate the same proposals that Shelley expresses in his exactly contemporary essay *Proposals for Putting Reform to the Vote:* Curran, for example, summarizes the moderate reformist position that Shelley, with Burdett, Kinnaird, Curran, and Hunt, endorses (with an exception from Shelley concerning annual parliaments):

> [Curran] had to say he respected the liberties of the people as much as any man could do, and he thought they ought to be extended, as far as this could be done with a view to their benefit; but if the words Universal Suffrage were acted upon to the extent of their meaning (which in his conscience he did not believe the people understood), he was satisfied there would be no representation at all. He however considered a substantial reform to be necessary, without which the Sovereign could not be safe, and the people must be oppressed (*Examiner* for March 2, 1817, p. 142).

In this same month, Shelley publishes his proposal, recommending exactly that position, except that he is a bit more radical, advocating annual parliaments while Curran, Burdett, and Leigh Hunt do not. "With respect to Universal Suffrage," he agrees, saying that "its adoption, in the present unprepared state of public knowledge and feeling [would be] a measure fraught with peril" (6:68). Shelley endorses the moderate proposal for a greater enfranchisement though not a universal suffrage: "I think that none but those who register their names as paying a certain small sum in *direct taxes* ought, at present, to send Members to Parliament." Where Shelley differs from Curran, Burdett, and Hunt is, in one sense, a relatively slight matter, given the substantial agreement on the character, extent, and necessity of parliamentary reform. Where Curran would postpone annual parliaments, Shelley sides with the more radical Cobbett: "Annual Parliaments have my entire assent. I will not state those general reasonings in their favour, which Mr. Cobbett and other writers have already made familiar to the public mind" (6:68). Here Shelley acknowledges a controversy among the advocates of reform: moderates (Leigh Hunt, Burdett, and Curran) advocate limited rather than universal suffrage; radicals (Cobbett and Major John Cartwright) advocate suffrage for all adult males or (in the case of Jeremy Bentham) all men and women; republicans advocate the dissolution of the institutions of monarchy and aristocracy altogether. Like Leigh Hunt, Shelley advocates a gradual progress of reform, the moderate position (with the single practical exception of the annual parliaments).

More generally, as Cameron has pointed out, what was for Shelley a measure of prudence and policy was for Hunt both policy and ultimate principle:

The distinction . . . between Shelley and Hunt must again be emphasized. Hunt looked for little beyond an extension of the franchise to the middle class and was indeed quite satisfied with the Reform Bill of 1832 (and his own consequent pension). Shelley not only favored in theory the universal suffrage demands of the radicals but wished to push beyond them into a republican and then an equalitarian state. He attacked Cartwright and the radicals, he made clear, not because he disagreed with their aims but because he felt that those aims could more safely be accomplished in two stages than in one.[24]

Thus Shelley's moderate program is merely provisional, a compromise with circumstances. He openly endorses the goals of the radicals, including universal suffrage: "Abstractedly it is the right of every human being to have a share in the government" (6:68). He goes even farther, endorsing the goals of the republicans, including the abolition of the monarchy and aristocracy: "A pure republic may be shewn, by inferences the most obvious and irresistible, to be that system of social order the fittest to produce the happiness and promote the genuine eminence of man" (6:68). His *Proposal* would not deny these goals, therefore, but rather postpone their accomplishment, thereby to assure it.

On the subject of this internal dispute among the reformists, Shelley repeats an argument from Burdett and the *Examiner* just as specifically as he repeats their proposals. Says Burdett,

Instead of looking at each other with captious feelings of jealousy, he hoped Reformers would abstain from mutual recriminations, no longer participating in that spirit of religious bigotry that illustrated its intolerance in proportion as it approximated in principle (*Examiner* for March 2, 1817, p. 142).

In his version of the argument, published in the same month, Shelley says exactly the same thing:

A certain degree of coalition among the sincere Friends of Reform, in whatever shape, is indispensable to the success of this proposal. . . . It is trivial to discuss what species of Reform shall have place, when it yet remains a question whether there will be any Reform or no (6:67).

The extent of Shelley's involvement in this public discourse, and the importance of his active daily participation in dialogue on the problems raised in his prose, might easily be forgotten in the course of a conceptual analysis of his philosophical prose; such an *oubliance* would be injurious for an understanding of Shelley. The substance, the form, and the timing of his political writing—and especially the *Philosophical View of Reform*—are powerfully conditioned by the immediate context within which Shelley works.

A second political pamphlet of the same year, *An Address to the People on the Death of the Princess Charlotte,* is equally parallel with polemics appearing simultaneously in the *Examiner* and in Thomas Jonathan Wooler's periodical *The Black Dwarf.*[25] Three working-class men—Jeremiah Brandreth, Isaac Ludlam, and William Turner—were leaders of a demonstration known as the Derbyshire Insurrection. On November 7, 1817, they were first hanged and then beheaded. On the preceding day, the Princess Charlotte had died. The absurdity and implicit injustice of a national mourning for the death of the princess coupled so closely with a brutal execution of victims of oppression made for an anomaly that Shelley, Hunt, and Wooler agreed in pointing out. "That the death of the Princess Charlotte should have been immediately followed by such a scene of blood as that exhibited upon the scaffold at Derby, is as shocking to the understanding, as it is abhorrent to the feelings," as *The Black Dwarf* says; Shelley agrees, but he extends the polemic in two ways. He supplies an additional contrast, comparing the national concern for the death of the princess with a national unconcern for the numerous deaths among the destitute: "Some have perished in penury or shame. . . . thousands of the poorest poor, whose misery is aggravated by what cannot be spoken now, suffer this. . . . Yet none weep for them" (6:73–74). It is not only Brandreth, Ludlam, and Turner but an entire social class—the politically and economically dispossessed—in whose behalf Shelley writes. Second, he adds arguments from his essay *On the Punishment of Death:* "What is death? Who dares to say that which will come after the grave?" (6:76). This sentence, like the frequent reports of executions in the *Examiner,* indicates that the *skepsis* of the earlier essay *On the Punishment of Death* was no abstract speculation but an engagement with an immediate and bloody reality.

As in the case of his *Proposal for Putting Reform to the Vote,* Shelley takes a topic, a general argument, and a substantial point of political agreement from the political journalists with whom he was in immediate contact, and he contributes his own essays to this forum of discussion; but it happens with some frequency that his particular arguments differ in their more radical character from those of the political writers to whom he was personally closest, and especially Leigh Hunt. Shelley's skeptical methods engage his polemic (even his apparently journalistic polemics on a reform of the vote, or on the execution of political prisoners) in philosophical structures. Shelley's issues are deepened, and conceptualized more philosophically, and his arguments' conclusions tend accordingly toward a more thorough and profound revolution than what the polemicists envision. Rather than an attack on one or many abuses, Shelley writes ideological critique, a more total challenge to the thought structure and political structure of his society.

SHELLEY AND THE *EXAMINER*

Consistently throughout his career, though most expansively in the *Philosophical View of Reform,* even Shelley's most minutely political polemics have metaphysical depth. That part of his corpus that is most obviously journalistic is also and simultaneously engaged with the ideological dimension of his more abstract arguments. And when Shelley left England, sailing to Calais on March 11, 1818, his ties with

Leigh Hunt, the *Examiner,* and the political circle to which they belonged were attenuated but not broken. His first letter from the Continent was to Hunt (on March 13). Shelley's continued activity as a writer on reform is shown repeatedly in the following months, as when he writes to Godwin that he is "exceedingly delighted with the plan you propose of a book illustrating the characters of our calumniated Republicans" (*Letters,* 2:21). On the same day, he writes to Peacock that he has received a letter in which Peacock reports the results of the parliamentary elections, including the elections of Samuel Romilly (the Shelley family lawyer) and Burdett. In the same letter, Peacock quotes for Shelley a sentence from the *Quarterly Review,* which Shelley subsequently echoes: "No country was ever in a more combustible state than England is at this moment."[26] After he receives the news of the Manchester massacre, Shelley says, "These are, as it were, the distant thunders of the terrible storm which is approaching" (2:119); again, in the *Philosophical View of Reform,* Shelley says that England has arrived "at a crisis in its destiny" (7:19); events are occurring—e.g., the Manchester massacre—"which might terminate in a civil war" (7:53).

The presence of a comprehensive ideological frame, rather than a merely topical concern, shows itself in that same letter: Shelley asserts a linkage of economic conditions with the political struggle and oppression: it is, he says, financial affairs that will precipitate the collision of the oppressed and the oppressors (2:119). This conjunction of economics and political change is repeated in the *Philosophical View.* It also derives from what Shelley had read in the *Examiner,* a journal that (as he tells Peacock) he has been receiving regularly. On August 29, Hunt had published an article attacking the inflationary programs that had devalued the currency, following this essay immediately with a reprint of Hazlitt's essay "On the Regal Character." One week earlier, Hunt had coupled the economic crisis with electoral reform in his essay "Disturbances at Manchester" (*Examiner* for August 22, 1819). On June 22, Hunt had printed an article, "The New Taxes," attacking financial policies and borough-mongering as associated abuses of power.

But Shelley did not merely read the political journalism of the period; he sought to continue contributing to it, as he had done in England with his *Proposal for Putting Reform to the Vote* and *Address to the People on the Death of the Princess Charlotte.* On February 25, he en-

courages Peacock to start a new political journal for the "staunch reformers" (*Letters,* 2:81). On September 9, he compares the revolutionary storm approaching in the wake of the Manchester massacre to
the French Revolution, and he asks Peacock to send him the "*earliest
political news*" (*Letters,* 2:119). The philosophical and even metaphysical depth of Shelley's interest in this political news appears recurrently: on November 6, he sends to the *Examiner* a contribution
for that journal, an essay on the trial of Richard Carlile for blasphemous libel: Carlile had published in 1818 the works of Thomas Paine,
and the charges concerned several passages in Paine's *Age of Reason.*[27]

Hunt did not publish Shelley's article on the trial of Carlile: it arrived long after Hunt had already published five articles on the subject, all sympathetic with Carlile as Shelley was and all of them linking the dogmatism of religion with the despotism of political tyranny,
as Shelley does.[28] But Shelley's essay, closing in an address to Hunt,
enunciates their common aims:

> These, my dear Hunt, are awful times. The tremendous ques-
> tion is now agitating, whether a military & judicial despotism is
> to be established by our present rulers, or some form of govern-
> ment less unfavourable to the real & permanent interests of all
> men is to arise from the conflict of passions now gathering to
> overturn them: *We* cannot hesitate which party to embrace; and
> whatever revolutions are to occur, though oppression should
> change names & names cease to be oppressions, our party will
> be that of liberty & of the oppre[ss]ed (*Letters,* 2:148).

Shelley repeats what he and Burdett had said in 1817: that reformists
should set aside their differences because of the urgent need for coop-
eration. He repeats, too, the fact that he is more radical in his principles than Hunt (Shelley advocates immediate annual parliaments,
eventual universal suffrage, and the complete abolition of the monarchy; Hunt advocates limited suffrage alone); but, as Shelley emphasizes in the *Letter to the Examiner,* these differences in theoretical principles do not affect his entire agreement on matters of political practice
(*Letters,* 2:148).

The union of the different levels of ideology—"legal, political, religious, aesthetic or philosophic," as Marx lists them[29]—was for Shelley
as for Marx a theoretical working hypothesis, a heuristic tool for the

analysis of history; but it was also a fact of daily life. On September 6, Shelley writes to the publisher Ollier that *Prometheus Unbound* is finished and is being transcribed to be sent for publication. In the same letter he says,

> The same day your letter came, came the news of the Manchester work, & the torrent of my indignation has not yet done boiling in my veins. I wait anxiously [to] hear how the Country will express its sense of this bloody murderous oppression of its destroyers. "Something must be done. . . . What yet I know not" (*Letters*, 2:117).

That quotation, which he applies here to the Manchester massacre and the revolutionary response to it that he anticipates, is a sentence from his own poetic drama *The Cenci*. His poetic work and his political interests and activities condition and reflect one another; what is more, Shelley shows that he understands this interpenetration, and he writes of this higher-level issue rather than topical, political, practical matters merely.

Two weeks later, Shelley tells Peacock that the *Examiner* is arriving regularly, he commends the radical leader Henry Hunt (no relation to Leigh Hunt), who had organized the Manchester demonstration, and he announces that "I have sent you my Prometheus" (*Letters*, 2:120). In the letter to Ollier in which Shelley says that he is "preparing an octavo on reform," he says again that he has been reading the *Examiner*, he has seen a review of his poem *The Revolt of Islam* ("the *beau ideal* as it were of the French Revolution" [*Letters*, 1:564]) in *Blackwood's Magazine*, and he commits his future poems to "dreadful or beautiful realities" (2:164); such realities, he says, are the subjects of the poem he has just written, *Julian and Maddalo*.

Consistently it is ideology—that which forms of thought have in common—that concerns Shelley. Incidents (the Carlile affair, and the Manchester massacre) exemplify structure. When Shelley describes his *Letter to the Examiner* on the Carlile trial, he makes a statement about politics, referring to his reading of Clarendon's *History of the Rebellion and Civil Wars in England* or Madame de Staël's *Considérations sur la Révolution française,* or perhaps to his own *Philosophical View of Reform;*[30] but in that same essay on the Carlile trial he writes also of

"Sir William Drummond, the most acute metaphysical critic of the age," and he compares the metaphysician Drummond with the radical Paine. To delineate the comprehensiveness of the thought structure (ideology) that he has in mind, Shelley compares Drummond (metaphysics) with Bentham (economics). Shelley argues that certain kinds of thinking appear alike in Drummond's metaphysics, Paine's critique of orthodox Christian religion, and Bentham's economic utilitarianism.

In this way, the ideological argument denies the autonomy of separate fields of thought, or spheres of activity. Simultaneously, such an analysis empowers a deepened interpretation of political events or reform. The "menaces of power," as Leigh Hunt had said, involve "dogmas legal as well as ecclesiastical" (*Examiner* for June 27, 1819, p. 401; October 17, 1819, p. 657). Shelley's analysis extends the argument for comprehensiveness: he perceives paradigms of oppression inscribed in the entire ideological superstructure, in literature, philosophy, and the arts, as well as institutions of church and state. The philosophical burden of *A Philosophical View of Reform* is an articulation of this ideological paradigm as it appears on all levels of the societal superstructure.

It is in fact at exactly this time, November 1819, that Shelley begins work on *A Philosophical View of Reform*. As Reiman shows, both internal and external evidence suggest that the essay was written between November 1819 and January 1820, and most of the writing was probably done during December, the month in which he wrote to Ollier about it. Shelley writes of the essay again, in May, in a letter to Hunt: "Do you know any bookseller who wd. publish for me an octavo volume entitled 'A Philosophical View of Reform' . . . ? It is intended for a kind of standard book for the philosophical reformers politically considered, like Jeremy Bentham's something [i.e., somewhat], but different & perhaps more systematic" (2:201). This description and question concerning his essay do not actually indicate that Shelley was still, in May, at work on it; it is more likely, given datable references in the essay, that he had finished the extant portions of it earlier, probably in January, but he obviously had failed to interest a publisher in the project.[31] Its composition, therefore, coincides with the *Letter to the Examiner* on the Carlile case, with Shelley's reading of the *Blackwood's* review of *The Revolt of Islam,* and with Hunt's publication in December 1819 of a series of articles entitled "Proposed

Despotic Measures." The Tory government, in response to the Manchester uprising, had proposed three repressive bills, regulating reform meetings to the point of prohibiting them, prohibiting meetings for the purpose of "military training," and empowering magistrates "to search for arms" (*Examiner* for December 5, p. 769; December 12, p. 785).

It was not only Shelley, Hunt, and the editors of the *Quarterly Review* who feared an armed insurrection: the proposed regulations forbidding citizens to meet for the purpose of training and practicing with weapons reflected the fact that the outraged radical poor were doing so. The language in Shelley's letters and Hunt's journals, about potential bloodshed and immediate risk of violent revolution, was not inflated rhetoric. And under this pressure of violent urgency Shelley writes his treatise. While his rhetoric acknowledges and addresses this immediate crisis, his arguments also, simultaneously, address the higher-level phenomena of superstructural paradigms that render the political acts intelligible.

A Philosophical View of Reform consists of three parts or chapters. The first part presents an interpretation of European history, arguing dialectically for the reciprocal determination of base and superstructure, or of material conditions and ideology.[32] This section explains an evolutionary theory of history; Shelley focuses on the progress of liberty as a conjunction of institutional realities and intellectual products. The second section of the essay analyzes the contemporary political and economic situation in England: Shelley considers concrete and particular facts of the immediate political present. Here, he articulates a principle of interestedness, assigning a great deal of efficacy to economic class interest. He analyzes the institutions of political power in their conjunction with institutions of capital. Thus, even his topical and politically specific discussion involves an argument of ideological determinism in the sense of conditioning forces. In the final section of his essay, Shelley turns to his recommendations, advocating particular reforms in the suffrage. Both immediate and ultimate goals are specified. The particular and general, or the given and the ideal, are simultaneously involved.

I do not think that it has ever been pointed out that Shelley's essay has thus the structure of a syllogism:

Chapter I. *Major premise:* a theory of history involving the conjunction of basic, superstructural, and ideological levels and forms, and celebrating the progressive ascendancy of the philosophical skepticism that Shelley finds in metaphysical writers.

Chapter II. *Minor premise:* particular facts and material conditions observable in the contemporary setting; facts to which both skeptical critique and ideological analysis can be applied.

Chapter III. *Conclusion:* a "therefore"-statement; application of the principles of Chapter I to the data of Chapter II, yielding imperatives for political action.

To analyze the statements contained within the three sections of the treatise is to discern the following crucial issues: Chapter I involves a concept of conjunction, whereby the political, religious, aesthetic, and philosophical levels or forms of human living are shown to be conditioned by one another. Particularly, the ascendancy of philosophical *skepsis* is seen as conjoined with progressive political evolution. Shelley's working concepts are determination 1 (condition) and determination 2 (limit) as the material and mental forms are related reciprocally. Then, Chapter II focuses more narrowly, not only on the economic and political facts of the moment but also on the limited concept of ideology as inversion, in the sense in which Marx was to explain it. Shelley articulates a form of economic reification of value that Marx also identifies, in *Capital*. Shelley aligns that economic reification with the religious inversion (superstition) and political inversion (tyranny), both of which are undermined by skeptical critique. Finally, in the third section of his essay, Shelley advocates particular actions. To do so, he finds a form of discourse committed to positive practical action but consistent with the negative principles of his epistemological skepticism.

The demystifications that such skepticism achieves concern, as I have shown, primarily the philosophical problem of knowledge. But the sense of ideology as inversion effects a similar demystification in a social and material frame. Shelley's argument is deepened, therefore, beyond those of his contemporaries. Uniquely, he explicates the nexus of (philosophical) skepticism and (political) ideology.

A PHILOSOPHICAL VIEW OF REFORM, CHAPTER I

In pages of the same notebook in which the *Philosophical View* appears, Shelley writes in *On Life* of the negative work of abstract philosophical criticism: "It destroys error, and the roots of error" (R&P, p. 477).[33] While he advocates a "strict scepticism concerning all assertions" (7:62), Shelley also makes positive statements intended for concrete responses in the world of hard fact. He is able to do so without vitiating that skepticism reflexively. In contrast to some later versions of Marxist dialectic, Shelley discovers a form of discourse whereby his positive political statements are not logically undermined by his negative epistemological method. Considered narrowly as historical writing, the primary accomplishment of the *Philosophical View* is the combination of the general theory of history with the contemporaneous political scene, as Cameron says; but considered philosophically, its primary accomplishment is the combination of the skeptical method with positive statements for action, without contradiction. Marx and Engels were later to attempt a similarly deepened ideological argument, but Shelley's more rigorous skepticism evades contradictions to which later dialectics are liable.

Shelley begins with a powerful generalization that shows how particular political occasions are to be fitted into an interpretive framework:

From the dissolution of the Roman Empire, that vast and successful scheme for the enslaving [of] the most civilized portion of mankind, to the epoch of the present year, have succeeded a series of schemes, on a smaller scale, operating to the same effect (7:5).

This kind of link between religion and politics did, demonstrably, persist "to the epoch of the present year," as Shelley says: his *Letter to the Examiner* on the Carlile trial for blasphemous libel emphasizes the point, and so does Leigh Hunt's interpretation of that trial in terms of "dogmas legal as well as ecclesiastical."

Shelley explains that appropriation of religion for political power in terms of class conflict. The Catholic Church is misunderstood when it is conceived as a system of religious doctrine; instead, Shelley says, the Catholic Church is "a plan according to which the cunning and selfish few have employed the fears and hopes of the ignorant many to the establishment of their own power" (7:5). The ideological inversion that appears as religious dogma is what Marx and Engels describe in *The German Ideology:* the projections of human intellectual activity are reified as deity and dogma. Like Marx and Engels, Shelley here argues that the reification (superstition) is used to install and support a materially political institution. The notion that religious belief systems are culturally relative and socially specific is at least as old as Pyrrho, and it is elaborated methodologically by Diogenes Laertius, Sextus, and virtually all influential skeptics including Montaigne and Drummond. Rather than the ancient response of quietude or indifference (*ataraxia*), both Shelley and Marx elicit a revolutionary ethos and impulse from this theoretical orientation.

In Marx's social and historical frame, a pattern of inversion is discerned: a product of human (mental) activity is reified into a supposed cause, or power, external to human beings. The same pattern appears, in Shelley, in an epistemological frame of reference; this pattern is what I have called nominalization:[34] a mere name is alleged to have a substantial referent in external actuality; then, the mere name has actual efficacy. The doctrines of Jesus Christ have nothing in them susceptible of the perversions of political oppression, Shelley says; "but the mere names" abstracted from Christ's system are wielded as tools in a concrete struggle. The products of intellectual construction are first mistaken as substantial entities and then used as tools of political domination. And here for Shelley, as later in *The German Ideology,* the oppressive illusion is located within a struggle for class domination. The trope of relativity is applied as a social–class differential. Further, as I have argued in connection with Drummond, Shelley's historicizing of the problem of power, treating that concept as a construction within social history, generates a radical critique.

What is implied is not, however, a one-directional chain of determination whereby the notional contents of religion and philosophy are said to be caused by the material foundation of wealth and power; instead, Shelley uses a multidimensional model of relatedness between the foundations of a society and its superstructural elements. Florence's resistance to the empire of the papacy is the cause to which "if to anything, was due the undisputed superiority of Italy in literature and the arts over all its contemporary nations": the importance of that qualifier ("if to anything") is emphasized in the same paragraph, where political conditions are placed "among other causes." Contemporary intellectual existence is related reciprocally and not causally with material conditions.[35] Shelley affirms the efficacy of political reality in determining (conditioning) intellectual products, but he simultaneously limits that formulation in two ways: he places the efficacy of politics "among other causes," and he admits that the political determinant was itself notional rather than material—it existed "in the bosoms" of the liberators, not in the material base alone. This distinction is crucially important: the commonplace conception of political struggle and institutions as concrete and real, in contrast to mental and ideal systems, is wholly repudiated. The institutions themselves are, at bottom, ideational things.

The Reformation is an instance of the linkage of politics and religion. Simultaneously a liberation from priest and from king, the Reformation defies comprehension by any scheme of unilinear cause. "The progress of philosophy and civilization" culminate in the material revolution; if the material base of power is put as a determinant of philosophy, so too philosophy is put as a determinant of political power. Shelley's conception is thoroughly dialectical, emphasizing the inextricable association and reciprocal efficacy of these levels of reality without dogmatizing on the cause.

In the epistemological frame of the skeptical tradition, the argument could be paraphrased in this way: the conjunction of the ideational forms (religious dogma) with the material conditions ("yoke of priests and kings") is a constant. But no cause is perceptible; the leap from conjunction, or constant condition, or association, to externalized cause is an indefensible dogmatism. Aenesidemus' tropes against etiology, rehearsed by Sextus and reformulated by Hume and then Drummond, make just this argument. Further, the alleged autonomy of idea and thing, the very distinction that manifests itself in the dichotomy of belief system (idea) and political reality (thing) is an illusion. The notion of class conflict is germane, because it explains or describes the motivated production of beliefs in the first place.

The Reformation, thus, like the origin of the Catholic Church, is explicable in terms of class conflict: "The poor rose against their natural enemies, the rich" (7:6). The phenomenon is not unique but paradigmatic. The insurrection of the peasantry is comparable to the insurrections of the black slaves in the West Indies, as class struggle: "For so dear is power that the tyrants themselves neither then, nor now, nor ever, left or leave a path to freedom but through their own blood" (7:6). The violence, bloodshed, and terror into which the French Revolution collapsed are, Shelley says, in his preface to *The*

Revolt of Islam, intelligible in the same way. The pattern of class conflict, as a repeatable paradigm, rather than the events themselves, is
what his argument here would adumbrate. The conception of history
is dynamic, offering a model of related stages of conflict rather than a
static sequence of discrete episodes. The fact that Shelley's political
discourse is about the conceptual paradigm, and not primarily the examples, distinguishes his polemic from other contemporaneous and
journalistic arguments in the reform movement; he writes no less
than a theory of history.

Shelley articulates here the comprehensive claim of his ideological
theory. At the time of the Reformation in England, "the exposition of
a certain portion of religious imposture [ideological inversion] drew
with it an enquiry into political imposture, and was attended with an
extraordinary exertion of the energies of intellectual power" (7:7).
The language expresses the weakest sense of determination, the notion of conjunction; poets and philosophers are "at once the effects of
the new spirit in men's minds, and the causes of its more complete
development" (7:7). The opposition of *skepsis* to dogmatism, the un-
veiling of authority as *doxa,* as fallible and time-bound opinion rather
than truth, and the concomitant release of mental power are all elements of the skeptical tradition that Shelley extends; but he invests
them with political urgency rather than disinterested or abstract implications alone.

The evolutionary concept of history in fact depends on that interaction of superstructural elements. The Revolution of 1688 was a compromise between the impulses of liberty and tyranny, whereby "aristocracy and episcopacy [superstructure 1] were at once established
and limited by law." But "the fruit" of that event was a matter of
theoretical principle [superstructure 2]—and that theoretical principle
is social-contract theory.

> Meanwhile those by whom [aristocracy and episcopacy] were
> established acknowledged and declared that the will of the People
> was the source from which these powers, in this instance, de-
> rived the right to subsist. A man has no right to be a King or a
> Lord or a Bishop but so long as it is for the benefit of the People
> and so long as the People judge that it is for their benefit that he
> should impersonate that character (7:7).

A primary concern with the fact of a political institution (monarchy, or the power of a particular king, or a case of injustice) would blind us to Shelley's point, which is entirely theoretical. "The solemn establishment of this maxim as the basis of our constitutional law, more than any beneficial and energetic application of it to the circumstances of this aera of its promulgation, was the fruit of that vaunted event": that maxim is the relocation of the criterion of right within experiential and intellectual space; power and political right are not externalities opposed to the idealizations of theory; they are themselves matters of judgment, experienced benefit, ideas, and a maxim.

Shelley's interpretation does not, however, dissolve the actualities of social relation into driving ideas: "intolerant and oppressive hierarchies" of the most actual sort subsisted, with most actual consequences. "Catholics massacred Protestants and Protestants proscribed Catholics, and extermination was the sanction of each faith within the limits of the power of its professors" (7:8). But while these actualities condition the expression of liberty and tyranny, Shelley is willing simultaneously to articulate conceptual bases that reach beyond circumstance: "The protesting against religious dogmas which present themselves to his mind as false is the inalienable prerogative of every human being" (7:8). This statement leads immediately to a celebration of philosophical skepticism.

Shelley's subversive logic here is comparable to what we have seen in Drummond's critique of Descartes. The fact of ideological relativity—that is, the conspicuous presence of differing and evolving belief systems—undermines the authority of any particular ideology. But Shelley adds a political dimension that Drummond did not make explicit in *Academical Questions*. Rather than a merely metaphysical critique, Shelley employs the trope of relativity to bring that metaphysical argument to bear upon the historically specific alliance of Catholic or Protestant church with monarchical power. The metaphysical illusions of church dogma are employed as tools of power, but beyond this point Shelley suggests that all levels of ideological superstructure, including the clergy and the monarchy, recapitulate internally the dynamic of inversion.

In Chapter I of the *Philosophical View*, Shelley comes close to saying that the dogmatic philosophies connected with orthodox Christianity are the ideological inversions of power structure, whereas skeptical methodology is the enabling force of political revisionism:

The new epoch was marked by the commencement of deeper inquiries into the forms of human nature than are compatible with an unreserved belief in any of those popular mistakes upon which popular systems of faith with respect to the cause and agencies of the universe, with all their superstructure of political and religious tyranny, are built (7:8).

Skepsis (inquiry) is the opponent of dogma ("unreserved belief"). In a theological frame, *epochē* displaces the dead letter of doctrine or absolute truth. But in a political frame, the solidification of fictional constructions into "unreserved belief" is cognate with tyranny. Shelley illustrates his assertion with a list of influential writers in the history of skepticism: "Lord Bacon, Spinoza, Hobbes, Bayle, Montaigne."

It is worth emphasizing what Shelley saw in the philosophical work of those writers. Bacon begins his *Great Instauration* with a statement of the relativity of knowledge that is similar to what Shelley found also in Godwin's *Political Justice:* "For no man can rightly and successfully investigate the nature of anything in the thing itself; let him vary his experiments as laboriously as he will, he never comes to a resting-place, but still finds something to seek beyond." [36] Ceaseless mental construction is a corollary of ideological relativity; a permanent "resting-place" is a dogmatism, and Bacon commits his method to resisting that fatal error.

Bacon attacks the commonsense criterion of universal consensus, as I have shown in an earlier section of this book. Bacon uses the madman hypothesis as Cicero and Drummond also use it: "Even if men went mad all after the same fashion, they might agree one with another well enough." [37] Bacon even presses the argument from relativity to the point of treating philosophical systems as illusions of the philosophers' creation, again as Drummond was to do: "In my judgment," says Bacon, "all the received systems are but so many stageplays, representing worlds of their own creation after an unreal and scenic fashion." [38]

Bacon names explicitly the philosophical context that he, Cicero, Drummond, and Shelley share: the Academic skeptics, the successors of Plato, "introduced *Acatalepsia,* at first in jest and irony, and in disdain of the older sophists. . . . their's is a fairer seeming way than arbitrary decisions; since they say that they by no means destroy all investigation, like Pyrrho and his Refrainers, but allow of some things to be followed as probable, though of none to be maintained as true."[39] Bacon's aphorisms in the *Novum Organum,* especially up to and including No. LXX, are devoted accordingly not to affirmations or positive claims but, like the intellectual system of Shelley and Drummond, to "purgings of the mind" and "the extirpation of Idols from the understanding."[40]

Shelley had earlier employed Bacon's concept of the idols of the mind, saying in the *Essay on Christianity* that "Every human Mind has, what Lord Bacon calls its 'idola specus,' peculiar images which reside in the inner cave of thought" (6:241). Bacon's formulation of the concept includes other terms and issues that, in the *Philosophical View,* become important in Shelley's thinking. These terms include "superstition," "imposture," and more generally the delusions inherent in language:

Idols are the deepest fallacies of the human mind. For they do not deceive in particulars, as the others do, by clouding and snaring the judgment; but by a corrupt and ill-ordered predisposition of mind, which as it were perverts and infects all the anticipations of the intellect. For the mind . . . is rather like an enchanted glass, full of superstition and imposture. Now idols are imposed upon the mind, either by the nature of man in general; or by the individual nature of each man; or by words, or nature communicative. The first of these I call Idols of the *Tribe,* the second Idols of the *Cave,* the third the Idols of the *Marketplace.* There is also a fourth kind which I call the Idols of the *Theatre,* superinduced by corrupt theories or systems of philosophy, and false laws of demonstration.[41]

The metaphor is powerfully inclusive, as Shelley points out; "Lord Bacon was a poet" (*Defence,* R&P, pp. 484–85). But it is also effective epistemologically, enclosing philosophical criticism within the circle of intensional reference that I have examined in Shelley's *Treatise.* Thus, Bacon says of the "final causes" of traditional philosophy that they "have relation to the nature of man rather than to the nature of the universe."[42]

The other thinkers in Shelley's list participate in the development and extension of exactly that line of thought. Spinoza is another important figure in the history of skepticism: he illustrates two ways out of an apparent absurdity that is threatened by the skeptical arguments. Unmitigated skepticism would appear to confine science and philosophy within a circle of illusion. Skeptical methods might, therefore, appear to make both science and philosophy meaningless, but Spinoza counters that charge in two ways. First, he substitutes the ancient criteria of clarity and adequacy of ideas for the criterion of extensional veridicality. Rather than warrant a knowledge claim by pointing to external facts, these criteria locate confirming evidence within the cognition itself, as we have seen in Descartes's system. Second, Spinoza anchors metaphysical discussion in the context of history. In place of Christian dogma, Spinoza offers an approach to the books of the Bible, for example, that Alasdair MacIntyre has summarized:

> The Old Testament is to be interpreted in two ways: as allegories of intellectual truth, and as fitted for the social, moral, and intellectual needs of a primitive people. . . . the philosophically enlightened man cannot accept what [the Hebrew prophets] said, if he is asked to treat it as a literal truth.[43]

That conception of the Old Testament books is also that which Drummond applies in his *Oedipus Judaicus* (1811). Shelley was familiar with the relevant principles and text specifically, and even translated one of Spinoza's tracts: "The qualification to prophecy," says Spinoza in Shelley's translation, "is rather a more vivid imagination than a profounder understanding than other men" (I&P, 7:274). In these ways, Spinoza, like Bacon, belongs in Shelley's list of influential skeptics, his metaphysical argument rehearsing the dynamic of liberation that Shelley traces in both political and philosophical contexts.

Hobbes, the next philosopher on Shelley's list, was a personal friend of the French skeptics who responded to Descartes. He went further than Spinoza in historicizing the problems of knowledge; as Popkin says, Hobbes "had admitted the force of the problem of finding *the* criterion for judging what was genuinely true, and he insisted that the solution was ultimately political."[44]

Pierre Bayle, whom Shelley mentions next, summarized and codified seventeenth-century European skepticism in the *Dictionary Historical and Critical,* which was already in a second edition in English translation by 1734. In an article in that work on Pyrrho, Bayle encapsulates the relationship of Academic and Pyrrhonic skepticism: Phyrrho's "opinions did not differ much from those of Arcesilaus; for he did almost teach, as well as he, the incomprehensibility of all things [*akatalepsia*]. He found in all things reason to affirm and to deny [*isostheneia*]; and therefore he suspended his assent [*epochē*] after he had well examined the arguments *pro* and *con,* and reduced all his conclusions to a *non liquet, let the matter be further enquired into.*" [45]

But it was Montaigne, with whose name Shelley concludes his list of philosophers, who was the most famous of the Renaissance skeptics. His *Essays* and especially the *Apology for Raimond Sebond* popularize the Pyrrhonism of Sextus; Montaigne had read the recent Latin translation of Sextus' works shortly before composing the *Apology*. Montaigne produces the classical arguments for the relativity of knowledge, including the variability of the senses, the variety of individual perceptions, and cultural relativity. The fideistic skepticism with which Montaigne concludes is almost exactly the same as that expressed by Eusebes in Shelley's theological dialogue, *A Refutation of Deism.*

The progress of skepticism illustrated by those philosophers was continued, Shelley says, in the subsequent period, and the intensification of the skeptical procedure was simultaneously the progress of political liberty:

> Berkeley and Hume, [and] Hartley [at a] later age, following the traces of these inductions, have clearly established the certainty of our ignorance with respect to those obscure questions which under the name of religious truths have been the watchwords of contention and the symbols of unjust power (7:9).

It was in the wake of this skeptical movement in philosophy, Shelley says, that the French Ideologues formulated their doctrines of mechanistic materialism, and Shelley emphasizes the determining pressures of the concretely political context within which those French writers worked:

> A crowd of writers in France seized upon the most popular portions of the new philosophy which conducted to inferences at war with the dreadful oppressions under which the country groaned, [and] made familiar to mankind the fals[e]hood of their religious mediators and political oppressors (7:9).

The relativity of truth is a principle Shelley found among the skeptical philosophers whom he names, but it is also a structural feature of his own interpretations. He does not polarize philosophies into those with which he agrees and those with which he disagrees, nor does he posit a global system of wisdom in which each philosophy makes up a small part; instead, he puts an organic conception whereby the determining occasion of a philosophical product expresses itself in the content and form of the historically relative systems:

> Considered as philosophers their error seems to have consisted chiefly of a limitedness of view; they told the truth, but not the whole truth. This might have arisen from the terrible sufferings of their countrymen inviting them rather to apply a portion of what had already been discovered to their immediate relief, than to pursue one interest, the abstractions of thought, as the great philosophers who preceded them had done, for the sake of a future and more universal advantage (7:9).

Metaphysics was thus "stripping Power of its darkest mask," demystifying the ideological inversions, the dogmas of church and state that had previously dominated thought. As a correlative development, "Political Philosophy, or that which considers the relations of man as a social being, was assuming a precise form" (7:9). Political philosophy "sprang from and maintained a connexion with" metaphysics; metaphysics was the "parent" of political philosophy. As the metaphysical arguments that Shelley identifies were consistently skeptical, the correlative development in social philosophy was precisely the movement toward social-contract theory and then a broad view of utilitarianism: "A thirst for accommodating the existing forms according to which mankind are found divided to those rules of freedom and equality which are thus discovered as being the elementary principles according to which the happiness resulting from the social union ought to be produced and distributed, was kindled by these inquiries" (7:9–10). The overturning of metaphysical authorities and traditions was connected with a social philosophy that similarly sought to overturn the ossifications of oppressive institutions. The direction of change moves the locus of value out of the transcendent heavens and into the world of human experience.

Shelley's sympathy with this progress is evident, and so is his sense of the constant conjunction of superstructural levels; "Contemporary with this condition of the intellect all the powers of man seemed . . . to develop themselves with uncommon energy" (7:10). At this point Shelley notices a discrepancy between the development of the "means and sources of knowledge," mechanical as well as literary and philosophical, and the institutional forms of society. The old social order fails then to correspond with the new social forces. In what is perhaps the argument of Shelley's that most closely resembles Marx's, Shelley states the discrepancy:

The benefit of this increase of the powers of man became, in consequence of the inartificial forms into which society came to be distributed, an instrument of his additional evil. The capabilities of happiness were increased [including commerce and mechanical science], and applied to the augmentation of misery. Modern society is thus a[n] engine assumed to be for useful purposes, whose force is by a system of subtle mechanism augmented to the highest pitch, but which, instead of grinding corn or raising water acts against itself and is perpetually wearing away or breaking to pieces the wheels of which it is composed (7:10).

The resemblance of that statement to Marx's is striking:

At a certain stage of their development the material forces of production in society come into conflict with the existing relations of production. . . . From forms of development of the forces of production these relations turn into their fetters. Then comes the period of social revolution.[46]

For Shelley as for Marx, an inversion occurs in material economic life, which is precisely cognate with the philosophical inversions unmasked by the skeptics. The means (material mechanisms) displace the end; what people made as a tool becomes a fetter; the invented machinery comes to control the inventors. As a fiction (mental construct) can be reified as a truth and can then subject its own producers, so too material mechanisms (forces and means of production) can, through mystification, come to oppress their own human makers. At this point in the *Philosophical View*, Shelley turns from philosophy to politics, from history developing in metaphysical systems to recent progress of political revolutions. He reads the American Revolution as an "illustration of the new philosophy" (7:10), again subordinating the manifestation to the conceptual structure that it manifests. He singles out for praise, in the American example, not only the republican form of government but also two ways in which that form is hostile to dogmatism. He commends the absence in America of an established church, an institution that wherever it exists, must be a "system of opinions" or *doxa* reified legally and politically. He associates *doxa* with "prosecutions" used to enforce it; his own essays on the trials of Eaton and Carlile show what kind of prosecution he has in mind. The evil avoided by the American example is not the error or abuse of this or that church institution; it is the reification and enforcement of opinion, fallible thought system, as fixity and truth.

Whereas previous governments have hypostatized their own rationales, called their own perspectives eternal truths, and shackled both present and future generations to the forms of government that they, the fallible and time-bound legislators, have contrived, Shelley commends the American constitution's reserving itself for amendment. (Obviously, Shelley is misinformed about the mandatory revision every ten years.) A legislative reification takes place, in cases of permanent constitutions conceived as binding on posterity: the principles of one class, constructed at one time, in one place, are treated as permanent universals; the Americans illustrate a way to overcome this reification, subjecting their own legislative construction to "contingent discoveries" and the "progress of human improvement" (7:12, 11). For *skepsis,* no question, no constitution, no case, is ever closed, finally; closure manifests ideological inversion and imprisons the maker of systems inside the parameters of his or her own system.

Shelley turns to the French Revolution, analyzing its failure according to two principles that he has already introduced: he applies a class analysis and he produces a concept of determination as limit. The feudal system had persisted in France long after the conditions of its institution had passed; as Marx was to argue later, Shelley says here that this discrepancy between the old social order and the new social forces produces revolution. The ruling class in France "called soldiers to hew down the people when their power was already past" (7:13). By maintaining the no-longer-adequate social order and by defending it with violent oppression, the ruling class acted as the aggressors.

Then the oppressed, having been rendered brutal, ignorant, servile and bloody by long slavery, having had the intellectual thirst, excited in them by the progress of civilization, satiated from fountains of literature poisoned by the spirit and the form of monarchy, arose and took a dreadful revenge on their oppressors (7:13).

The revenge executed by the oppressed upon the oppressors was "a mistake, a crime, a calamity," but it was determined by exactly that system of oppression against which it was aimed. Both enhancement and deprivation of intellect, morality, philosophy, art, and political action are specifically conditioned and limited by the social world in which those products arise. This method of interpretation shifts the discourse from the limited factual occasion, the Reign of Terror, to the conceptual and ideological structure whereby it is intelligible.

Accordingly, Shelley characterizes the French philosophers of the Revolutionary and pre-Revolutionary period, including Condorcet, Voltaire, and Holbach, as "weak, superficial, vain, with little imagination, and with passions as well as judgments cleaving to the external form of things" (7:13–14). These deficiencies do not arise from the nature of the French or from the nature of these writers; they arise from the conditioning social relations. "Their institutions made them what they were." The superstructure 1 (institutional system) reacts efficaciously on the material base, as in the case of Napoleon's usurpation of Empire and the subsequent restoration of the Bourbons. The ideological form of the French Ideologues and the ideological structure of the reactionary Empire are equally "shapes" in which a reciprocal and intelligible relationship "clothed itself" (7:14).

As in his treatment of metaphysical systems, Shelley does not polarize right from wrong, good from evil; these values, frozen as absolutes, render the sort of dogma that Engels was to challenge, for example, in Dühring. The topic of cultural relativity that Shelley and Engels share with skeptical tradition empowers a more complex analysis. Shelley places political institutions, like metaphysical systems, within their determining contexts, but he detects and celebrates a progressive evolution. Like the Cromwellian revolution in England, where blood was also shed brutally, the French Revolution enacted reforms and improvements, though imperfect. "The authors of both Revolutions proposed a greater and more glorious object than the degraded passions of their countrymen permitted them to attain"; these passions were degraded by the oppressive institutions. "But in both cases abuses were abolished which never since have dared to show their face" (7:15).

Shelley then turns to the other nations of Europe, to South America, India, Persia, Syria, Arabia, and the West Indian islands (using information from the weekly columns of "Foreign Intelligence" printed in the *Examiner*). In each case he finds revolution or progress toward it, acknowledging the limits and imperfections conditioned by the concrete circumstances in the specific countries. But the effect of his list of progressive development around the world is a rhetorical crescendo that rises to this announcement: "Meanwhile England, the particular object for the sake of which these general considerations have been stated on the present occasion, has arrived, like the nations which surround it, at a crisis in its destiny" (7:19).

Shelley's notion of progress and political evolution is not utopian in the dogmatic sense: the current political crisis cannot culminate in the best of all possible worlds, nor will a successful issue of the current struggles do away with the need for skeptical revisionism. Like Godwin's notion of perfectibility, Shelley's argument of progressive improvement implies a development of relative systems of thought and of political order; he emphatically resists any reading of history that would come to a teleological stop, closure representing the antithesis of *skepsis,* and a teleological end constituting a premature stop to the (dialectical) progress that *skepsis* engenders.

Shelley's explanation of the current crisis among European institutions applies two concepts: the interpenetration of the various superstructural levels, and the conflict between an old social order and a new set of social forces, including social consciousness. Marx says, in the preface to *A Contribution to the Critique of Political Economy,* that it is in legal, political, religious, aesthetic, and philosophical forms that human beings become conscious of such a fundamental conflict. Shelley here anticipates that observation: "The literature of England, an energetic development of which has ever followed or preceded a great and free development of the national will, has arisen, as it were, from a new birth" (7:19). Shelley's statement includes an *isostheneia* that is more effective philosophically than are some rigidly deterministic versions of Marxism: literature follows *or* precedes those national developments. Shelley cannot insist on a statement of determination as cause, as already in 1812 he had seen that such a sense of determination is untenable. That concept was an error of the French Ideologues, and in its place Shelley puts a more thorough reciprocity; he acknowledges the conditioning efficacy of national institutional change and of ideational developments; he puts an *epochē* in response to the question of causal priority, saying that poetry may be the cause, effect, or companion of changes in national forms:

> We live among such philosophers and poets as surpass beyond comparison any who have appeared in our nation since its last struggle for liberty. For the most unfailing herald, or companion, or follower, of an universal employment of the sentiments of a nation to the production of beneficial change is poetry (7:19).

Individual mentality is assimilated to the social order. The spirit (mind) of these philosophers and poets is "less their own spirit than the spirit of their age" (7:20). In the case of the current political pressure for reform in England, as earlier in the analysis of the French Revolution, Shelley says that a discrepancy between ossified institutions and the dynamic forces of the life that is constrained by those institutions is the precipitating condition of revolution. Pressure for reform or revolution, he says, expresses "a desire of change arising from the profound sentiment of the exceeding inefficiency of the existing institutions to provide for the physical and intellectual happiness of the people" (7:20). With that point Shelley ends the first part of his treatise, and he summarizes the concepts of superstructural interpenetration that form the structural center of his theory of history: "Poets and philosophers are the unacknowledged legislators of the world."

A PHILOSOPHICAL VIEW OF REFORM, CHAPTER II

The second chapter of *A Philosophical View of Reform* is an analysis of the contemporary political situation in England. It is chiefly devoted to the large-scale economic conditions that Shelley presents as limiting or conditioning that political situation. Passing from his general view of European history to the particular facts of the present, Shelley does not in fact turn away from his theoretical arguments but rather anchors and applies them in the concrete data of the moment. Such a connection among theoretical and circumstantial matters is obviously implied in the theoretical argument itself, and it had also been a commonplace of long standing in the Shelley circle and in the polemics of British liberalism.

In terms of the essay's internal logic, this structure reproduces the form of a syllogism: Chapter I presents a major premise (general principle); Chapter II states a particular case (minor premise) to which the general principle can be applied; and Chapter III will then articulate a relevant conclusion (a "therefore"-statement) in the form of imperatives or instructions for action. To summarize Shelley's syllogism baldly: I. History is an ongoing and ceaseless dialectic of two mental modes: *skepsis,* with its acts of mental construction, and reification, or ideological inversion, with its concomitant institutions of tyranny. II. The political and economic conditions of England, at the present time, constitute a specific articulation of tyranny founded upon a particular system of ideological illusion. III. Therefore, the legal and political superstructures should be transformed to accommodate and to express the shifting volition of a liberated population; the act of ideological construction should be set in motion, not to establish an alternative system but to mobilize, to develop, and to free the constructive powers of humanity.

This simplification of the argument may distort it by elision, but my point concerns the form of reasoning: in contrast to political polemic or journalism, Shelley's argument concerns first and last the conceptual frames that interpenetrate with the political forms, facts, conditions, and goals. Ideological or ideational structure encloses the origins, aims, and data of Shelley's analysis. Dialectic, as I have said in connection with Engels, is a feature of reality and not of propositions merely. Shelley's argument, involving the forms of thought with the facts of political life, distinguishes itself thus from the sort of political writing—Hunt's, for example, or Cobbett's—that would accumulate facts as if they alone would yield inductively the needed conclusions. Shelley as dialectician probes further, into the models of mind in which facts are constituted, understood, and interpreted in the first place.

The issue of Hunt's *Examiner* that prints Shelley's "Hymn to Intellectual Beauty" contains also an article on reform and a speech on that subject by John Philpot Curran, as I have said, but it includes also an article, "Mr. Pitt—Finance—Sinking Fund," that treats the same economic problem to which Shelley turns in his treatise. The *Examiner* article is largely a review of a book, *An Inquiry concerning the Rise and Progress, the Redemption, present State and Management, of the National Debt of Great Britain, by Dr. Hamilton, Professor of Natural Philosophy, Aberdeen.* This book argues that "a Sinking Fund which borrows what it pays, if the operation be without loss or gain, is nugatory: If with loss, absurd."[47] The effects of the national debt are said, in the *Examiner* review, to include the prospect of a "hardy, industrious, and ingenious population, transformed into paupers, and indignant at the change" (p. 37). The political crisis, including the prospect of revolution, is associated with an economic crisis, and that economic crisis is in turn associated with the form of capital investment known as the sinking fund and the national debt. The critical article in the *Examiner* takes these data as given, and its analysis is inductive ("factual") rather than intellectually critical of the relevant theoretical modes.

Certainly, both political and economic crises had intensified by 1819, when Shelley writes the *Philosophical View.* Shelley had read in the *Examiner* of June 13 of the worsening economic depression and the consequent political unrest:

> At the moment when the people are absolutely lying down and panting under their burdens,—when the partial reliefs from the war-incumbrances have not given them time enough to recover from the galling soreness,—when in order to soothe them they have been told over and over again how much lighter their situation would become every day,—and when the manufacturing districts, one after the other, are roused almost to madness,—at such a moment the placemen, pensioners, and sinecurists, come forward to saddle them with a permanent peace taxation of *three millions of money!* (p. 369)

As Shelley explains, this new burden of taxation was a means of enriching the already wealthy investors of capital, by paying them compound interest on the national debt. And Shelley defines the national debt as "a debt contracted by the whole of a particular class in the nation towards a portion of that class" (7:40). The redress of the economic oppression, like the redress of political tyranny, is a matter of class struggle, as Shelley makes even clearer in other paragraphs of his essay.

Shelley says that a reform is resisted by "those interested in maintaining the contrary" (7:21). These conservatives argue that a large-scale political reform would entail "popular violence"; "But as those who argue thus derive for the most part great advantage and convenience from the continuance of these abuses, their estimation of the mischiefs of uprising [and] popular violence as compared with the mischiefs of tyrannical and fraudulent forms of government are likely . . . to be exaggerated" (7:21). The disenfranchised class views tyranny and economic exploitation as a series of evils greater than the risk of popular uprising; the small class of the rich and economically empowered think the reverse.

This explanation according to economic interestedness also anticipates a Marxist argument of determination; in both cases, however, the idea is not crudely deterministic (money-lust explains everything) but rather dialectical: "The economic situation is the basis, but the various elements of the superstructure . . . also exercise their influence upon the historical struggles and in many cases preponderate in determining their *form.*" [48]

Shelley uses the argument of historical determination to relativize both poles of the conflict, rather than to take sides simply in a one-dimensional definition. The poor, he says, are "incapable of discerning their own genuine and permanent advantage," because of the "degraded condition which their insurrection would be designed to ameliorate" (7:21). Because they are right about the wrongs they have suffered, they would be wrong in their methods of setting things right. At this point, Shelley deepens his analysis beyond the contemporary journalism on which he relies. He associates the data with the correlative structures of thought that constitute them.

Shelley enumerates among the class whose interestedness determines them to reactionary opinions the following: "All public functionaries who are overpaid either in money or in power for their public services," from king or Regent to turnkey (7:21–22); all members of the House of Lords; and a majority of the House of Commons. The interests of these sets of functionaries have been bought; they are tools of the rich, whose services have been procured by that wealthy class, as they are paid "several millions yearly of the produce of the soil for the service of certain dogmas" (7:22). The opinions, policies, and actions of these functionaries are attributable neither to their own convictions nor to the dogmas they serve, but to the class-based interest that they have been induced to serve.

Shelley is not reductive or mechanical in his application of the principle of interestedness: he refuses to apply a one-dimensional motivism to "every person whose interest is . . . concerned in the maintaining things as they are" (7:336n.). For one thing, judgments can be overdetermined; relative degrees of intellectual and moral development are germane, and so are particularities of experience and circumstance. It is a general description of class action that Shelley offers, not a rigid law of nature.

Nor are the phenomena Shelley describes static or episodic; they are part of an organic development of history. The progressive industrialization and economic development of England since the seventeenth century has increasingly defined and polarized class interests:

> Population increased, a greater number of hands were employed in the labours of agriculture and commerce, towns arose where villages had been, and the proportion borne by those whose labour produces the materials of subsistence and enjoyment to those who claim for themselves a superfluity of these materials began to increase indefinitely (7:22–23).

The "unrepresented multitude" increased in proportion to the enfranchised property owners. This political change is, again, conditioned by the economic developments of industrialization and capital economy: those who own decrease as a percentage of the population, as those who work for owners increase.

Then Shelley entangles the political and economic contexts in yet more complex ways. At the Revolution of 1688, the nobility found the royalty to be its ally and the people to be its enemy. At this point, both monarchy and the oligarchy of aristocracy become mere representations of "the interests of the rich" (7:24). A mystification takes place, because the aristocratic and monarchic institutions drape themselves under the impressive cloaks of right, justice, and power, but the power belongs in fact to the wealthy rather than the ornamental nobles and kings. "The name and office of king is merely the mask of this power. . . . Monarchy is only the string which ties the robber's bundle" (7:25). This argument illustrates ideological inversion in the narrowly Marxist sense: a fiction ("mask") and rationale (notions of divine right) are constructed by interested human beings and subsequently mistaken for originary forces.

The fiction, spuriously invested with significance, acquires efficacy as a tool of power. Such an inversion is what Shelley (following Hunt in the *Examiner*) calls "imposture," and the correlative rationales that are generated around the imposture are the opinions determined by the economic base. Such an oligarchy, employing the monarchy as its ideological mask, is worse than an absolute monarchy, "because it reigns both by the opinion generated by imposture, and the force which that opinion places within its grasp" (7:25). Both the forms of social consciousness and the material machinery of power are employed as tools in the maintenance of such an oligarchy.

In Shelley's philosophical view of reform, the point does not concern primarily the particular people now purveying particular falsehoods. His argument does not suggest what a literal reading might suppose: that these people in power are saying what is false in order to do what is wrong, but that they might and should say what is true, and do what is right. The point is far more incisive and methodological: Shelley's argument concerns the nature and structure of human thought about political structures in general. Relativity and interestedness, and the mental dynamic of reification and inversion, are more to his point than the examples here produced.

Public credit is, Shelley says, a device in a machinery of class power. It was employed, from the Revolution of 1688, "less as a resource for meeting the financial exigencies of the state than as a bond to connect those in the possession of property with those who had . . . acceded to power" (7:25). Under pretense of meeting national financial obligations, the system of national borrowing was invented for the actual purpose of consolidating power in the ruling class; those possessed of industrial and investment capital form a coalition with those possessed of hereditary political power. "The rich, no longer being able to rule by force [because of the limitations entailed in the Revolutionary settlement of 1688], have invented this scheme that they may rule by fraud" (7:25).

This fraud represents another ideological inversion, the reification of capital. This theory is based on a labor theory of value: "All property is the produce of labor" (7:31). This pre-Marxist conception is related to Adam Smith's arguments in *An Inquiry into the Nature and Causes of the Wealth of Nations:*

> The real price of every thing, [or] what every thing really costs to the man who wants to acquire it, is the toil and trouble of acquiring it. . . . Labour was the first price—the original purchase-money that was paid for all things.[49]

David Ricardo's version of the formulation introduces a refinement or complexity that is important in Shelley's argument:

> The value of a commodity . . . depends on the relative quantity of labour which is necessary for its production, and not on the greater or less compensation which is paid for that labour.[50]

To consider value as a relational function accommodates new complexities: "The principle that the quantity of labour bestowed on the production of commodities regulates their relative value" is, Ricardo says, "considerably modified by the employment of machinery and other fixed and durable capital" (1:30). Capital value comes to predominate over use value (1:11). A class conflict ensues when capitalists take as profit some of the product of labor or some of the value that labor has generated: "There can be no rise in the value of labour without a fall of profits" (1:35). Unless labor is compensated less than it earns, or unless the value of labor exceeds what the laborer is paid, profit is not generated. And Ricardo makes the point emphatically that by way of a class stratification, the modern economy comes to be driven by profit rather than productivity:

> In all rich countries, there is a number of men forming what is called the monied class; these men are engaged in no trade, but live on the interest of their money, which is employed in discounting bills, or in loans to the more industrious part of the community (1:89).

The argument is important in Shelley's essay because here the paradigm of ideological inversion appears in an economic example. Capital value arises in the first instance as a measure of real (labor) value.

This fabricated and merely nominal form of value acquires a spurious autonomy, until it is reified as the only, or as the predominant, conception of value. The money measure of value is a form of superstition; the wealth of the unproductive exists only, like the emperor's new clothes, because others accede to the fiction.

This confusion of fiction as hard fact appears, as Ricardo points out, in the case of paper money: "Neither a State nor a Bank ever have had the unrestricted power of issuing paper money, without abusing that power" (1:356). The problem is that the paper is a nominal substitute for actual gold but (like capital value) tries to take on autonomous existence and power, spuriously and by way of delusion. A control is necessary, Ricardo says, and he recommends "subjecting the issuers of paper money to the obligation of paying their notes, either in gold coin or bullion" (1:356).

Printed money, Shelley says, represents its holder's "right to so much gold, which represents his right to so much labour" (7:26). When the mere sign is by a trick allowed to displace that which it supposedly signifies, an inversion takes place: "A man may write on a piece of paper what he pleases; he may say he is worth a thousand when he is not worth a hundred pounds. If he can make others believe this, he has credit for the sum to which his name is attached" (7:26). This is what the national government has done: rather than alloy the gold of the coins (which would amount to the same thing), the government in England substituted a paper currency for the gold coin; "they have merely fabricated pieces of paper" and then ruled that the persons who held office for redeeming those promissory papers could not be forced to do so (7:27).

Shelley's argument here is closer to Cobbett's than to Ricardo's; Cobbett had published his *Paper Against Gold* in 1817, the year before Shelley left England for Italy. As Shelley was to do, Cobbett attacks the issue of paper money with skeptical demystification, with an argument of superstitious inversion, and with a concept of nominalization. Some people, Cobbett says, "seem to regard the Bank of England as being as old as the Church of England, at least, and some of them appear to have full as much veneration for it" (p. 8). Cobbett applies to this economic illusion the same kind of critique that Shelley had applied (in *A Refutation of Deism* and *Essay on Christianity*) to theological illusion:

The Bank of England is a mere human institution, arising out of causes having nothing miraculous, or supernatural, about them. . . . both the institution and the agents who carry it on, are as mortal as any other thing and any other men, in this or in any other country.[51]

To treat the institution as an illusion, as a mental attribution, is to enclose it in subjectivity:

The Bank Company . . . at no time could have in hand gold and silver enough to pay off *all* their notes at once; nor was this necessary as long as the people regarded those notes as being equally good with gold and silver (p. 11).

This scheme depends upon opinion and on delusion: "'Public Credit,' as it has been called . . . may more properly be called, *The credit of bank notes*"; it "has been emphatically denominated, 'SUSPICION ASLEEP'" (p. 14).

The delusion is collective rather than personal, but as Drummond (among other skeptics) had pointed out, the collective sharing of a delusion does not make it less a delusion. The relevant analysis is psychological, and the relevant category is nominalization, transposed here from a metaphysical frame (such as Shelley gives it in *On Life* and *Treatise on Morals*) into an economic frame:

These funds, or stock . . . have no bodily existence, either in the shape of money or of bonds or of certificates or of any thing else that can be seen or touched. They have a being merely in *name* (Cobbett, *Paper Against Gold,* p. 21).

Again,

We have now seen what the Funds and the Stocks *really are:* . . . we have blown away the mist in which we had so long been wandering; . . . the financial Ark is now no more in our sight than any veritable box made of real boards and nails; . . . there is nothing mystical in the words Funds and Stocks . . . [and] far from meaning *a place where a great quantity of money is kept,* they are not the name of any place at all, nor of any thing which has a corporeal existence, and are the mere denominations, or names, of the several classes, or parcels, of Debt (Cobbett, *Paper Against Gold*, p. 22).

The fetishistic reification of a mere name is applied to theological illusion (in *A Refutation of Deism*), and to personal identity (in *On Life*), and to the Hegelian Absolute Idea (in *The German Ideology*). This conceptual form is applied to the skeptical critique of capital (in Marx's argument on surplus value in *Capital*), and—by Shelley as by Cobbett—it is this same conceptual form that is brought to bear on the problem of paper money.

The national debt is a part of this contrivance. A holder of a largely fraudulent promissory piece of paper (e.g., a fund-holder) lends the piece of paper to the government, with the understanding that it will be returned to him with yet more such fraudulent paper (interest payment). The government procures all these additional pieces of promissory paper from the working poor, by taxing them. Those who labor, producing goods, suffer taxation; those who do not labor enjoy payment from those who do (7:36).

The system of inflationary paper currency and the system of national debt is, Shelley says, a scheme whereby fund-holders can, without producing a thing, "enjoy the profit of the labour of others" (7:27). This scheme is an imposture that makes one class (the laboring class) pay what another class "neither received by their sanction nor spent for their benefit" (7:36). The point concerns the structure of illusion: "At the bottom it is all trick" (7:28); the currency is a fiction, the taxation is a fraud, and the earned interest of the fund-holders is "a mere hypothesis" (as Hunt says in the *Examiner* for January 19, 1817). But despite its basis in illusion and deception, this system of public credit has painfully concrete results:

That is, to increase the labours of the poor and those luxuries of the rich which they supply. To make a manufacturer [i.e., laborer] work 16 hours where he only worked 8. To turn children into lifeless and bloodless machines at an age when otherwise they would be at play before the cottage doors of their parents. To augment indefinitely the proportion of those who enjoy the profit of the labour of others as compared with those who exercise this labour (7:27).

This argument of Shelley's about the "imposture" and "trick" of capital value abstracted from labor value is closely similar to Marx's arguments, in *Capital,* about the fetishism of capital. What is probably one of the clearest summaries of this complex theory is by G. A. Cohen, and Cohen's explanation elucidates Shelley's theory as well:

> In religious fetishism an activity of thought, a cultural process, vests an object with apparent power. . . . The religious fetish does not really acquire the power mentally referred to it. But if a culture makes a fetish of an object, its members come to perceive it as endowed with the power. What is mistakenly attributed to it is experienced as inhering in it.

In that sense, fetishism is an example of ideological illusion of the type described in *The German Ideology.* The phenomenon appears in philosophy and in the idealizations of religion, as Marx and Engels point out. In economic terms,

> Commodities possess exchange-value, and capital is productive. But these powers belong to them only by grace of the material labour process. Yet they appear to inhere in them independently of it. That appearance is fetishism. . . . The illusion is that [the economic fetish] has the power inherently, whereas it is in fact delegated by material production.[52]

Two principles in this theory appear exactly in Shelley: the economic fetishism is a repetition, with a difference, of the ideological inversion that converts the fictions of religion into tools of political oppression. Power attributed to a fetish is (unjustifiably) experienced as belonging to it; an illusion is solidified and wielded as a tool in the material play of power.

Among ancient skeptics, Carneades explained religious illusion as such an attribution.[53] So does Shelley: human beings, he says in *A Refutation of Deism,* "have . . . adored under various names a god of which themselves were the model" but which they project outward. The mental projection is then politicized in the *Essay on Christianity:* "Mankind . . . attribute to the universal cause a character analogous with their own"; an illusion of a "paternal Monarch" originates in "the idle dreams of the visionary or the pernicious representations of impostors," and then the illusion is solidified and exploited as political and economic machinery of oppression. The mental dynamic of illusionistic projection reappears in the *Philosophical View of Reform* as the imposture of paper currency and the fraud of national debt; it appears in Marx's *Capital* as the specious abstraction of surplus value. The philosophical point to be made about Shelley's essay is that this structure of argument, involving the ideological illusions of attribution, is a tool applicable equally in economic as in theological discourse.

Shelley distinguishes, as Marx does, two kinds of property or bases of value: "Labour, industry, economy, skill, genius, or any similar powers honourably and innocently exerted are the foundations of one description of property" (7:37). The second kind of property, however, "has its foundation in usurpation, or imposture, or violence"; at bottom it is all trick. Transmitted over generations, such property "acquires, as property of the more legitimate kind loses, force and sanction" (7:39). The basis of this value is confirmed by successions of people who seem to believe in it; it is illusion, but it acquires power (as any fiction does) when a society bestows power on it—when, as Cobbett says in 1817, suspicion falls asleep.

Shelley returns in this section of the *Philosophical View* to religion as another example of ideological inversion, and he analyzes similarly the mystification of alleged laws of nature thought to be the determinants of the social order. Shelley admits that the poorer classes—who "eat less bread, wear worse clothes, are more ignorant, immoral, miserable and desperate"—are victims of what Labriola was later to call an ideological envelope. Though it is the case that religious superstition is a contrivance employed for the oppression of the multitude, part of the efficacy of this inversional institution lies in the fact that the multitude internalize the illusion. "They are more superstitious, for misery on earth begets a diseased expectation and panic-stricken faith in miseries beyond the grave" (7:30).

An illusion with entirely different content exhibits the same structure. It sometimes happens that miseries that attend upon a human policy, upon human decisions and acts, are ascribed to alleged laws of nature; in theories like those of Malthus, for example, such an inversion takes place. Malthus argues that "population, when unchecked, increases in a geometrical ratio. Subsistence increases only in an arithmetical ratio."[54] Malthus reifies that description into an allegedly inescapable law:

> Necessity, that imperious all pervading law of nature, restrains [creatures] within the prescribed bounds. The race of plants and the race of animals shrink under this great restrictive law. And the race of man cannot, by any efforts of reason, escape from it (Malthus, p. 72).

As usual an illusionistic reification takes place. The fictional law is invented, and then human beings are subjected to it, as though it determined them, rather than the other way around. And as usual the reification has concrete results in hard economic terms: in this case, Malthus lets the allegedly inescapable law become an argument against the possibility of equalitarian reform:

> No fancied equality, no agrarian regulations in their utmost extent, could remove the pressure [of the alleged "law which pervades all animated nature"]. And it appears, therefore, to be decisive against the possible existence of a society, all the members of which should live in ease, happiness, and comparative leisure (Malthus, p. 72).

Shelley and radical reformers would imagine a society in which all persons "should live in ease, happiness, and comparative leisure"; Malthus and other apologists for the ruling class would imagine laws to prevent it. Shelley perceives that this reification of existing social relations into a law of nature simply cloaks repressive policy under the mystification of an abstract principle. He also perceives that the inversion is based on class interest.

In both principles of his critique—the demystifying of Malthus's reified law and the argument of class conflict—Shelley accompanies Godwin and anticipates Marx and Engels. In 1820, contemporaneously with Shelley's *Philosophical View of Reform*, Godwin writes *Of Population: An Enquiry concerning the Power of Increase in the Numbers of Mankind, Being an Answer to Mr. Malthus's Essay on that Subject.*[55] In this volume Godwin makes the same dual critique that Shelley had made in *Philosophical View of Reform*. First he exposes the ideological illusion whereby a fiction is mistaken as a given and inexorable fact:

> What is it . . . that causes any man to starve, or prevents him from cultivating the earth, and subsisting upon its fruits . . . ? Mr. Malthus says, it is '*the Law of Nature*' (Godwin, *Of Population*, p. 18).

"But," says Godwin, "it is not *the Law of Nature*. It is *the Law of very artificial life*" (p. 20). Shelley's skeptical demystification of this superstition resembles Godwin's, but Shelley joins it to the similar critique, on similar grounds, of paper currency, national debt, theological illusion, and paternalistic monarchy.

Godwin also produces the argument that Malthus's theory is overdetermined by class interest: Malthus's "law . . . 'heaps upon some few with vast excess' the means of every wanton expence and every luxury, while others, some of them not less worthy, are condemned to pine in want" (p. 20). Godwin devotes an entire chapter (Book VI, Chapter 1) to treating Malthus's *Essay* as an attack on "systems of equality," and here again Shelley's argument is comparable. Shelley generalizes this principle whereby policies favorable to one class's interest are hypostatized as laws of nature. The working class, he admits, know, obviously, that they "are destitute and miserable, ill-clothed, ill-fed, ill-educated" (7:31). And he acknowledges that the majority among them may tend to believe "that all they endured and all [they] were deprived of arose from the unavoidable condition of human life"; "this belief being an error," every enlightened person, Shelley says, ought to demystify it, bringing the majority "to the temperate but irresistible vindication of their rights" (7:31-32). This vindication depends on expanded consciousness, on the exposure of the illusions by which the reigning structures of power not only rule but also enlist the support of their own victims.

Marx and Engels were to produce both of these principles—the claim that Malthus's theory involves ideological illusion and the claim that this illusion is overdetermined by class interest. Engels calls Malthus's theory a "specious excuse" for ruling-class hegemony; Marx calls it an "antidote to the teachings" of French revolutionary thinkers and a defense of the "English oligarchy." Malthus's book had the practical aim of proving, in the interests of the then English government and landed aristocracy, that the doctrines of perfectibility of the French Revolution and of its supporters in England were 'economically' utopian. In other words, it was a panegyrical tract, in favour of the existing state of affairs as against historical development, and in addition a justification of the war against revolutionary France.[56]

The political point is obvious enough, in Shelley, Godwin, and Marx-Engels; but the philosophical interest of Shelley's version is the reproduction in the Malthusian example of the skeptical methods that he articulates in other and more abstract contexts. An imagining mind projects phantoms (gods, debts, surplus value, paper currency, laws of nature) to which that mind believes it is then subjected. To disclose the fictitious ontological status of the reification is to liberate the subjected populace, imaginatively and economically, and it is to release that populace's energetic productivity. At the center of the structures of both liberation and enslavement is a form of thought, not because thought rehearses action, rather because thought and action are equally contained within one epistemological circle.

Shelley ends the second chapter of his treatise with a discussion of parliamentary reform, the necessity of which rests upon this principle: "that no individual who is governed can be denied a direct share in the government of his country without supreme injustice" (7:40). This reasoning, Shelley says, warrants the justice of universal suffrage and, beyond that, the abolition of monarchy and aristocracy, the leveling of inordinate wealth, and a widespread distribution of land, "including the Parks and Chases of the rich" (7:41); and yet Shelley proposes none of these reforms as an immediate political goal. For reasons that he had explained in 1817, those purposes can best be served by a postponement of their enactment: " A Republic, however just in its principle and glorious in its object, would through violence and sudden change which must attend it, incur a great risk of being as rapid in its decline as in its growth" (7:41).

Shelley's proposal is that of the moderate reformers, including Leigh Hunt and Sir Francis Burdett, but he turns to the particular proposal in the subsequent chapter. He ends the second chapter of the *Philosophical View of Reform* not with a proposal for action but with a reminder of principle: the efficacy of oppressive institutions is such that the oppressed, who have been long degraded by destitution and ignorance, cannot be expected to institute their own liberty at once. This insight invests the issue with ideological (rather than circumstantial, economic, or narrowly political) force and depth. But even as he says so, Shelley endorses as principles for the ordering of social life a radical set of changes including economic and political equalities. How Shelley can assert such values, with statements about their basis in "the true state of the case" (7:32), without contradicting his own arguments about the relativity of knowledge and truth, is a matter to be worked out in the third chapter of his treatise, where he articulates those values as a plan of action.

A PHILOSOPHICAL VIEW OF REFORM, CHAPTER III

Chapter III, the conclusion of Shelley's syllogism, begins with a political principle (the House of Commons should reform itself) and the political question of the "Probable Means" of effecting a reform: "That Commons should reform itself, uninfluenced by any fear that the people would, on their refusal, assume to itself that office, seems a contradiction." It appears that Commons must be presented with an ultimatum. Otherwise, "what motive would incite it to institute a reform" (7:42)?

Shelley then repeats the rationale of a reform, which is in fact a rationale for universal suffrage. Shelley advocates enfranchisement for "every individual of mature age"; and he assumes the first principles of social-contract theory, finding the final cause of government to be for the advantage of the governed, who thus can be said to have instituted the government in the first place. The mandate for absolute and total equality of enfranchisement, of course, distinguishes the radical character of Shelley's position more than the principle of the social contract, which he shares with all the reformers, including the most modest and cautious among them.

From those principles follows an imperative for action: "A government that is founded on any other basis is a government of fraud or force and ought on the first convenient occasion to be overthrown" (7:42). Here Shelley repeats that the bases of despotic power are false ("fraud or force"). That sentence summarizes the critique of ideological inversion from Chapter II, and it joins that critique to an ethical injunction (an "ought"-statement). A set of logical problems arises. The critique of ideological illusion involves an argument of relativity. That argument in turn suggests that no solutions, practical or intellectual, are final. Here, however, in the conclusion of his own argument, Shelley enunciates principles (social-contract theory, equality of natural rights, and utilitarianism) as if they were truths. In Chapter I he presents an "ought"-statement as a rule "established":

The result of the labors of the political philosophers has been the establishment of the principle of Utility as the substance, and liberty and equality as the forms according to which the concerns of human life ought to be administered (7: 10).

In Chapter III, he calls "equality in possessions" a moral truth (7:42). If these principles are truths, then it is not clear that they, like the ideological illusions that he attacks, are time-bound, relative, and intensional. A stronger claim seems to be made for these principles that Shelley commends. To say of a claim that it is a truth seems to be saying more than a "strict scepticism concerning all assertions" would allow. Shelley seems at this point to be culpable of the same kind of contradiction that appears in some forms of Marxist dialectic, as I have shown. Such an argument disallows truth claims and then makes one. Such a statement undermines the absolute veridicality of any statement and then gratuitously exempts itself. In such a case, the critique is at fault or the truth is faulty; it is logically impossible that both the critique and the truth could be valid. And yet Shelley seems to offer both a comprehensive ideological critique, entailing the relativity of all knowledge and of all knowledge claims, and then, second, a truth.

One possible way out of the contradiction would be to suppose that under the press of circumstance, it is best to affirm, believe, and act upon the most likely version of truth that is available. The endless disputation of a metaphysical dialectic simply must be put aside (so we might argue) so that we can act. To be dogmatic would be to claim Universal Truth for our propositions, and all that we need (all that Shelley offers) is the most likely guess. So let us proceed with what is probably true, assuming it is so and in any case acting as if it were so. This is the "provisional truth" version of some of Shelley's interpreters, and I argue that it is wrong because it claims too much. To say of a proposition that it is probably true is not, in the context of Shelley's philosophical skepticism, to say that it is likely that the proposition is veridical. Probability (*to pithanon*) does not imply that a statement's object of reference is extensionally as affirmed. "Probable" (*pithanon*) means "persuasive." Persuasiveness is a property of a concept, not of a natural or extensional object.

Alternatively, one could argue that Shelley is expressing something like volition rather than something like facticity. He could be voicing a wish, a desire, and not a description of the truth. Admittedly (so this interpretation might proceed) his own use of the word "truth" is a bit odd, given this explanation; but Shelley does mention the sort of object "which is, because we will it" (7:43), and Mary Shelley does, in her note to *Prometheus Unbound,* summarize as a doctrine of Shelley's the moral claim that mankind had only to will that there be no more evil, and then there would be none. I also contend that this, the wish-fulfillment school of Shelley interpretation, is wrong: it tends to overlook the fact that both Mary and Percy Bysshe Shelley refer to collective and societal configurations of thought and feeling, to total cultural modes of understanding; neither Shelley is referring to delusions entertained individualistically in the privacy of one's own head. To suppose that the conclusion of Shelley's most sustained philosophical argument is simply a case of his closing his eyes, crossing his fingers, and wishing with all his heart is to portray unphilosophical imbecility.

Instead, Shelley overcomes the apparent contradiction that dialectic is heir to, and he does so with a philosophical sophistication that, as far as I know, has yet to be appreciated. First, he distinguishes two kinds of truth, according to the nature or status of their constitutive objects. Then, he distinguishes two kinds of statement, according to their intentional purpose or (what is in effect the same) the kind of response that would be pertinent. The first distinction concerns objects; the second concerns statements about objects. The outcome of these two distinctions includes the discovery and the use of a form of discourse that is valuable for philosophy of action but also compatible with a "strict scepticism concerning all assertions." Shelley can make, use, and value assertions and expect them to be heeded, without violating the constraints of his own epistemological circle.

Shelley distinguishes between moral and political truth. "The broad principle of political reform is the natural equality of men, not with relation to their property but their rights" (7:42). That is, equality in respect of rights is a "political truth"; equality in respect of property is another kind of matter. The "equality in possessions which Jesus Christ so passionately taught is a moral rather than political truth." These kinds of truth involve not the properties of the sentences expressing them but rather the properties of objects of reference themselves. What distinguishes them is the sort of object of reference that attaches to the assertion: a political truth admits of instantiation; it is something we should do, a state of affairs we should bring about concretely. In contrast, a moral truth is true though it is not and even perhaps should not be instantiated. Equality in possessions is a moral truth, and yet for social institutions to secure such a condition would incur "mischief." The truth of such a truth cannot be a case of its being a wish, commendable or otherwise; Shelley expressly does not wish for an institution of equality of possessions, at least not as a relevant response to his statement. In what, then, if not in the world and not in a wish, can such a truth consist?

Again, it is not the statement that is said to be true but rather the object of its reference, that which it says. P. F. Strawson explains what sort of entity the object is:

> What a proposition is about is often a particular natural thing, what falls under a concept or exemplifies or instantiates a universal is generally a particular thing or occurrence in nature; but these relations of "falling under," "exemplifying," "instantiating," or "being about" are not relations themselves exemplified in nature, i.e. not relations between one natural thing and another. The non-natural abstract entities I speak of—if indeed there are such things—are sometimes called "intensions" or "intensional entities."[57]

Political truths are exemplifiable in the most positivistic sense; they refer to actions we can see people performing and states of affairs that we can witness. Moral truths, alternatively, are not exemplifiable in that way; their notional content is not necessarily what could be witnessed in the observable world of action. Again, I want to emphasize that these truth properties, in Shelley's account, belong to the notional objects themselves and not to the statements that express those notional objects.

Second, Shelley distinguishes two kinds of statements: one kind ("is"-statements) describes an object, condition, or action. These are the statements of science, requiring a "minute and accurate attention to facts" (7:63). These statements denote and record those facts. A second kind of statement, however, proposes to itself a different sort of task. Rather than record, reflect, or represent pictorially a prestatemental fact, a moral statement enjoins action. It does not report a state of affairs but rather prompts one. The two different kinds of statements differ so widely that it is, as Shelley says in the *Treatise,* an absurdity to require a metaphysical (factual) reason for a moral (imperative) action, and it is equally absurd to demand a moral reason for a mathematical or metaphysical fact (Tokoo, p. 25; I&P, 7:79). The one sort of statement produces a picture, like a camera; its truth is a matter of descriptive accuracy. The other sort of statement produces instead an impulse, an action, like a torch beneath straw.

Now, the first kind of statement can describe either kind of truth. That is, a report of fact could be a description of extensional fact—for example, naming an object that occupies space and is visible. Alternatively, a statement could be of the first (descriptive) kind and yet take a notional and entirely intensional object. In such a case, the statement could be factually correct, though its object of reference could not, or should not, or will not, be instantiated. But if the reference of a statement is to a thing that cannot be shown to exist, then it might be said by some that the statement is without a meaning, or that the statement means nothing. Shelley's argument requires that a descriptive statement with entirely intensional objects of reference be allowed to have a meaning, and a warrant for that kind of statement does in fact exist, as a simple example can show.

My friend Calvin used to compose his essays with a dictating machine. He would pace, and speak his sentences into a recording device. Later, a secretary (Maxine, I think it was) would type those sentences onto 8½″ × 11″ paper. Subsequently, a typesetter would produce large sheets (galleys) bearing the same sentences. Eventually, a book or journal would appear. It is clear that (aside from revisions that Calvin or an editor may have introduced) what Calvin spoke aloud (A1) and what Maxine typed (A2) and what the typesetter made (A3) and what appeared between hard covers on the library shelf (A4) had something in common (A). Certainly the items (A1, A2, A3, A4) are not at all the same. They occupy different space, for instance, appear at different times, and are not of the same material substance. And yet A surely is affirmed to exist, when we agree that (barring typographical errors) Maxine's typescript says the same thing as Calvin's tape-recorded version. What they have in common is A, and that is usually called their propositional content.

The case becomes a bit more complicated, because what Calvin said in A1—the object of his sentence's reference—may have been false. He may have affirmed that unicorns will enroll as college freshmen, at a rate sufficient to compensate for a temporary reduction in the number of eighteen-year-old human beings. But the falsehood of his sentence in no way affects the existence of his intensional object. "Falsehood" here would mean a failure of correspondence between his sentence and a prestatemental fact. An assertion about A1, A2, A3, A4, or their relationships requires no such correspondence. What is more, things can be said of A (the propositional content) that may be true though A be false. For example, I could say truly that A is false.

Descriptive assertions of notional objects can be accurate without respect to the existence, in the world, of anything like the notional content. What Shelley calls a moral truth is an intensional object and therefore free of the requirement of exemplification in the world of particular observable entities. Assertions can be made about such nonexemplifiable objects, and the assertions can be both accurate and pertinent, though the object have no instance whatsoever.

Further, some statements ("ought"-statements) do not even require that much descriptive veridicality. They incite, they do not describe; they impel, they do not record. They do not even record a wish on the part of the speaker (such would be the claim of the wish-fulfillment school of Shelley interpreters). They define the relevant range of responses to themselves, not as facts of mind or nature but rather as actions. The absurdity to which Shelley refers is the absurdity of confusing these ranges of relevant responses. For example, if I were to say, "Please pass the oleo," and my companion were to reply, "Thank you," we would have perpetrated just such an absurdity. My sentence was not true or false but rather inefficacious. It had defined the range of relevant responses to itself in such a way that my companion's response fell outside that range. The result is absurdity. But that is not to say that my sentence or its object of reference did not exist.

One intensional object of Shelley's reference in the *Philosophical View of Reform* is equality in possessions. What is named by that noun phrase is a truth, Shelley says, though it does not exist in any recognizable naturalistic sense of the word "exist." And yet there is no absurdity in calling it a truth, given Shelley's categories of reference. Further, there is no absurdity in saying things about this nonexemplifiable intensional object: "Equality in possessions, must be the last result of the utmost refinements of civilization; it is one of the conditions of that system of society, towards which with whatever hope of ultimate success, it is our duty to tend" (7:43). It is worth emphasis that this system of society and this condition of it, as also our duty with respect to these objects, do not depend upon their ever coming into being. The phrase, "with whatever hope of ultimate success," includes the possibilities of partial, complete, or no success. A total failure of outcome does not affect the truth value of the moral statement. And this is the case, not because of a transcendental moral absolute (like Kant's, for example) but rather because the object of reference was notional to begin with. The range of the statement's reference includes only action, and not description.

What Shelley has stated and implied about language and about morality may well be liable to two kinds of critique or dismissal, and I wish to obviate both. A hostile critic of Shelley could reply in this way: despite Shelley's enjoyment of notional fictions, no object can be said to exist that is not potentially verifiable by the senses. This positivist would no doubt dismiss Shelley's moral truths with contempt, because they mean nothing, as they mean nothing observable or exemplifiable. Further, for the positivist, morality does not work that way: moral injunctions that do not result in concrete instances are not worthwhile, he or she might say. And Shelley's utilitarianism in any case has committed him to an ethic of outcome, measuring the goodness or evil of acts according to their consequences.

Shelley had met such hostile positivists, and he had much to say to them, as in the *Defence of Poetry:*

It is admitted that the exercise of the imagination is most delightful, but it is alleged that that of reason [of "reasoners and mechanists"] is more useful. Let us examine as the grounds of this distinction, what is here meant by Utility. Pleasure or good in a general sense, is that which the consciousness of a sensitive and intelligent being seeks, and in which when found it acquiesces. There are two kinds of pleasure, one durable, universal, and permanent; the other transitory and particular. . . . In the former sense, whatever strengthens and purifies the affections, enlarges the imagination, and adds spirit to sense, is useful (R&P, p. 500).

In the *Defence,* Shelley specifies as the leaders of the school of mechanistic utility the same French writers whom he accused, in the *Philosophical View of Reform,* of a "limitedness of view," and whom he dismisses in *On Life* as superficial. In the *Treatise on Morals* Shelley produces the facts of mind as objects of analysis, and he shows that the distinction of real from false according to the dichotomy of internal and external is itself merely notional. The promoters of the limited and mechanistic sense of utility base that moral position on the kind of materialistic mechanism that Shelley refutes in all three essays (*On Life, Treatise on Morals, Defence of Poetry*).

Another possible misconstruction of Shelley's argument is not hostile but rather perniciously favorable. A religious mystic, for example, or even a nonmystical believer in transcendent spiritual realities, might rejoice that Shelley's truths must refer to spiritual realities, since they do not involve naturally existing things. Such a thinker might posit a world of Being, above the world of human existence as we know it, and might say that the objects of Shelley's reference exist there (with God or with some version of God such as Pure Spirit or First Cause, or with the apparently nontheistic Absolute of Being). He or she could produce the "white radiance of eternity" and other phrases from the poetry that his or her predecessors in piety had misinterpreted as statements of transcendental beliefs. People who have wanted to assert transcendental truth have always preferred Shelley's poems to his prose. These readers have disfigured his argument as they sought to admire it.

Shelley's prose also provides refutation of that spiritualistic interpretation, just as he anticipates positivistic objections. It is enough here to point out that any extensional object of reference, spiritual or material, in this world or in a World Beyond, would make up a descriptive statement of an extensional truth. The distinction that Shelley makes first is a distinction between such descriptions and this other kind of statement that he has in mind, the kind whose object is a moral truth independent of extensionality altogether. Nothing is changed by making the extensional referent invisible or ethereal or spiritualistic. Shelley's second class of truths (intensional) simply includes nothing of the kind, by definition.

What he does include among moral truths are these: universal suffrage, abolition of monarchy and aristocracy, and equality of property (by equal dispersal rather than by collective ownership). Feasible or infeasible (Shelley considers them infeasible), these truths certainly have nothing mystical about them, nothing requiring an ontological plane of the pure spirit. Rather, each is an "elementary principle" belonging to thought, because we think it. Shelley predicates three things of such a notional object: (1) it "is, because we will it"; (2) it "may be, because we hope and desire it"; and (3) it "must be if succeeding generations of the enlightened sincerely and earnestly seek it" (7:43). But only one of these predicates is a positive assertion—1, a notional object exists because we will it. The other predicates indicate first what it may be, i.e., may or may not be—a statement of possibility, not truth, or of what may be imagined, rather than what is; and then what it must be if something else is the case. That last is a hypothetical syllogism, not a description of a positive fact. All that Shelley positively says, therefore, in his definition of notional objects, or moral truths, is that their existence consists in our willing them.

"But our present business is with the difficult and unbending realities of actual life, and when we have drawn inspiration from the great object of our hopes [equality of property, universal suffrage] it becomes us with patience and resolution to apply ourselves to accommodating our theories to immediate practice" (7:43). Here, Shelley enthusiasts proudly point to a sign that the ineffectual angel can turn to "unbending realities of actual life," but the narrow-minded positivist replies that Shelley here confesses the vanity of his idealistic metaphysics and admits the urgency of the real world. And the positivist puts for the real world an external, material thing.

But the concept of facticity—the independence of a perception from volition—does not lend the slightest support to such a materialism of externality. "Real" does not equal "external." It is not even clear that because an object of thought is "unbending," it is therefore real; but in any case a philosophical skeptic can readily concede that this or that object of perception arises without our will and does not submit readily to the demands of our will. The principle of facticity has nothing to do with materiality or externality.

But it does turn Shelley from the volitional conceptions of intensional moral truths to the practical matter of political truths—objects of institutional instantiation. And it is here, at his most immediately practical level of reference, that Shelley produces what is, in my judgment, the most powerful contribution to skeptical method in the entire essay.

Shelley says, "If reform could begin from within the Houses of Parliament, as constituted at present, it appears to me that what is called moderate reform, that is a suffrage whose qualification should be the possession of a certain small property, and triennial parliaments, would be principles—a system in which . . . all reformers ought to acquiesce" (7:46). We have already seen that Shelley favors universal suffrage and annual parliaments (i.e., elements of a radical reform) rather than those moderate goals. But he says that these moderate measures should be taken "for the sake of obtaining without bloodshed or confusion ulterior improvements of a more important character" (7:46). This political truth is then followed by a moral claim that warrants it. "Towards whatsoever we regard as perfect, undoubtedly it is no less our duty than it is our nature to press forward." I call this a moral claim not because it concerns what is right but rather because its object of reference is not tied to exemplification, belonging rather to notionality: "This is the generous enthusiasm which accomplishes not indeed the consummation after which it aspires" (7:46).

What follows from this conjunction of the moral claim with the political proposal is an illustration of a general rule. Shelley overcomes a contradiction to which dialectic is liable: he does not say that his injunctions are true (an injunction is not true or false), and he does not say that his understanding of history, politics, or human life is exempt from the relativizing constraints of skeptical methodology. Instead he elicits a value from within those constraints. Human powers can be "developed by a delusion" (7:46).

If, as Cicero, Bacon, and Drummond had suggested, any system of cognition may be illusion, then, Shelley recognizes, his own system of understanding may be delusional as well as those systems whose delusive character appears to him. But he finds a warrant for action and also for taking seriously the underlying descriptions, and this warrant does not require veridicality.[58] A statement can be valuable if it is an incentive rather than a report, and as such it cannot be false. But even as a description, a statement can have a kind of validity other than veridicality: it can develop powers of thought, action, or feeling. As the last principle of morality that Shelley has discovered is the utilitarian principle, and as that principle concerns "whatever strengthens and purifies the affections, enlarges the imagination, and adds spirit to sense" (*Defence,* R&P, p. 500), he need not cross the epistemological circle, even in his descriptions of matters of fact. Utility broadly defined imposes a circumference coextensive with the epistemological circle. Statements—even statements descriptive of fact—can be subjected to the criterion of utility (enhancement of human development) rather than to the criterion of extensional veridicality.

To summarize: a statement of fact can be validated because it promotes human development. With the criterion of utility in its broadest intellectual sense, this validation can warrant an utterance.

Shelley's moral claim is protected against the charge of impracticality: there is nothing "durable" or "permanent" about a delightful but foolish fancifulness. Whatever comforts I may derive from a pleasing delusion, both the comforts and the delusion are likely to run afoul of the requirement of durability. If I fail to acknowledge the facticity of things (phenomena), I shall face harm, or perhaps incur harm for numbers of others.

Shelley's ethic of the heuristic illusion is thus protected against the charge of solipsistic self-entertainment. His principle of total equality of benefits would rule out narcissistic behavior as a permanent plan. Shelley's readers are enjoined to struggle toward certain objects of collective importance; Shelley calls this struggle a duty.

On a series of particular issues—women's suffrage, the property qualification, and a revolutionary struggle—Shelley constructs hypothetical arguments. That is, if "the Houses of Parliament obstinately and perpetually refuse to concede any reform to the people, my vote is for universal suffrage and equal representation" (7:47). Shelley observes that Bentham and others "have urged the admission of females to the right of suffrage"; to Shelley, this proposal seems not wrong but ill-timed; "Should my opinion be the result of despondency, the writer of these pages would be the last to withhold his vote from any system which might tend to an equal and full development of the capacities of all living beings" (7:44).

Because Shelley designs *A Philosophical View of Reform* as a manual for political reformers, engaged in actual legislation, he introduces here a temporizing limit to his feminism: universal suffrage is his choice, if parliament were to act in those ways; given his assessment of the legislative actualities of Regency politics, he despairs of this goal as an immediate action, advocating women's suffrage by way of historically sequential steps, or mediations in a political program to be launched (and achieved) over time, in the frame of political expediency. What appears as a limit to Shelley's feminism, therefore, is instead the hardheaded efficacy of a political radical. The aim of his recommendation is his unswerving conviction (voiced also in his *Discourse on the Manners of the Ancient Greeks*) that sexual inequality, in ideological or in legal form, is an injustice and an evil; it constitutes an impediment to the development of human power and capacities.

With two more particular issues, the unfinished manuscript of *A Philosophical View of Reform* ends. Shelley recommends massive nonviolent resistance, explaining in the essay what he had already voiced in the poetic rhetoric of "The Mask of Anarchy."[59] The prose, however, analyzes several moods of response, going farther than the pacifist poem. The rationale for nonviolent resistance might, or could, warrant other forms of insurrection as well. The evil of war is in the *Philosophical View* assimilated to the paradigm of ideological inversion: "War is a kind of superstition; the pageantry of arms and badges corrupts the imagination of men" (7:53). The conceptual form that Shelley drew out of metaphysical argument, in Chapter I, and applied to economic theory in Chapter II is again elicited from another range of reference. The evil of war is "imposture," like the so-called national debt or like the anthropomorphisms of older and orthodox theologies. As a great good involves an exertion and enlargement of imagination (R&P, p. 500), so too a great evil inheres in a corrupting of that faculty (I&P, 7:53). In both cases, the good and evil do not lie solely in the results or consequences of imagination, as if a healthy mind will conceive a salubrious state of affairs and is thus valuable for the state of affairs that it might help to bring about; instead, in the framework of the experiential and epistemological circles, the free and energetic exertion of mind, in imagining, *is* a great good, and the corruption of that cognitive act is a great evil.

To contextualize the argument as Shelley does in the *Philosophical View* is to return to Shelley's notion of social determination, or "the inevitable connection between national prosperity and freedom." This connection appears in a metaphysical frame when the *skepsis* of Bacon and his successors culminates in a philosophical and political liberation after the English Reformation, as Shelley had argued in Chapter I; it appears in an economic frame when delusions of capital value enslave and constrain the populace; and the principle of connection appears again here, in the conclusion of Shelley's fragmentary treatise. His theory of history is a way of conceptualizing that connectedness, and by virtue of this comprehensiveness of vision, as well as the dialectical form of his argument, Shelley's essay is one of the most advanced and sophisticated documents of political philosophy in the nineteenth century.

A Philosophical View of Reform is also the most sustained exposition of Shelley's philosophical skepticism. Rather than the abstract discourse of the *Treatise on Morals* or the essay *On Life,* it is in the political treatise, with its ostensible reference to the Revolution of 1688, to the national debt, and to reform of the franchise, that Shelley's philosophical system—his "intellectual system"—finds its fullest fruition.

Relativity, constant conjunction, epistemic nominalization, facticity, intensionality, and the epistemological circle: all these terms name more than concepts cuiled from philosophical tradition, though they carry that history and relevance too. In *A Philosophical View of Reform,* as later in *The German Ideology,* these concepts and methods have become tools for the analysis of social life.

NOTES

1. Stuart Curran has recently suggested that "the extent to which Shelley still appears in general criticism with this label [Platonic] pinned to his shirt suggests how long exploded conceptions can persist and how tempting it is for humanists to resolve the flux of things by categories and niches." I agree with Curran that British empirical tradition—including Locke, Berkeley, Hume, Godwin, and Drummond—constitutes a body of philosophical literature that Shelley knew and that he assimilates with classical skepticism; see my introductory essay in the facsimile edition of Sir William Drummond's *Academical Questions* (Delmar, NY: Scholars' Facsimiles & Reprints, 1984). The dialogical elements of Greek philosophy involve the Socratic denial of knowledge, and Shelley's use of Plato entails such a dialogical skepticism rather than alleged transcendent truths. Curran's brief remarks in his review essay call for a historical exposition of the Platonic and post-Platonic forms of Academic philosophy in which skepticism comes to the foreground, and an analysis of its complex development in subsequent skeptical tradition, toward Shelley: the present book includes such an exposition and analysis. See Curran's chapter on Shelley in *English Romantic Poets: A Review of Research and Criticism,* 4th ed., ed. Frank Jordan (New York: Modern Language Association, 1985), pp. 620–21.

I. SHELLEY AND PHILOSOPHICAL SKEPTICISM

1. These quoted phrases appear in a fragmentary essay, *On Life,* on which I shall be drawing frequently in this book. The essay was composed late in 1819—an important year for Shelley, because in it he also composed *Prometheus Unbound, A Philosophical View of Reform, The Cenci,* and other important works. *On Life* was written, in fact, in the same notebook as that in which Shelley wrote his most sustained philosophical work, the *Philosophical View of Reform.* The pages containing *On Life* were subsequently separated from the rest of this notebook (a fate that has befallen other Shelley essays as well, posing problems for editors in the assembly of accurate and complete texts). The manuscript pages are now located in the Pierpont Morgan Library in New York City. The manuscript is especially important, because the essay was not published in Shelley's lifetime, appearing in print only in 1832 and then again in a corrected version (by Mary Shelley) in 1840. The text that I shall be citing is that of Donald H. Reiman and Sharon B. Powers, in *Shelley's Poetry and Prose,* pp. 474–78. This edition includes "several important changes from previous texts" (p. 475n.).

2. What I cite as the *Treatise on Morals* is a compilation of manuscript fragments that were first published by Mary Shelley in *Essays, Letters from Abroad, Translations and Fragments,* 2 vols. (London: Edward Moxon, 1840). She published these fragments as two incomplete treatises—"Speculations on Metaphysics" and "Speculations on Morals." Roger Ingpen published them in that form in I&P, vol. 7. P. M. S. Dawson has concluded that "they should be considered as intended for a single work" (*The Unacknowledged Legislator: Shelley and Politics* [Oxford: Oxford University Press, 1980], p. 238). David Lee Clark had published them in that form in 1954 (in *Shelley's Prose, or the Trumpet of a Prophecy* [Albuquerque: University of New Mexico Press]). Kenneth Neill Cameron has said that there is insufficient evidence for determining that these fragments do belong together in one single work (see *SC,* 4:733–44). In my judgment, while Cameron doubts, the case is not closed. For the sake of discussion, I have chosen to refer to the fragments as if they were at least loosely connected, and for convenience I use the title *Treatise on Morals.* But I do not rest any argument on a textual or otherwise factual claim in this matter.

Concerning the date of the fragments: they were apparently begun in late 1816 or in 1817, and the latest passages were composed in 1821. "The Bodleian manuscript [on morals] was probably not begun until at least September 10, 1816, and was certainly completed by March 10, 1818. As the . . . Pforzheimer manuscript is a continuation of [that portion of] the Bodleian, the same dating span also applies to it"; other portions (the parts placed by I&P under "Plan of a Treatise on Morals" and "Chapter II") were probably "written later than January 1821" (Cameron, *SC,* 4:742–43). See also Dawson, *Unacknowledged Legislator,* pp. 238–39.

The source of the text is this series of manuscripts: in the Bodleian Library, ms. Shelley d. 1, ff. 2r–6v, ff. 114v rev.–111v rev., ff. 110r rev.–109v rev.; ms. Shelley adds. c. 4 ff. 183r–185v, ff. 190r–195; in the Carl H. Pforzheimer Library, ms. *SC,* 339; a manuscript first printed by H. Buxton Forman in 1880 (in *The Works of Percy Bysshe Shelley* [London: Reeves and Turner], 6:286–90); and manuscripts edited by Mary Shelley (in *Essays, Letters . . .*) but now lost. My citations will locate the quoted passages in I&P, but wherever possible my quotations will actually be taken from manuscript transcriptions.

3. See Roy R. Male and James A. Notopoulos, "Shelley's Copy of Diogenes Laertius," *RES,* 54 (1959):10–21, and *Letters,* 1:380.

4. For lists of Shelley's reading, which are especially useful because they are dated very precisely, see two works of Frederick L. Jones: *Letters,* 2:467–88, and *Mary Shelley's Journal,* ed. Jones (Norman: University of Oklahoma Press, 1947).

5. See essays by Pierre Couissin and David Sedley in *The Skeptical Tradition,* ed. Myles Burnyeat (Berkeley: University of California Press, 1983).

6. Shelley met Sir William Drummond in April 1819, when the philosopher and statesman visited Shelley in Rome (see Mary Shelley's note to Shelley's letter to Peacock from Rome, April 6, 1819). Much earlier (at least by Janu-

ary 1813), Shelley had read Drummond's *Oedipus Judaicus,* an allegorical interpretation of the Bible (see Thomas Jefferson Hogg, *The Life of Percy Bysshe Shelley,* with intro. by Edward Dowden [London: George Routledge and Sons, 1906], p. 375; Hogg cites a Shelley letter from Tanyrallt, Tremadoc, January 26, 1813). Shelley had read *Academical Questions* in Edinburgh in 1813 (*Letters,* 1:433); he, Mary Shelley, or both read it again in December of 1814 (*Mary Shelley's Journal,* p. 29—entry for December 11, 1814). It was late in 1819 that Shelley called Drummond "the most acute metaphysical critic of the age" (*Letters,* 2:142); thus, Shelley read, reread, and commended Drummond's work for a period that virtually encompasses his own philosophical work.

7. Cicero's *Academica* was published in 1553 under the title *Academicarum quaestionum* (Parisiis: A. Turnebus), and again in 1594 (Heidelbergae: Comelinum). It appeared in English translation by C. D. Yonge, as *Academic Questions* in 1853 (London: H. G. Bohn), and again in 1867, 1870, and 1872.

8. This tradition is sketched in a series of expositions and arguments that make up *The Skeptical Tradition,* ed. Burnyeat, an important book to which I am much indebted.

9. An excellent discussion of these tropes and their significance in skeptical tradition is "The Ten Tropes of Aenesidemus," by Gisela Striker, in *The Skeptical Tradition,* ed. Burnyeat, pp. 95–115. See also Julia Annas and Jonathan Barnes, *The Modes of Scepticism: Ancient Texts and Modern Interpretations* (Cambridge: Cambridge University Press, 1985), pp. 19–30.

10. Drummond, *Academical Questions* (London: W. Bulmer, 1805). Rpt. with intro. by Terence Allan Hoagwood (Delmar, NY: Scholars' Facsimiles & Reprints, 1984).

11. In 1812, Shelley composed a pamphlet on the trial and sentencing of Daniel Isaac Eaton, who was sentenced to prison and pillory for publishing a part of Thomas Paine's *Age of Reason.* Shelley had his pamphlet printed in Barnstaple, but the printer destroyed most of the copies, perhaps fearing the apparently seditious contents. I&P includes a text based on the surviving copy that is located in the Bodleian Library (5:279–94).

In October 1819, Richard Carlile was tried for blasphemous libel, also for publishing Paine's *Age of Reason.* In November 1819 Shelley composed for the *Examiner* an essay on this topic; Hunt did not publish this letter, having already published polemical accounts on the topic, similarly sympathetic with Carlile and similarly treating the case as an instance of a larger political oppression that was intensifying at the time. Shelley's letter to the *Examiner* appears in *Letters,* 2:136–48.

12. Between November 1819 and (probably) January 1820, Shelley composed the existing portions of *A Philosophical View of Reform.* The Manchester massacre (often called Peterloo) and the continued pressure in England for reform had apparently prompted Shelley to undertake this political project. It remained unfinished, however, and long unpublished. (Though Mary Shelley made a transcript of Shelley's manuscript sometime before 1839, she did not publish it with other prose works by Shelley in her 1840 edition.) In 1920 it

was first published, in an edition with an introduction by T. W. Rolleston. In 1930, Walter E. Peck prepared the text of *A Philosophical View of Reform* for the I&P edition; he used the Shelley holograph in the collection of Carl H. Pforzheimer. In 1973, Donald H. Reiman published an exact transcription of that holograph ms. in *SC* 6. Reiman also compared the holograph with a microfilm of Mary Shelley's transcript, and his notes to his transcription record the significant variants (see *SC*, 6:951–61). Reiman finds that "the uncancelled portions of Shelley's treatise have been adequately presented through Peck's improvement of Rolleston's text"; but Reiman's transcription and notes contribute significantly to an understanding of the essay, and so, while my text will be taken from I&P, I shall also cite occasionally the *SC* text on special points of textual interpretation.

13. DL, I,409–11; Pierre Bayle, *The Dictionary Historical and Critical of Mr. Peter Bayle,* with intro. by Burton Feldman (New York: Garland, 1984), 4:653. This edition is a reprint of the second edition of this translation (London: J. J. and P. Knapton, 1734–38).

14. Earl R. Wasserman, *Shelley: A Critical Reading* (Baltimore: Johns Hopkins University Press, 1971), pp. 462–502.

15. Ibid., pp. 134, 136.

16. Michel Frede, "Stoics and Skeptics on Clear and Distinct Impressions," in *The Skeptical Tradition,* ed. Burnyeat, p. 87.

17. Shelley identifies the "intellectual system" with Drummond's *Academical Questions;* Drummond, in turn, cites Ralph Cudworth, *The True Intellectual System of the Universe* (London: Printed for Richard Royston, 1678). There is no documentary evidence that Shelley had read Cudworth's book, but by way of Drummond it offers to him an interesting backdrop for some of his own arguments. Like Drummond, Cudworth begins with an account of ancient philosophical systems from which he culls both skeptical arguments and elements of the "Atomical Philosophy" (p. 12). Cudworth summarizes, for example, the ancient view that Plato's allegory of the cave "is a description of the State of those Men, who take Body to be the only Real and Substantial thing in the World, and to do all that is done in it; and therefore often impute Sense, Reason and Understanding, to nothing but Blood and Brains in us" (p. 19). As Drummond was to do, Cudworth identifies a modern controversy concerning empirical epistemology, and he shows how the paradigmatic argument appeared in ancient philosophy: "*Aristotle* somewhere also censures that other Fundamental Principle of the Atomical Physiology, That the sensible *Ideas* of Colours and Tastes, as Red, Green, Bitter and Sweet, formally considered, are only Passions and Phansies in us, and not real Qualities in the Object without" (p. 9). Obviously, Cudworth is locating the modern arguments about "secondary qualities" of objects within a classical context of debate, and that was exactly what Drummond was subsequently to do.

For an account of this philosophical crux in Locke and eighteenth-century British philosophy, see Terence Allan Hoagwood, *Prophecy and the Philoso-*

phy of Mind: Traditions of Blake and Shelley (University, AL: University of Alabama Press, 1985), pp. 16–24; that account tries to show how this problem leads to the skeptical critique by Hume.

18. C. E. Pulos, *The Deep Truth: A Study of Shelley's Scepticism* (Lincoln: University of Nebraska Press, 1954).

19. Lloyd Abbey, *Destroyer and Preserver: Shelley's Poetic Skepticism* (Lincoln: University of Nebraska Press, 1979).

20. This essay has an odd and troubled history, which Claude Brew summarized in 1977, when he put the text together. One fragment, to which Shelley assigned no title, was first published by Frederick L. Jones in 1948; Jones gave the fragment the title "On the Christian Religion." Another fragment had been published earlier, in I&P; Shelley had not entitled this fragment either, and Ingpen and Peck called it "On Miracles." One reason these two fragments continued to be considered as separate works is that, like the pages of *On Life,* the manuscript pages of one essay were separated and dispersed sometime between Shelley's death and the editing of the *Complete Works.* What Brew has reassembled and entitled "Essay on Miracles and Christian Doctrine" was written by Shelley on four folio sheets; somehow, two were set into a notebook of Mary Shelley's and found their way, finally, to the Library of Congress, where that notebook is now kept. The two other pages that made up this essay were not set into that notebook, and went elsewhere: they are now located in the Bodleian Library at Oxford. Jones had suggested in 1948 that the fragments belonged together, but not until Brew's work in 1977 were they actually edited and published as one essay: see *Keats-Shelley Memorial Bulletin,* 28 (1977): 22–28.

21. "As it was for the ancient skeptical probabilist Carneades, the ground of likely truth for Shelley is the degree or intensity of belief" (Wasserman, *Shelley,* p. 151). Wasserman points precisely to the pertinent context for the pertinent issue; more important, however, neither Carneades nor Shelley confused the category of interior conviction with the category of likely truth. It is this finer distinction, and not the contextual agreement, that I mean to press here.

22. Couissin, "The Stoicism of the New Academy" (1929), rpt. in *The Skeptical Tradition,* ed. Burnyeat, pp. 31–63.

23. Ibid., p. 32.

24. Arcesilaus left no written works; the accounts of his teaching are PH, DL, and Ac. See also Couissin, "The Stoicism of the New Academy," pp. 32–42.

25. Ibid., p. 46.

26. Like Arcesilaus, Carneades left no written works; the accounts of his teaching are, chiefly, Sextus Empiricus (*PH* and *Against the Dogmatists*), DL, and Ac. See also David Sedley, "The Motivation of Greek Skepticism," in *The Skeptical Tradition,* ed. Burnyeat, pp. 9–23.

27. *A Refutation of Deism* is a dialogue "in 101 pages of large print," published in 1814 (Hogg, *Life of Shelley,* 1:484). Few copies survive. Ingpen records that the British Museum purchased one, Sir Percy Shelley presented one to

Richard Garnett, T. J. Wise's copy was given to the Reverend Stopford A. Brooke by Lady Jane Shelley, and Dowden bought a copy "off a perambulating book-cart for twopence"—see I&P, 6:349n.

In the dialogue, Eusebes presents skeptical and fideistic arguments, and Theosophus presents deistic and naturalistic arguments. Doubt rather than decision results, judgment being suspended in the clash of viewpoints. The quoted passage is spoken by Theosophus.

28. An important interpretive problem should be raised here: the statements that I have quoted from *A Refutation of Deism* are not made by Shelley in *propria persona;* they are spoken by Theosophus, a fictional character, and *A Refutation of Deism* is wholly a dialogue. This form of argument, the dialogue, is a generic commonplace in the history of skepticism: besides Cicero's philosophical dialogues, Shelley saw the form used to skeptical purpose in Hume's *Dialogues Concerning Natural Religion,* in Bayle's *Dictionary* (in the article on Pyrrho, where Bayle expounds classical skepticism), and in Drummond's *Academical Questions,* in the dialogue on natural religion, pp. 218–81. I am tempted to treat the sentences I have quoted as Shelley's, because they resemble so closely statements that he makes in his own voice at the same time or earlier: see *An Address to the Irish People* (I&P, 5:222), *Declaration of Rights* (5:274), and *A Letter to Lord Ellenborough* (5:285). This similarity, however, is local; there is no global position articulated in *A Refutation of Deism* that could be assigned to Shelley. The genre of skeptical dialogue suspends assent and commitment among conflicting perspectives.

29. *On the Punishment of Death* (I&P, 6:185). This essay is of uncertain date, though Ingpen and Peck indicate 1814 as a probable date of composition. It was first published in Mary Shelley's edition, *Essays, Letters . . .* in 1840. As *A Refutation of Deism* was printed in 1814, it is reasonable to suppose that no wide gap separates the ways of thinking expressed in these two essays; to align Shelley's scale of probability with what he says he admires in Hume and the "modern Academy" is warranted when what Hume treats is exactly the same issue, probability.

30. David Hume, *A Treatise of Human Nature,* ed. L. A. Selby-Bigge (1888; rpt. Oxford: Oxford University Press, 1973), p. 181. This edition is a reprint of the 1739 edition (London: John Noon), to which Selby-Bigge has added an analytical index.

31. Ibid., pp. 181–82. For a similar account of Hume's reasoning on probability, see Robert J. Fogelin, "The Tendency of Hume's Skepticism," in *The Skeptical Tradition,* ed. Burnyeat, pp. 397–412.

32. I&P put "power" for the manuscript's "force"—7:59.

33. Pulos, *The Deep Truth,* p. 39.

34. See especially Burnyeat's "Carneades Was No Probabilist," in *Riverside Studies in Ancient Skepticism,* ed. David K. Glidden, forthcoming; cited by Burnyeat, in *The Skeptical Tradition,* p. 8n.

35. Wasserman, *Shelley,* p. 134.

36. Pulos, *The Deep Truth,* p. 50.

37. In a different context Lucien Goldmann makes a similar complaint: Marx-

ism, says Goldmann, "is a monist philosophy which rejects all the false alternatives characteristic of idealism and of mechanism." These "false alternatives" include, according to Goldmann, "subject-object, determinism-freedom, continuity-discontinuity, mind-matter, etc." (*Power and Humanism* [Nottingham: Bertrand Russell Peace Foundation, 1970], p. 4). It is obvious that these antitheses belong to the structure of language (most obvious, perhaps, in the case of the subject-object antithesis). Goldmann's point is a commonplace, but I cite it from him to emphasize both its connection with Marxist dialectic and the conjuncture of this skeptical trope with practical commitment to action.

38. In *Prophecy and the Philosophy of Mind*, pp. 23–35, I offer a different account of Berkeley's arguments on the existence of external objects, and Hume's subsequent advancement of them. That account is in no way contradicted by that which appears here, in this book; but in *Prophecy and the Philosophy of Mind* I was concerned with a different set of relationships (i.e., those between the writers on epistemology and writers on visionary theory), and so a different approach and a different set of emphases were called for.

39. George Berkeley, *A Treatise Concerning the Principles of Human Knowledge*, in *The Works of George Berkeley*, ed. A. C. Fraser, 4 vols. (Oxford: Clarendon Press, 1901), vol. 1.

These quotations are taken from sections 2 and 18 of the *Treatise*, and subsequent quotations from this work will be identified conventionally by section (or numbered paragraph) rather than by page.

40. Ibid., 18.

41. Benson Mates, *Skeptical Essays* (Chicago: University of Chicago Press, 1981), pp. 102–3.

42. See, for example, Richard H. Popkin, "Berkeley and Pyrrhonism" (1951), rpt. in *The Skeptical Tradition*, ed. Burnyeat, pp. 377–96; and Fogelin, "The Tendency of Hume's Skepticism."

43. The others who thus misdirected them include, I would point out, not only the "ordinary-language or common-sense type of dogmatist," as Mates mentions (*Skeptical Essays*, pp. 112 and 169n.) but also, alas, no less an authority than Samuel Johnson: see James Boswell, *The Life of Samuel Johnson Together with Boswell's Journal of a Tour to the Hebrides and Johnson's Diary of a Journey into North Wales*, ed. G. B. Hill, rev. G. F. Powell (1934–50; rpt. Oxford: Oxford University Press, 1971), 1:471.

44. Hume, *Treatise*, p. 187.

45. I do not wish to submerge the fact that debate still exists about the nature of Hume's philosophical project. Some scholars (like Popkin) agree with the kind of interpretation that I am offering here, with others (including D. C. Stove) dissenting. See Popkin's concise account in *The Encyclopedia of Philosophy*, ed. Paul Edwards (1967; rpt. New York: Macmillan, 1971), s.v. "Skepticism"; and contrast Stove, *Probability and Hume's Inductive Scepticism* (Oxford: Oxford University Press, 1973), p. 33.

46. Spencer Hall, "Shelley, Skepticism(s), and Critical Discourse," *Southern Humanities Review*, 18 (1984):65–74.

47. Fogelin, "The Tendency of Hume's Skepticism," in *The Skeptical Tradition,* ed. Burnyeat, p. 398.
48. Hume, *An Enquiry Concerning Human Understanding,* in *Enquiries Concerning Human Understanding and Concerning the Principles of Morals,* 3d ed., ed. L. A. Selby-Bigge, rev. P. H. Nidditch (Oxford: Oxford University Press, 1975), p. 151.
49. In *Prophecy and the Philosophy of Mind,* I take the argument over the existence of external objects back to Locke and show how it is reasonable for Shelley (as well as Berkeley) to take Locke in that way: see pp. 15–31.
50. Ludwig Wittgenstein, *Über Gewissheit [On Certainty],* ed. G. E. M. Anscombe and G. H. von Wright, with trans. by Denis Paul and G. E. M. Anscombe (1969; rpt. New York: Harper and Row, 1972), no. 103.
51. George Santayana, *Scepticism and Animal Faith: Introduction to a System of Philosophy* (1923; rpt. New York: Dover, 1955), p. 15.
52. See Pulos, *The Deep Truth,* p. 38.
53. I am aware that although Shelley does not make much of his discussion of the problem of the existence of the individual mind, Shelley studies *have* made a great deal of it, following Wasserman's undeniably brilliant exposition (in *Shelley: A Critical Reading*). Wasserman makes much of it by capitalizing two letters in a phrase that Shelley applies to a person ("one mind") and then transforming that phrase into a confession of virtually religious faith; this is the One Mind concept that Wasserman elaborates with impressive complexity but with almost total impertinence to Shelley's actual statements. In *On Life* (where the phrase "one mind" appears), Shelley is concerned to enclose the terms of the argument within epistemological and even linguistic limits; Wasserman, in contrast, lunges into a religious impulse and an assertion of *x* beyond *y* (Being beyond existence). As Charles E. Robinson has observed, "Shelley uses the phrase 'one mind' to designate not the ontological unity into which all human minds are subsumed, but rather the epistemological unity of thoughts in an individual mind"—see *Shelley and Byron: The Snake and Eagle Wreathed in Fight* (Baltimore: Johns Hopkins University Press, 1976), p. 246.
54. See Mates, *Skeptical Essays,* p. 103, for a related account.
55. On this point I am indebted to Professor James Lesher of the Department of Philosophy at the University of Maryland; from Lesher's learned conversations on Hume and the concepts of cause I have benefited substantially.
56. The date at which the essay *On a Future State* was composed is uncertain. A portion of it was published in 1832 by Thomas Medwin, and then in 1840 Mary Shelley published the essay in *Essays, Letters* . . . . She does, in her preface, quote a passage from Shelley's journal that refers to an incident in 1814, and the essay may in fact date from that year.
57. *Proposals for an Association of those Philanthropists, Who Convinced of the Inadequacy of the Moral and Political State of Ireland to Produce Benefits Which Are Nevertheless Attainable Are Willing to Unite to Accomplish Its Regeneration.* By Percy Bysshe Shelley. Dublin: Printed by I. Eton, Wintavern-Street. 1812. In February 1812, Shelley went to Dublin, "principally to forward as much

as we can the Catholic Emancipation," as he explained to Godwin before departing (*Letters*, 1:231). In Dublin, he had three political works printed, *An Address to the Irish People, Declaration of Rights,* and *Proposals for an Association.* For an account of the essay, see below.

58. Both "constant conjunction" and "necessary connection" are Hume's phrases, of course, which Shelley is here borrowing: see, e.g., *Treatise of Human Nature*, pp. 77, 155ff.; *Enquiry*, pp. 59, 61.

59. For an account of this work of political philosophy, its logic and context, see my introductory essay in Drummond's *Philosophical Sketches of the Principles of Society and Government* (Delmar, NY: Scholars' Facsimiles & Reprints, 1986), pp. 3–11.

60. In the *Euthyphro,* Socrates subjects to critical revision every definition that Euthyphro offers of good and evil, or piety, or the principle on which Euthyphro decides how to act. Forcing Euthyphro to discard each definition in turn as unsatisfactory, Socrates shows that Euthyphro does not know or understand these concepts. The dialogue ends when Euthyphro leaves in an impatient and ignorant hurry, to act without knowing the principle on which he acts. The dialogue thus offers the sort of inconclusive conclusion that Shelley prescribed for dialectic generally: "It destroys error, and the roots of error. It leaves, what is too often the duty of the reformer in political and ethical questions to leave, a vacancy" (*On Life,* R&P, p. 477).

61. Plutarch, *Reply to Colotes;* quoted in Sedley, "The Motivation of Greek Skepticism," in *The Skeptical Tradition,* ed. Burnyeat, pp. 15–16.

62. *Ancilla to the Pre-Socratic Philosophers: A Complete Translation of the Fragments in Diels, "Fragmente der Vorsokratiker,"* trans. Kathleen Freeman (1948; rpt. Cambridge, Mass.: Harvard University Press, 1983), pp. 104, 120; *Ac.,* I,45.

63. Shelley's statement about probability belonging to logic and dialectics appears in his *Essay on Miracles and Christian Doctrine.* His definition of dialectics appears in his marginal annotation to Diogenes Laertius (see Male and Notopoulos, "Shelley's Copy of Diogenes Laertius," p. 17).

64. Professor Eugene Schlossberger of the Department of Philosophy at Louisiana State University points out to me that there are problems in this argument of Shelley's: I am the depository of my genes, for example, but it does not follow that I have therefore certain knowledge about my genes.

65. See Terence Allan Hoagwood, introduction to Drummond's *Academical Questions* (Delmar, NY: Scholars' Facsimiles & Reprints, 1984), pp. iii–xi.

66. George Stanley Faber, *A Dissertation of the Prophecies,* 5th ed., 2 vols. (London: Printed for F. C. and J. Rivington, 1814), 2:114; Joseph Priestley, *Letters to the Right Honourable Edmund Burke, Occasioned by His Reflections of the Revolution in France, &c.* (London: Printed by Thomas Pearson and sold by J. Johnson, 1791), pp. 143–44.

67. Michael Frede, "Stoics and Skeptics on Clear and Distinct Impressions," in *The Skeptical Tradition,* ed. Burnyeat, p. 65.

68. Evidently this ancient argument has the same structure as the critique by Berkeley and Hume that Mates summarizes, in *Skeptical Essays,* pp. 100–104.

69. Frede, "Stoics and Skeptics on Clear and Distinct Impressions," in *The*

Skeptical Tradition, ed. Burnyeat, pp. 79–81; Frede offers a different but useful summary of the Stoic doctrine.

70. Nicholas Rescher, *Scepticism: A Critical Reappraisal* (Totowa, NJ: Rowman and Littlefield, 1980), p. 12.

71. Couissin, "The Stoicism of the New Academy," in *The Skeptical Tradition,* ed. Burnyeat, p. 36.

72. Popkin, "Skepticism in Modern Thought," in *Dictionary of the History of Ideas,* ed. Philip P. Wiener, 4 vols. (New York: Charles Scribner's Sons, 1973), 4:242.

73. Gisela Striker, "The Ten Tropes of Aenesidemus," in *The Skeptical Tradition,* ed. Burnyeat, p. 96.

74. Karl Mannheim, *Ideology and Utopia: An Introduction to the Sociology of Knowledge,* trans. Louis Wirth and Edward Shils (New York: Harcourt, Brace and World, 1936), p. 6.

75. Popkin, *The History of Scepticism from Erasmus to Spinoza* (Berkeley: University of California Press, 1979), p. 3. Popkin cites Luther from *Documents of the Christian Church,* ed. Henry Bettenson (New York: Oxford University Press, 1947), pp. 271–72.

76. Popkin, "Erasmus," in *The Encyclopedia of Philosophy,* ed. Edwards, 3:43.

77. Erasmus, *The Praise of Folly,* trans. Leonard Dean (Chicago: Packard and Co., 1946), p. 84. See Popkin, *The History of Scepticism from Erasmus to Spinoza,* p. 84.

78. On Luther, Erasmus, and the problem of the criterion, see Popkin, *The History of Scepticism from Eramus to Spinoza,* pp. 1–8.

79. Montaigne, *An Apology for Raimond Sebond,* in *Essays of Montaigne* (New York: Modern Library, 1933), p. 544. On this argument in Montaigne, see Rescher, *Scepticism,* pp. 10ff.

80. Pyrrho was said to advocate compliance with reigning customs, and Sextus Empiricus occasionally articulates a similar conservatism; but this conservative disposition is one of the points that distinguishes the position ascribed to Pyrrho from the more disputative skepticism of the Hellenistic Academy: see *PH,* pp. 139–43; DL, IX,108.

81. Kai Nielsen, *Scepticism* (London: Macmillan, 1973), p. 3.

82. What is conventionally called the *Essay on Christianity* is a fragment published with that title by Lady Shelley in *Shelley Memorials* (Boston: Ticknor and Fields, 1859), pp. 273–308. The manuscript (a set of fragments in a notebook) is located in the Bodleian Library. Its date is not certain, but the most probable conjecture is 1817—see A. H. Koszul, *Shelley's Prose in the Bodleian Manuscripts* (London: Henry Froude, 1910), pp. 9–11; Reiman, *Percy Bysshe Shelley* (New York: Twayne, 1969), p. 60; Kenneth Neill Cameron, *Shelley: The Golden Years* (Cambridge, Mass.: Harvard University Press, 1974), p. 163; and Dawson, *Unacknowledged Legislator,* p. 283. For accounts of the *Essay on Christianity,* see Cameron, *Shelley: The Golden Years,* pp. 163–69; and Michael Henry Scrivener, *Radical Shelley: The Philosophical Anarchism and Utopian Thought of Percy Bysshe Shelley* (Princeton: Princeton University Press, 1982), pp. 87–107.

83. *Dictionary of National Biography* (1917; rpt. Oxford: Oxford University Press, 1960), 8:148.
84. Thomas Goodwin, *The Vanity of Thoughts Discovered* (London: Printed by M.F. for R. Dawlman and L. Fawne, at the signe of the Brazen Serpent, 1638).
85. See Bernard Williams, "Descartes's Use of Skepticism," in *The Skeptical Tradition*, ed. Burnyeat, pp. 347–48.
86. Popkin, *History of Scepticism from Erasmus to Spinoza*, p. 172.
87. Bernard Williams, "Descartes," in *The Encyclopedia of Philosophy*, ed. Edwards, 2:344.
88. Nicholas Copernicus, *On the Revolutions*, trans. Edward Rosen, ed. Jerzy Dobrzycki (Baltimore: Johns Hopkins University Press, 1978), p. xvi. This foreword to Copernicus's book was published anonymously; it was written by Andreas Osiander.
89. Popkin, *History of Scepticism from Erasmus to Spinoza*, pp. 174–75; and Williams, "Descartes," *Encyclopedia of Philosophy*, 2:344.
90. Descartes, *Meditations*, trans. John Veitch, in *The Rationalists* (Garden City, NY: Doubleday, 1960), pp. 102–3. All quotations from the *Meditations* will be taken from this text. Quotations from Descartes's *Discourse on Method*, however, are taken from the translation by Laurence J. Lafleur, 2d ed. (Indianapolis: Bobbs-Merrill, 1956).
91. Burnyeat, Introduction to *The Skeptical Tradition*, p. 3.
92. One excellent recent discussion of the dreamer argument in Descartes's *First Meditation* is Barry Stroud, *The Significance of Philosophical Scepticism* (Oxford: Oxford University Press, 1984), pp. 6–13.
93. See Bernard Williams, "Descartes's Use of Skepticism," in *The Skeptical Tradition*, ed. Burnyeat, p. 341.
94. Popkin, *History of Scepticism from Erasmus to Spinoza*, p. 178.
95. Williams, "Descartes," *Encyclopedia of Philosophy*, 2:346.
96. Williams, "Descartes's Use of Skepticism," in *The Skeptical Tradition*, ed. Burnyeat, p. 347.
97. Williams, "Descartes," *Encyclopedia of Philosophy*, 2:345.
98. Reiman records that Shelley wrote but cancelled the following phrase: "delusion which is not a delusion" (*SC*, 6:1051). The apparent equivocation that Shelley cancelled is a philosophical crux of some importance, as I shall argue below.
99. Francis Bacon, *Of the Dignity and Advancement of Learning*, in *The Works of Francis Bacon*, ed. James Spedding, Robert Leslie Ellis, and Douglas Denon Heath (New York: Hurd and Houghton, 1864), 9:98–99.
   On Bacon in the context of skepticism, see Henry G. van Leeuwen, *The Problem of Certainty in English Thought, 1630–1690* (The Hague: Martinus Nijhoff, 1963), especially pp. 1–10.
100. This argument over universal assent persists in contemporary philosophical criticism, though it speaks by other oracles, as Drummond once said. This is a controversy that has recently received clarification from Jonathan Culler: "The appeal to consensus and convention—truth as what is validated by our accepted modes of validation—works to treat the norm as a foundation" (*On*

Deconstruction: Theory and Criticism after Structuralism [Ithaca, NY: Cornell University Press, 1982], p. 153).

This extension of the dreamer argument leads directly, as I shall show, to important political applications, but it arises from the same epistemological circle that Drummond had articulated in metaphysical terms.

101. These traditional arguments appear in *PH*, I,180–86; in Hume's *Treatise*, Book I; and in Hume's *Enquiry*, sections 48–61.

102. Hoagwood, *Prophecy and the Philosophy of Mind*, pp. 30–35.

103. See John W. Wright, *Shelley's Myth of Metaphor* (Athens, GA: University of Georgia Press, 1970), pp. 34–35, 55–56.

104. Jean Hall, *The Transforming Image: A Study of Shelley's Major Poetry* (Urbana: University of Illinois Press, 1980), p. 57.

105. Wasserman, *Shelley*, pp. 231–38.

106. Rescher, *Scepticism*, p. 41.

107. Mary Mills Patrick, *The Greek Sceptics* (New York: Columbia University Press, 1929), pp. 169–70.

108. Quoted in Christopher Kirwan, "Augustine Against the Skeptics," in *The Skeptical Tradition*, ed. Burnyeat, p. 216.

109. Leslie Tannenbaum, *Biblical Tradition in Blake's Early Prophecies* (Princeton: Princeton University Press, 1982), p. 77.

110. On the relation of Berkeley to the skeptical tradition, see Popkin, "Berkeley and Pyrrhonism" (1951), rpt. in *The Skeptical Tradition*, ed. Burnyeat, pp. 377–96; and Mates, *Skeptical Essays*, pp. 100–105.

111. Couissin, "The Stoicism of the New Academy," p. 32.

112. According to Shelley, he had read Reid's *Inquiry* even before he had read Godwin's *Political Justice*—see *Letters*, 1:303.

113. Thomas Reid, *Inquiry into the Human Mind*, in *Philosophical Works with Notes and Supplementary Dissertations by Sir William Hamilton* (Hildesheim, Zürich, and New York: Georg Olms Verlag, 1983), p. 117.

114. Terry Eagleton, *Literary Theory* (Minneapolis: University of Minnesota Press, 1983), p. 128.

115. Jacques Derrida, *Of Grammatology*, trans. Gayatri Spivak (Baltimore: Johns Hopkins University Press, 1976), p. 157.

116. Hume, *Treatise of Human Nature*, pp. 252–53.

117. Reid, *Essays on the Intellectual Powers of Man*, in *Philosophical Works*, p. 421.

118. Priestley, *Disquisitions Relating to Matter and Spirit, to Which Is Added the History of the Philosophical Doctrine Concerning the Origin of the Soul*, 2d ed., 2 vols. (London: Printed by Pearson and Rollason, for J. Johnson, 1782), 1:iv.

119. Paul Henri Thiry, Baron d'Holbach, *The System of Nature; or, Laws of the Moral and Physical World*, trans. H. D. Robinson (1835; rpt. Ann Arbor: University Microfilms, 1963), p. 50.

120. Priestley, *An Examination of Dr. Reid's Inquiry into the Human Mind . . . Dr. Beattie's Essay on the Nature and Immutability of Truth, and Dr. Oswald's Appeal to Common Sense in Behalf of Religion* (London: Joseph Johnson, 1774; rpt.

New York: Garland, 1978), pp. 123–24. Reid cites this response of Priestley's: see Reid's *Essay on the Intellectual Powers*, p. 421.
121. Striker, "The Ten Tropes of Aenesidemus," in *The Skeptical Tradition*, ed. Burnyeat, pp. 95–115.
122. *Ancilla to the Pre-Socratic Philosophers*, trans. Freeman, p. 104.
123. Scrivener, *Radical Shelley*, p. 91.

2. SHELLEY AND HISTORICAL DIALECTIC

1. Cameron, *Shelley: The Golden Years*, p. 149; Michael Henry Scrivener, *Radical Shelley*, pp. 95–96.
2. See Edward Aveling and Eleanor Marx Aveling, *Shelley's Socialism* (1888; rpt. London: The Journeyman Press, 1975); and Cameron, "Shelley and Marx," *The Wordsworth Circle*, 10 (1979):234–39.
3. *Karl Marx: Early Texts*, ed. David McLellan (Oxford: Basil Blackwell, 1971), p. 12.
4. Roy Edgley, "Philosophy," in *A Dictionary of Marxist Thought*, ed. Tom Bottomore et al. (Cambridge, Mass.: Harvard University Press, 1983), p. 371.
5. Marx, Preface to *A Contribution to the Critique of Political Economy*, in *Karl Marx and Friedrich Engels: Basic Writings on Politics and Philosophy*, ed. Lewis S. Feuer (Garden City, NY: Doubleday, 1959), pp. 43, 44. Whenever possible, subsequent quotations from the works of Marx will be taken from this volume, hereafter abbreviated as *MEBW*.
6. Louis Althusser, "La Filosofia como arma de la revolucion," *Cuadernos de Pasado y Presente* (1970); quoted in Jorge Larrain, *Marxism and Ideology* (Atlantic Highlands, NJ: Humanities Press, 1983), p. 170.
7. Raymond Williams, *Marxism and Literature* (Oxford: Oxford University Press, 1977), p. 78.
8. Aveling and Marx-Aveling, *Shelley's Socialism*, p. 16.
9. Karl Marx, quoted in Aveling and Marx-Aveling, *Shelley's Socialism*, p. 4.
10. Cameron, "Shelley and Marx," p. 234.
11. Ibid., p. 235; Aveling and Marx-Aveling, *Shelley's Socialism*, p. 13.
12. Ibid., pp. 16–17.
13. I quote from Reiman's transcription of *A Philosophical View of Reform*, in *SC*, 6:963.
14. Bertrand Russell, *Sceptical Essays* (1956; rpt. London: Unwin, 1977), pp. 19, 23–24, 46.
15. Cameron, "Shelley and Marx," p. 237; and see Cameron, *Shelley: The Golden Years*, p. 135.
16. Cameron, "Shelley and Marx," p. 238.
17. I am aware that this distinction is heuristic rather than absolute, and that already, by selecting texts and methods of analysis, I have expressed commitments. But there is a more complete kind of confusion that I have sought to avoid: the truth content of Cameron's discourse, for example, depends not

only on Shelley's text, or Marx's, but on whether his account of social determinism and the derivative character of human thought is veridical. In contrast, my argument will arrive at conclusions that require less, though I pay the price of achieving less: my claims concern concepts of the world, and not (otherwise) the world.

18. Engels, *Herr Eugen Dühring's Revolution in Science (Anti-Dühring)*, trans. Emile Burns and ed. C. P. Dutt (1939; rpt. New York: International Publishers, 1966), p. 95.

I do not mean to suggest, by these comparisons, any direct influence between Shelley and Engels, though Engels knew at least some of the work of Shelley, referred to Shelley as "the genius," and emphasized the class content of Shelley's thought and work: see Engels's *Condition of the English Working Class* (1845; rpt. London: Panther, 1969), p. 265.

On Marx's mastery of classical skepticism—the generic point of contact that lies at the basis of my comparison—see *Karl Marx: Early Texts*, trans. McLellan, p. 12. Marx's dissertation was a comparison of the philosophies of Democritus and Epicurus: Democritus "concluded that either nothing is true or at least the truth is hidden from us," to quote Gisela Striker; and Epicurus adopted the Pyrrhonian *ataraxia* as an ethical ideal. Marx defined his plan in terms that specify Greek skepticism as a system of thought that he wishes to describe: "This treatise should be considered as only the preliminary to a larger work in which I will describe in detail the cycle of Epicurean, Stoic, and Sceptic philosophies in their relationship to the whole of Greek speculation" (*Karl Marx: Early Texts*, p. 12).

On Democritus and skepticism, see Striker, "The Ten Tropes of Aenesidemus," in *The Skeptical Tradition*, p. 111; on Epicurus, see DL, IX,64; and Sedley, "The Motivation of Greek Skepticism," in *The Skeptical Tradition*, ed. Burnyeat, p. 15.

19. Scrivener's *Radical Shelley* offers a sustained exposition of Shelley's thought in relation to Godwin's, an account to which I am indebted in the present chapter, though my focus is on a different set of conceptual relationships, and not Shelley's sources.

20. William Godwin, *Enquiry Concerning Political Justice and Its Influence on Morals and Happiness*, ed. F. E. L. Priestley (Toronto: University of Toronto Press, 1946), 1:92–93.

21. Cameron, *Shelley: The Golden Years*, pp. 131–33.

22. *Political Justice*, 2:500.

23. Albert William Levi, *Philosophy as Social Expression* (Chicago: University of Chicago Press, 1974), p. 19.

24. Friedrich Engels, *Ludwig Feuerbach and the End of Classical German Philosophy*, in *MEBW*, p. 199.

25. On the early Marx's linkage of thought and action, or theory and institution, in the concept of *praxis*, see *Karl Marx: Early Texts*, trans. McLellan, p. xiv.

26. Scrivener, *Radical Shelley*, p. 13. See Godwin, *Political Justice*, 1:343–44.

27. Godwin, *Political Justice*, 2:231–32.

28. Marx and Engels, *The German Ideology*, in *MEBW*, pp. 246–47; my italics.

29. *MEBW*, p. 408.
30. Antonio Labriola, *Essays on the Materialistic Conception of History*, trans. Charles H. Kerr (1903; rpt. New York: Monthly Review Press, 1966), pp. 106, 102.
31. Terry Eagleton, *Marxism and Literary Criticism* (Berkeley: University of California Press, 1976), p. 8.
32. See Sedley, "The Motivation of Greek Skepticism," in *The Skeptical Tradition*, ed. Burnyeat, p. 11.
33. For a short and professedly skeptical account of nonself-applicable properties, see Benson Mates, *Skeptical Essays*, pp. 3–8. For Mates, such problems lead to what Sextus calls *isostheneia*—the balancing of equally good arguments on both sides of a question, and to *epochē*—a suspension of judgment on the question. My point about Shelley's defensiveness and apologetic tone is precisely that he recognizes that the argument calls for a suspension of assent, but that instead he reports an assent.
34. Fredric Jameson, *The Political Unconscious: Narrative as a Socially Symbolic Act* (Ithaca, NY: Cornell University Press, 1981), p. 9.
35. Neil McInnes, "Marxist Philosophy," in *Encyclopedia of Philosophy*, ed. Edwards, 5:175.
36. The "total concept of ideology"—referring not to particular distorted ideas but to a totality of falsehood affecting all consciousness—is both explained and endorsed by Franz Jakubowski, whose account also points to the underlying absurdity of such a conception. A "whole world of ideas is ascribed to their location in being." Since "there is a particular kind of . . . ideology for every social position," it follows that "all the knowledge and thought corresponding to each of these social positions must be regarded as ideology." Further, "ideology means, first of all, a false consciousness which is not in accord with reality," so that all consciousness is false consciousness. As Jakubowski admits, "This, of course, raises the problem of what 'reality' actually is," and further, how, if consciousness is by definition false, Jakubowski's own claims could be true.

Jakubowski responds by retreating from his own premises: it turns out, in his account, that it is only the totality of someone else's ideas (other than those that Jakubowski would advocate) that are ideological. The consciousness of the proletariat is not "ideological" but "correct." The demonstration of this fact consists primarily of the further premise that the proletariat is "a kind of society outside bourgeois society." The thought of the bourgeoisie is ideological (false); since the thought of the proletariat is (allegedly) different, it is correct. See Jakubowski's *Ideology and Superstructure in Historical Materialism*, trans. Anne Booth (New York: St. Martin's, 1976), pp. 98–100.
37. Althusser, *For Marx* (Harmondsworth: Penguin, 1969), pp. 227–36.
38. Karl Popper, *The Philosophy of Karl Popper,* ed. Paul Arthur Schilpp (La Salle, IL: Open Court, 1974), pp. 31–33.
39. Sidney Hook, *Marxism and Beyond* (Totowa, NJ: Rowman and Littlefield, 1983), p. 24; Martin Seliger, *The Marxist Conception of Ideology* (Cambridge: Cambridge University Press, 1977), pp. 123–25.

40. Marx and Engels, *The German Ideology*, in *MEBW*, p. 247.
41. Eagleton, *Marxism and Literary Criticism*, p. 6.
42. Ibid., pp. 6–7.
43. Engels, letter to Joseph Bloch, in *MEBW*, p. 398.
44. Marx, *The Eighteenth Brumaire of Louis Bonaparte*, in *Selected Works of Marx and Engels* (London: Lawrence and Wishart, 1968), 1:272–73.
45. Marx, Preface to *A Contribution to the Critique of Political Economy*, in *MEBW*, p. 43.
46. Engels, letter to Joseph Bloch, in *MEBW*, p. 398.
47. E. P. Thompson, "The Poverty of Theory," in *The Poverty of Theory and Other Essays* (New York: Monthly Review Press, 1978), p. 4.
48. Karel Kosík expresses and advocates the doctrine of reciprocity and unification of consciousness and reality: "Materialist epistemology, as the spiritual reproduction of society, captures the *two-fold* character of consciousness which both positivism and idealism miss. Human consciousness is at once a 'reflection' and a 'project,' it registers as well as constructs and plans, it both reflects and anticipates, is both receptive and active." Kosík says what no psychologist of perception would dispute: "Elementary sensory knowledge is not the result of passive perception but of perceptual activity." Materialist epistemology, he then says, is based on a conception of reality that overcomes the thought-thing dichotomy in a recognition of activity and motion as reality, not merely as predicates ascribed to substances. The "movement of the thing, or the thing in motion, is the 'substance.'" The epistemological position that correlates with this ontological position is simply this: "All degrees of human cognition, sensory or rational, as well as all modes of appropriating reality, are activities"; the "praxis of mankind" is objective, and objects are in action; the form, act, and nature of knowledge participate in this activity.

　　See Kosík, *Dialectics of the Concrete: A Study on Problems of Man and World*, trans. Karel Kovanda with James Schmidt (Dordrecht, Holland: D. Reidel, 1976), pp. 10–13.
49. For this analysis of the three senses of "superstructure," I am indebted to Williams, *Marxism and Literature*, pp. 76–77.
50. Perhaps the first full-length exposition of the concept was Destutt de Tracy, *Projet d'eléments d'idéologie à l'usage des écoles centrales de la République française*, 4 vols. (Paris: n.p., 1801–18).
51. Jorge Larrain presents that argument in two important books: *The Concept of Ideology* (London: Hutchinson, 1979) and *Marxism and Ideology* (London: Macmillan, 1983). See also Larrain's article "Ideology" in *A Dictionary of Marxist Thought*, ed. Bottomore.
52. Engels, letter to Franz Mehring, in *MEBW*, p. 408.
53. Jerome J. McGann, *The Romantic Ideology* (Chicago: University of Chicago Press, 1983), p. 155.
54. Jakubowski, *Ideology and Superstructure in Historical Materialism*, pp. 98–100.

55. Seliger, *The Marxist Conception of Ideology*, p. 26.
56. McGann, *The Romantic Ideology*, p. 155; Larrain, *Marxism and Ideology*, p. 110.
57. Jürgen Habermas, *Toward a Rational Society*, trans. Jeremy J. Shapiro (Boston: Beacon, 1970), pp. 100–114.
58. Larrain, *Marxism and Ideology*, p. 170.
59. Larrain, "Ideology," in *A Dictionary of Marxist Thought*, p. 222.
60. Daniel Bell, *The End of Ideology* (Glencoe, IL: The Free Press, 1960), pp. 370–71.
61. A. A. Trew, in *Language and Control*, by R. G. Fowler, G. R. Kress, R. Hodge, and Trew (London: Routledge and Kegan Paul, 1979), pp. 95–96; and see Aers, Cook, and Punter, *Romanticism and Ideology: Studies in English Writing 1765–1830* (London: Routledge and Kegan Paul, 1981), p. 2.
62. Mannheim, *Ideology and Utopia*, p. 56.
63. Such a concept is Talcott Parsons': "An ideology . . . is a system of beliefs, held in common by the members of a collectivity, i.e., a society, or a sub-collectivity of one—including a movement deviant from the main culture of the society" (*The Social System* [Glencoe, IL: The Free Press, 1951], p. 349).

   This total concept thus transcends the limits of any particular consciousness, to include the thought systems of all classes: "The first thinker who posed the problem as to whether Marxism is an ideology was [Eduard] Bernstein. His answer is that although proletarian ideas are realistic in their direction . . . they are still thought reflexes and therefore ideological. . . . Marxism must be an ideology" (Larrain, "Ideology," in *A Dictionary of Marxist Thought*, ed. Bottomore, p. 221).
64. Larrain, "Base and Superstructure," in *A Dictionary of Marxist Thought*, ed. Bottomore, p. 42.
65. Engels, letter to Joseph Bloch, in *MEBW*, p. 398.
66. Marx, *Capital*, III, chapter 47, section 2; quoted in Larrain, "Base and Superstructure," in *A Dictionary of Marxist Thought*, ed. Bottomore, p. 43.
67. Williams, *Marxism and Literature*, p. 80.
68. Larrain, *Marxism and Ideology*, pp. 179–80. Franz Mehring puts a chronological sense on "determine" to explain "that economics is the basis of historical development, instead of philosophy" (*On Historical Materialism*, trans. anon. [London: New York Publications, 1975], p. 17). That Mehring understands this priority as a case of raw chronological order is made explicit: "Men must be able to eat, drink, live and must clothe themselves first before they can think and write poetry" (p. 17).
69. Althusser, *For Marx*, p. 213; N. Poulantzas, *Political Power and Social Classes* (London: New Left Books, 1973), p. 14; and E. Balibar, "On the Basic Concepts of Historical Materialism," in Althusser and Balibar, *Reading Capital* (London: New Left Books, 1970), p. 220. See Larrain, *Marxism and Ideology*, pp. 180–81 and n.
70. Unless otherwise indicated, all quotations from Shelley's poems are taken from *Shelley: Poetical Works*, ed. Thomas Hutchinson and rev. G. M. Matthews (London: Oxford University Press, 1970).

71. Shelley's sentence about the "dominion of the world power" refers not to Christian but pagan Roman power structure. The ideological state apparatus, his essay goes on to show, is the same in kind.

72. McGann, *The Romantic Ideology*, p. 157.

73. Ibid., p. 155.

74. Ibid., p. 154.

75. Ibid., p. 161.

76. Williams, *Marxism and Literature*, p. 78.

77. Cameron, "Shelley and Marx," p. 239.

78. Ibid., p. 238.

79. G. A. Cohen, *Karl Marx's Theory of History: A Defense* (Princeton: Princeton University Press, 1978), pp. 244–45. Cohen cites in this connection A. Goldman, "Towards a Theory of Social Power," *Philosophical Studies* (1972).

80. In *Shelley: The Golden Years*, Cameron quotes the preface to *A Contribution to the Critique of Political Economy:* "The mode of production of the material means of existence conditions the whole process of social, political, and intellectual life" (cit. p. 131). But in his paraphrase, Cameron uses "causes" where Marx uses "conditions." (The German is "*bestimmen.*") The difference between what Marx says and what Cameron says is significant: it is the difference between the nondogmatic "determine" in sense 1 and the dogmatic "determine" of sense 3. As usual, Cameron is exactly right about what Shelley says—"On the question of which of the two [i.e., social or intellectual forces] is primary, he [Shelley] does not commit himself but is content with simply stating the fact of interconnection" (p. 135).

3. SHELLEY'S PHILOSOPHICAL PROSE

1. Both Tatsuo Tokoo and Clark publish the fragments as parts of one larger treatise; Cameron, in contrast, points out that "the content of the two sets does not suggest a unified work" (*Shelley: The Golden Years*, p. 599n.; and see *SC*, 4:733–44). Cameron concludes "that the manuscripts are just what they seem—two sets of unfinished essays on two different though related subjects, ethics and metaphysics, written at various times."

2. Cameron, *Shelley: The Golden Years*, p. 65; *SC*, 4:733–44.

3. The *Examiner*, Feb. 27, 1820, pp. 137, 141–43, 177–78; E. P. Thompson, *The Making of the English Working Class* (1963; rpt. New York: Random House, 1966), pp. 614–15, 700–706; Cameron, *Shelley: The Golden Years*, pp. 117, 590–91n.

4. See Cameron, *Shelley: The Golden Years*, p. 592n.

5. Here Shelley also says of the Irish people, "Intemperance and hard labour have reduced them to machines. The oyster that is washed and driven at the mercy of the tides appears to me an animal of almost equal elevation in the scale of intellectual being" (*Letters*, 1:268).

6. Hume, *Treatise*, p. 624.

7. See Shelley's letter to Godwin, June 11, 1812—*Letters*, 1:307.

8. See the article on Vanini in *The New Columbia Encyclopedia,* ed. William H. Harris and Judith S. Levey (New York: Columbia University Press, 1975), p. 2863.
9. See the article on Vanini in *The Encyclopaedia Britannica,* 11th ed., 27:895.
10. Vanini, *De Admirandis Naturae Reginae Deaeque Mortalium Arcanis* (Lutetiae: Apud Adrianum Perier, 1616).
11. On Vanini and skepticism, see John Owen, *The Skeptics of the Italian Renaissance,* 2d ed. (London: Swan Sonnenschein, 1893), pp. 343–419.
12. Cf. *Political Justice,* 1:393: we should "look upon punishment with no complacence, and at all times prefer the most direct means of encountering error, the development of truth." All of Book 7 of *Political Justice* is devoted to the topic of punishment, arguing for that claim.
13. See, for example, *Ac.,* II,104.
14. I quote from Byron's journal entry for February 18, 1814, in *Byron's Letters and Journals,* ed. Leslie A. Marchand (Cambridge, Mass.: Harvard University Press, 1973–82), 3:244.
15. Byron, letter to Annabella Milbanke, March 3, 1814; *Byron's Letters and Journals,* 4:78.
16. Dawson, *Unacknowledged Legislator,* p. 230.
17. William Hazlitt, *Essay on the Principles of Human Action,* in *The Complete Works of William Hazlitt,* ed. P. P. Howe (London: Dent, 1930–34), 1:8.
18. Patrick, *The Greek Sceptics,* p. 165.
19. Hume, *Treatise,* p. 385.
20. Ibid.
21. See Male and Notopoulos, "Shelley's Copy of Diogenes Laertius," p. 19.
22. Hume, *Treatise,* p. 363.
23. The *Examiner,* January 19, 1817, p. 41.
24. Cameron, *Shelley: The Golden Years,* p. 124.
25. Cameron points out this same fact: see *Shelley: The Golden Years,* p. 126.
26. *Quarterly Review,* quoted in *Letters,* 2:24.
27. Carlile's trial took place on October 12, 1819. He was convicted, and he was sentenced to a fine of £1,500 and to imprisonment for three years in the jail at Dorchester; see *Letters,* 2:136n.
28. The *Examiner,* May 23, May 30, June 27, October 17, and October 24, 1819.
29. Marx, Preface to *A Contribution to the Critique of Political Economy,* in *MEBW,* p. 44.
30. Jones says that the sentence in the letter to John and Maria Gisborne is Shelley's first reference to *A Philosophical View of Reform* (*Letters,* 2:150n.). Reiman doubts that interpretation and suggests instead that Shelley refers here to those books by Clarendon and De Stael that Shelley had in fact been reading, as Mary Shelley's journal attests: see *SC,* 6:952–53.
31. Reiman, *SC,* 6:953–54.
32. Scrivener, *Radical Shelley,* p. 213.
33. At some later time the pages that contain *On Life* were separated from the main body of the notebook that contains *A Philosophical View of Reform;* the pages containing *On Life* are now at the Pierpont Morgan Library; the re-

mainder of the notebook, including the *Philosophical View of Reform*, is in the Pforzheimer Library, and its contents have been published in *SC*, vol. 6.

34. The term "nominalization" is used by linguists in a narrower but related sense: see, e.g., Roger Fowler, *Literature as Social Discourse: The Practice of Linguistic Criticism* (Bloomington: Indiana University Press, 1981), pp. 30–31.

35. Kimberly Hoagwood points out to me that the phrase "if anything" implies the possibility "maybe nothing," and that this construction is thus open-ended to embody a skeptical notion.

36. Bacon, Preface to *The Great Instauration*, in *The Works of Francis Bacon*, ed. James Spedding, Robert Leslie Ellis, and Douglas Denon Heath, new ed. (1870; rpt. New York: Garrett Press, 1968), 4:17.

37. Ibid., 4:51.

38. Ibid., 4:55.

39. Ibid., 4:69.

40. Ibid., 4:70, 72.

41. Ibid., 4:431.

42. Ibid., 4:57.

43. Alasdair MacIntyre, "Spinoza," in *The Encyclopedia of Philosophy*, ed. Edwards, 7:540.

44. Popkin, "Skepticism," in *The Encyclopedia of Philosophy*, ed. Edwards, 7:454.

45. Pierre Bayle, *The Dictionary Historical and Critical of Mr. Peter Bayle*, 2d ed. (1734–38; rpt. New York: Garland, 1984), 4:653.

46. Marx, Preface to *A Contribution to the Critique of Political Economy*, in *MEBW*, pp. 43–44.

47. The *Examiner*, January 19, 1817, p. 36.

48. Engels, letter to Joseph Bloch, in *MEBW*, p. 398.

49. Adam Smith, *An Inquiry into the Nature and Causes of the Wealth of Nations* (1776), ed. Edwin Cannan (London: Methuen, 1904), 1:32.

50. David Ricardo, *On the Principles of Political Economy and Taxation* (1817), in *The Works and Correspondence of David Ricardo*, ed. Piero Sraffa (Cambridge: Cambridge University Press, 1951), 1:11.

In 1810, Ricardo had published a pamphlet, *The High Price of Bullion: A Proof of the Depreciation of Bank Notes*, in which his argument about depreciated value is related to an issue that Shelley treats; both blame the problem on the Bank of England's issuing too much currency, spuriously. Ricardo's language sometimes suggests that he writes purposefully of delusion as a central problem: e.g., "I trust the day is not far distant when we shall look back with astonishment at the delusion to which we have so long been subject, in allowing a company of merchants, notoriously ignorant of the most obvious principles of political economy, to regulate at their will the value of the property of a great portion of the community" (Ricardo, *Reply to Mr. Bosanquet's Practical Observations in the Report of the Bullion Committee;* quoted in Joseph M. McCarthy, in *Biographical Dictionary of Modern British Radicals*, ed. Joseph O. Baylen and Norbert J. Gossman [Sussex: Harvester Press, 1979], p. 404).

51. William Cobbett, *Paper Against Gold* (London: W. Molineux, 1817), pp. 8–9.
52. Cohen, *Karl Marx's Theory of History*, pp. 115–16.
53. Patrick, *The Greek Sceptics*, pp. 169–70.
54. Thomas Robert Malthus, *An Essay on the Principle of Population*, ed. Antony Flew (1970; rpt. Harmondsworth: Penguin, 1982), p. 71.
55. Godwin, *Of Population* (London: Longman, Hurst, Rees, Orme, and Brown, 1820). Usefully, this work has been reprinted (New York: Augustus M. Kelley, 1964).
56. *Marx and Engels on Malthus*, ed. Ronald L. Meek (London: Lawrence and Wishart, 1953), pp. 69, 83, 121–22.
57. P. F. Strawson, *Skepticism and Naturalism: Some Varieties* (New York: Columbia University Press, 1985), pp. 70–71.
58. George Santayana has articulated a similar aim and strategy: dialectical criticism is able "to entertain the illusion without succumbing to it" (*Scepticism and Animal Faith* [1923; rpt. New York: Dover, 1955], p. 7). A concept under analysis is rendered "non-deceptive" by the skeptical procedure of "forbidding it to claim any sort of being but that which it obviously has"—i.e., phenomenal presence. The reification known as phenomenalism can collapse back into another dogmatism at this point, but need not do so. Shelley, like Santayana, simply draws a linguistic circle around the terms of skeptical discourse and an epistemological circle around its methods of analysis.
59. For a useful discussion of "The Mask of Anarchy" with which this argument accords fully, see Ronald Tetreault, *The Poetry of Life: Shelley and Literary Form* (Toronto: University of Toronto Press, 1987), pp. 197–210.

INDEX